16 5101

Professional Design Techniques

with **ADOBE® CREATIVE SUITE® 3**

DEVELOP EXPERT DESIG[N]
USING INDESIGN, PHOTO[SHOP]

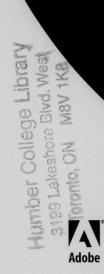

Adobe

Professional Design Techniques with Adobe Creative Suite 3

Scott Citron

This Adobe Press book is published by Peachpit. For information on Adobe Press books, contact:

Peachpit
1249 Eighth Street
Berkeley, CA 94710
510/524-2178
510/524-2221 (fax)
www.adobepress.com

To report errors, please send a note to errata@peachpit.com

Peachpit is a division of Pearson Education

Project Editor: Karyn Johnson
Development Editor: Judy Walthers von Alten
Production Editor: Becky Winter
Compositor: Kim Scott, Bumpy Design
Interior design: Scott Citron
Copyeditor: Kim Wimpsett
Proofreader: Suzie Nasol
Indexer: Jack Lewis, j & j indexing
Cover design: Scott Citron and Charlene Charles-Will

ISBN-13 978-0-321-49569-3
ISBN-10 0-321-49569-1

9 8 7 6 5 4 3 2

Printed and bound in the United States of America

*To my parents, Louise and Al, who supported and
indulged my interest in the arts when I was young.
To Jen, who continues to support and indulge my interest
in the arts now that I'm old. I love you all.*

Acknowledgments

Although I'd love to take all the credit for this book, the fact is I had help. Lots of help. Surprised? Me too. Whether directly or indirectly, the following people all share a part in the making of this book. Had it not been for their efforts, support, guidance, hand-holding, chastising, or goading in some way, this book wouldn't exist.

Thanks first to the phalanx of folks from Peachpit Press. My editors Karyn Johnson and Judy Walthers von Alten, design manager Charlene Will, production editor Becky Winter, and compositor Kim Scott all deserve medals of honor for their patience and support. In those darkest of days when I thought this book would finish me before I finished it, these five women stuck by my side and helped ferry my bruised and battered ego over the river Styx. Special thanks goes to Peachpit's Pam Pfiffner, good friend and cheerleader who conned, I mean convinced, me into writing the book in the first place. Without her initial oomph there would be no book.

Of course without Adobe itself there would also be no book. Never before have I had the good fortune to be associated with such kind and compassionate people as those whose names I now have the pleasure of singling out: Olav Martin Kvern, Ashwini Jambotkar, Patty Thompson, Camille Hoffman, Ginna Baldassarre, Kathryn Chinn, Will Eisley, Mary Lachapelle, Chad Siegel, Jim Ringham, Courtney Spain, Lisa Jensen, Lisa Niday, Stacy Sison, Lynly Schambers, and Whitney McCleary. Although some of those mentioned are no longer with Adobe, their contributions live on despite their absence.

And of all the great people at Adobe, a special thanks and a lifelong debt of gratitude goes to my personal cedar of Lebanon, Noha Edell. If you think people just don't care anymore you haven't met Noha. Not only is she passionate and dedicated to her work, but her life is an inspiration to those of us who whine when the cable goes out.

Not only did Claudia McCue serve as this book's technical editor, but she also pitched in to help write Chapter 7 when the riptide of work threatened to drag me out to sea. Having written her own book for Peachpit entitled *Real*

World Print Production, Claudia also provided a soothing shoulder to cry on when only a good sobbing would do. So too did the amazing Michael Murphy. Michael threw me a line in the form of writing most of Chapters 6 and 8. Not only is Michael a great designer himself, but his understanding of InDesign is matched only by the clarity with which he communicates his knowledge to others. Expect to see Michael's own book before long, which promises to be a sure thing.

It's an honor to count David Blatner, Sandee Cohen, Mordy Golding, Anne-Marie Concepción, Chris Murphy, Diane Burns, James Wamser, and Barry Anderson among my friends and colleagues. Their friendship and generosity has never wavered and I'm not only proud but lucky to have them in my corner.

Last, but not least, it's a thrill to be able to publicly acknowledge some of my oldest and truest friends. All four are part authors of this book because of the pivotal roles each played in getting me where I am today. Thank you True Sims, Sascha Schneider, Jeffrey Bloom, and Richard Stern.

—Scott Citron, New York City, 2007

Colophon

This book was produced entirely in Adobe Creative Suite 3. Book layout and production was created using Adobe InDesign CS3. Headlines, subheads, and captions were set in ITC Franklin Gothic Std. Body text was set in Garamond Premiere Pro. Both fonts are from the Adobe OpenType Font Folio. Final editorial corrections and markup were done using Adobe Acrobat 8 Professional. All photographs (except where indicated) are by the author.

Contents

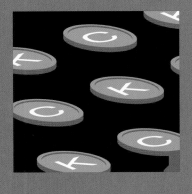

3

Designing a Corporate Identity System 65

4

Creating Newsletters and Forms 107

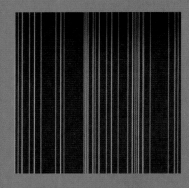

5

Designing Magazines and Newspapers

6

Books and Longer Documents

7

Designing Annual Reports

8

The Personal Portfolio and Interactive PDF

9

Making Your Workflow Work 265

Introduction

Despite being accepted many years ago to the Rhode Island School of Design, I never went to art school. Instead, I went to film school for two years in the mid-70s when all I wanted to do at the time was make movies. Afterward, I worked on and off as a post-production supervisor and producer for more than ten years, mostly on a string of unsuccessful TV pilots and series.

Although the TV business provided me with a better than average income, I eventually left the industry when I realized that much of my adult life might be remembered only by the show I had worked on at the time. I have no complaints, though: those years were mostly good. I worked with lots of great people, many of whom are among my best friends today. In fact, were it not for those years working in TV, I probably wouldn't be here writing this book.

It was the TV business that brought me to New York ten years ago where, by serendipitous accident, I became not only a professional print designer but also an Adobe Certified Instructor, which is how I make my living today.

Shortly after moving to New York, I worked part-time in the production department of a boutique book publisher. My job involved various kinds of noncreative drudgery, and I envied those designers whose days were spent creating handsome coffee-table books for equally handsome coffee tables. But how does one learn to design a book? I thought. Where do you begin? How do you choose fonts or colors? Why use a grid? There must be a book that'll tell me how, I figured.

I read all kinds of computer books and magazines and watched video tutorials. Lots of them. This really isn't a problem for me. Whereas for many reading a computer book runs a close second to standing in line at the DMV, for me reading such books has always been pure pleasure. What a joy it was (and still is) to learn some great new tip or technique to use in Adobe Photoshop or Adobe Illustrator. Call me crazy, but spending hours in front of a computer learning how to make it sing never ceases to thrill me.

Why This Book?

Although many an excellent book taught me the mechanics of using Photoshop or Illustrator in the general context of design, few of those books taught me good design techniques and principles. For those books that did explain the theory and philosophy of book design, none of them described the practice in the context of specific software. Now that many of the designer's tools have been combined into one amazing suite, Adobe Creative Suite 3, there is an even greater need for designers to learn good print design fundamentals in the context of the tools they use every day.

And here's where this book comes in. By taking a "best practices" approach, *Professional Design Techniques with Adobe Creative Suite 3* explains how to get the most out of the components of the suite while turning mountains of images, illustrations, and text into visually striking books, magazines, catalogs, brochures, business collateral, annual reports, newsletters, and more.

With the release of Creative Suite 3 and its inclusion of former Macromedia powerhouses Dreamweaver and Flash, Adobe continues to find even more ingenious ways to integrate the components so that switching from one to the other is more seamless than ever.

The integration of products is a great notion, but in reality, how is a designer to choose? No longer is Photoshop simply image-editing software: now it can be useful for setting type, too. But is Photoshop the best tool for your particular typesetting job? Well, that depends.

How do you as the designer know when to set type in Photoshop or when to use Adobe InDesign? Or Illustrator? The answer is that you don't—unless you have a complete, global understanding of each Creative Suite component. That is why I wrote this book—to help designers take greater advantage of the amazing power of Creative Suite. For example, most users don't know that an object in Illustrator can have more than one stroke. Or multiple fills. Or that InDesign can create an interactive PDF complete with movies, audio, and flexible navigation.

Some tasks previously done only manually now can be batch processed. Tools have improved to aid the designer. For example, Illustrator has an Actions panel like Photoshop that allows users to record and play back a complex series of steps in seconds. Adobe Bridge comes with many powerful tools such as batch renaming, automated InDesign contact sheet generation, and a number of image-processing scripts. New in InDesign CS3 are text variables (see Chapter 6, "Books and Longer Documents") that can be used to automatically populate a chapter header or footer with the name of the chapter.

Professional Design Techniques with Adobe Creative Suite 3 will show you how the tools interoperate within Creative Suite and how and when it makes sense to switch between the components for your projects. Within the context of good design, I'll take you through workflows that make sense, whether you're designing business collateral or printing the final piece.

How This Book Is Organized

For me I always learn best when working through a project. My friend Richard Stern, who got me started in digital design, always told me to design something, anything, regardless of whether it was ever printed. I took Richard's advice, and during those years when I wasn't working in TV I must have redesigned my business card umpteen times. Yes, design exercises are fine and dandy, but there's something about creating a project that makes learning less theoretical and more practical.

With this approach in mind, *Professional Design Techniques with Adobe Creative Suite 3* is based on a series of eight typical projects. Beginning with Chapter 2, "Creating Effective Typography," all chapters open with a number of key design and software concepts followed by a project that has been created to demonstrate how you might apply those concepts in the real world.

Although the book begins with simpler projects and progresses on through harder ones, you do not need to read it from cover to cover. You can skip around and dive into those projects that interest you most.

I've written *Professional Design Techniques with Adobe Creative Suite 3* for advanced beginning to intermediate designers who are designing materials mainly for print, although I cover techniques that can be applied to designing in general.

Chapter 1, "Getting Started," is mostly theoretical and discusses the principles of good design and work methods to achieve better results. It also introduces you to Bridge for keeping your projects organized and synchronizing color settings across your workflow, as well as setting preferences for the various Creative Suite components. Beginning with Chapter 2, "Creating Effective Typography," the chapters open with a number of design and software concepts—what to think about as you start and evaluate a design, what makes a good newsletter/magazine/book, and so on—followed by a project that demonstrates how those concepts might be used in the real world. Projects progress from the simple to the more sophisticated:

Chapter 2, "Creating Effective Typography," is about type. You'll create a simple yet compelling invitation as you learn about the ins and outs of typography, with additional tutorials on creating a pattern, applying displacement maps, and using lighting effects in Photoshop, with detours for Live Color, Smart Objects, and Smart Filters.

In Chapter 3, "Designing a Corporate Identity System," you'll create business collateral including a logo, a business card, and stationery. In the process, you'll learn to use Data Merge to automate adding data to business cards.

Chapter 4, "Creating Newsletters and Forms," shows how to create newsletters and forms. You'll learn how to create an identity for the piece at the same time you learn about table and cell styles in InDesign and how to create electronic forms in Adobe Acrobat 8 Professional.

Chapter 5, "Designing Magazines and Newspapers," addresses magazine and newspaper design. In the process, it introduces kuler, the Flash-based interactive color picker; shows how to color-correct a Photoshop image that will be added to the layout; and covers typographical issues including type and tone.

In Chapter 6, "Books and Longer Documents," you'll develop long, book-length documents in InDesign. You'll learn about setting up master pages and object and text styles, and you'll learn how to automate various tasks including updating folios and headers with text variables, generating a table of contents, and preflighting the file in preparation for printing.

Chapter 7, "Designing Annual Reports," covers the essentials of creating an annual report, including balancing the creativity of the design with the essentials of presenting and updating the numbers. Tasks include customizing a workspace, numbering sections in InDesign, using Live Paint in Illustrator, working with Smart Objects and Smart Filters, and working with InDesign tables.

In Chapter 8, "The Personal Portfolio and Interactive PDF," you'll learn how to create an interactive PDF in InDesign and Acrobat that's suitable for the Web, for a client presentation, or for your portfolio, with such interactive features as hyperlinks, movies and sound, and buttons.

Chapter 9, "Making Your Workflow Work," wraps up the book by covering the workflow, from start (monitor calibration, color settings, and synchronization in Bridge) to finish, of a printed piece—in this case, a CD package.

Although all the screen shots were taken using Adobe Creative Suite 3 for the Macintosh, the fact is they could just as easily have been taken in Windows. Gone are the days when there was a huge difference between working on one platform or another. Today, with fast Intel-based computers and cross-platform OpenType fonts, the gap between Macs and Windows-based computers is more in the mind than on the screen.

In procedures where commands or keyboard shortcuts appear, the Mac OS command appears first, followed by its Windows equivalent, like this:

Hold down Option (Mac OS) or Alt (Windows), and drag the text frame.

About the Companion Web Site

The chapters lead you through the process of creating real-world designs while teaching you the concepts and tools of Adobe Creative Suite 3. The projects in the book have files available for you to use at the book's companion Web page: www.peachpit.com/prodesignCS3. You can follow the lessons using the files supplied, or you can do the lessons using your own artwork and files. At the Web site, you'll also find a list of resources I find useful and have mentioned within the book.

The assets used in the project are for educational purposes only. Most of the photographs I took and all of the graphics I created, many of them specifically for this book. Use these assets to learn and grow, but please be respectful of the copyright for this book and do not use the files for other purposes.

Let's Get Started

I'm very excited to invite you to read my first book for Adobe Press. Here's hoping the excitement that allowed me to write this book translates to those of you who are taking the time to read what I have to say. In that regard, I wish you good luck in your own careers.

Chapter 1 | Getting Started

"THE COMPUTER CAN'T TELL YOU THE EMOTIONAL STORY.
IT CAN GIVE YOU THE EXACT MATHEMATICAL DESIGN, BUT
WHAT'S MISSING IS THE EYEBROWS." — Frank Zappa

To be graphic designers, we must think like musicians. This means we must understand the harmony of balance, the rhythm of shape, the staccato of tension, and the grace notes of type. Plus, as if this weren't enough, we have to know which keys to press and which commands to choose to make our computers play the right notes to produce our visual symphony.

Yet when most designers sit down to create a layout, I doubt many think about these principles. I know I don't, at least not consciously. Yet when I'm struggling, when things aren't coming together, or when I'm fighting the page or the screen, it's usually because one or more of these concepts is missing. The key then is to train yourself to recognize these concepts—not worry about them too much but understand how to use them to create design. In this chapter, you'll learn the basic principles of design and discover which Creative Suite 3 component to reach for when beginning a project. Armed with this knowledge, the job of what to place where suddenly becomes a lot less stressful and a lot more fun. So, without further ado, let the music play on!

The Principles of Graphic Design

At its simplest, good graphic design is the result of the organization of text, objects, and images on a page or other medium. Because design is organization, those most fluent in the language of visual communication are its most successful practitioners.

Although there's no definitive consensus on the subject, the principles of graphic design are often broken down into the following basic concepts.

Balance

Nature is balance. Night balances day, winter balances summer, and death balances life. Graphic balance occurs when dark objects are next to light, large objects are next to small, or hot colors are next to cool. Balance can be achieved when only one object occupies a page, such as the object on the left in Figure 1.1. Notice the difference in the image in the center. Here the purple disk is just slightly off the vertical and horizontal axes, making the composition unbalanced. To correct the problem of the off-center purple disk, you can add a smaller purple disk, such as the one added for the image on the right. Can you feel how graphic equilibrium returns once again to our composition?

Figure 1.1 Notice how the small disk balances the larger disk in the image to the right. Compositional balance is restored.

Any discussion of balance must include a reference to the concepts of symmetry and asymmetry. *Symmetry* refers to objects of equal size or weight that together create balance. *Asymmetry* is the opposite. Both symmetry and asymmetry can feel balanced, and ultimately it's the artist's job to decide which form best serves the composition.

Rhythm

When George Gershwin wrote "I've Got Rhythm," he probably wasn't talking about graphic design. Yet rhythm is an essential component of effective visual communication. In Western society, rhythm tends to be harmonious and somewhat predictable, but too much predictability is boring and static. This is not

Figure 1.2 Hemingway and Dos Passos battle it out on the cover of this play.

to say that predictability in art is always bad. Humans take comfort in a certain amount of predictability. As much as I dread the sultry days of summer, I know for a fact that, before long, fall will bring cool breezes.

Unpredictability isn't good either. It creates feelings of unease or negative tension. The same goes for art. When the rhythm of design is completely unpredictable, we find it disquieting or upsetting.

So, the job of the designer is to strike a rhythmic balance between what's predicted and what's not. Often a component of good design is the element of surprise: that little something that breaks expectations without causing discomfort. None of us likes a joke that we don't get. It makes us feel dim or inadequate. But when we understand a joke, that's different! We feel smart. We're cool—part of a special club.

Design can have the same effect, although in a more unconscious way. Shown in Figure 1.2, the cover I designed for a play pits literary giants Ernest Hemingway

NOTE: Although this cover was created with Adobe Illustrator, it could just as easily have been done using Adobe InDesign.

and John Dos Passos against each other; the title letters were used as horns or antlers sprouting from two warring bulls. Adding to the effect is that the type-face, Trixie, looks much like the letter forms Hemingway and Dos Passos might have pounded out on their typewriters in the 1920s.

The visual conceit is just enough to make viewers experience that brief moment of "aha!"—that joyous instant when we get the joke.

Proportion

When an artist draws his subject's head too big, we say it's out of proportion. We're uncomfortable; our sense of rhythm and balance is upset. Have you ever seen a layout where the designer chose type that's too big or too small? Again, the culprit may be a lack of proportion.

Proportion is the relationship between objects. In good design, the law of pro-portion works to convey movement or importance in the visual hierarchy. In a predictable composition, large objects are more important than small, and objects in front are more important than those in back. But what about designs that place large, unimportant objects in front and small, important objects in back? In Figure 1.3, note the large purple disk in the lower-left foreground. The disk is incomplete and appears to exist partly outside the composition. Because of its placement and position, your eye looks past the larger object and toward the smaller disk behind. In creating this composition, you as the artist also estab-lish an unconscious relationship or hierarchy, which communicates to the viewer which object is more important or dominant.

Dominance

So, what does hierarchy have to do with design? Objects that are dominant tend to have more weight or importance. They assume greater dominance in the pecking order, or hierarchy, of objects on the page or screen. What makes objects dominant? Typically, dominant objects are larger, more colorful, and closer to the front in a design. But as you see in Figure 1.3, visual dominance can also be achieved by just the opposite. Here the dominant object is smaller and behind the large, frontmost object. In this composition, the smaller object has more visual weight, or dominance.

Unity

The law of unity says that like objects attract and unlike objects repel. Like the principle of rhythm, good design tends to use unity to create predictable and coherent visual rhythm. In Figure 1.4, the three purple circles are scattered around the page. They lack unity and rhythm. No one object dominates. Yet

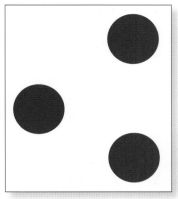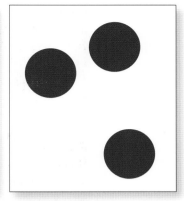

Figure 1.3 A large foreground object acts like a frame, directing your eye toward the smaller, more important background object.

Figure 1.4 These three circles carry equal weight, each pulling away from the other. The result: the composition lacks unity.

Figure 1.5 Two circles placed close together achieve the unity, dominance, and rhythm that is lacking in the Figure 1.4 example.

by grouping two circles closer together and balancing them against one smaller circle, the design now has balance, rhythm, proportion, dominance, and unity (Figure 1.5).

Tell Me a Story: Sequencing, Relating, and Pacing

Up until now, our discussion of design principles has focused on single-page compositions, whether on screen, canvas, or paper. Yet much of the graphic designer's job is to create multipage documents such as books, magazines, brochures, or pamphlets. Although the same principles of balance, rhythm, proportion, dominance, and unity apply, designing documents longer than one page pose their own special challenges (Figure 1.6).

In his book, *Inside/Outside Design: From the Basics to the Practice of Design*, noted designer Malcolm Grear speaks about the visual poetry of books and the importance of sequencing, relating, and pacing when it comes to design. "If a book has a weak or muddled visual structure, its information loses force." The same can be said for a story; writing that's weak and muddled also has no punch and no strength. A symphony that has all the drama in the opening overture and saves nothing for the finale, disregarding the importance of pace, is one dull piece of music. Like the Olympic swimmer who goes out fast at the gun only to lose to another who takes it easy midway through the race and then explodes with a last kick down the final stretch, pacing is everything.

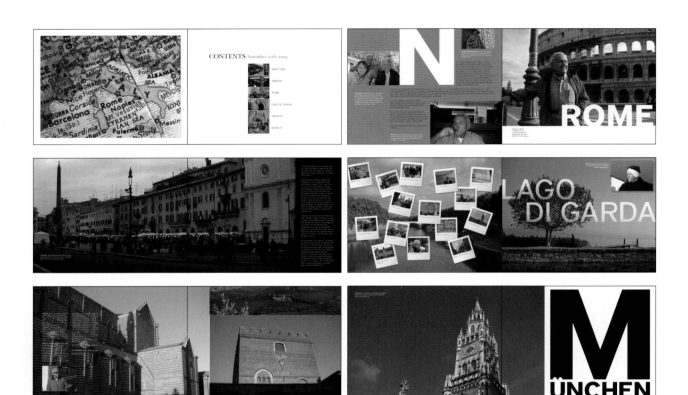

Figure 1.6 From left to right: Balance, rhythm, proportion, dominance, and unity are exemplified in these spreads from a project you'll create in Chapter 8, "The Personal Portfolio and Interactive PDF." Although each page stands on its own compositionally, when combined in a spread, the two pages present a more unified and cohesive design. This flow from page to page, spread to spread, is what designer Malcolm Grear refers to as *sequencing*.

One of the problems of designing books on computers is that the designer has a hard time seeing pages in the context of the pages around it. Without this kind of perspective, evaluating sequencing and pacing is tough if not impossible. To combat this difficulty, Grear suggests laying a book's pages down a long corridor or hall, side by side. At least this way the designer can "walk the book" to get a feel for how pages play off one another. If lack of space prevents you from laying out pages as Grear suggests, at least make it a habit to periodically print out sections at a time for evaluation. More than once have I thought how perfect a layout looks on the screen only to discover much later that the font's too clunky, the captions are too small, or the pacing is too bland.

Use Grids to Add Structure

Imagine trying to dig a tunnel from opposite sides of a mountain only to have the tunnels not meet in the center. Would you build a house without a blueprint? Assemble a model airplane with no plans? Write a novel with no outline?

You get the picture. Although not impossible, creating almost anything without some kind of plan or underlying structure is usually a recipe for disaster.

Graphic design often uses grids to structure a composition visually and hold it together. Yet why does even the mention of grids send many designers running for cover?

Over the years grids and the idea of preplanning or structure has unfortunately gotten a bum rap. Designers who react badly to the G-word usually complain that the imposition of grids acts to stifle or constrict their creativity, and often they're right. When grids are too rigid, followed too dogmatically, the spontaneity and freshness of the design does suffer. But like the jazz pianist who never loses sight of the melody, properly understanding and using grids can be a huge help not only to the artist but also to the audience by providing a hidden yet powerful structure that makes clarity out of chaos.

Grids in Nature

Whether you consciously use grids to build structure into your work, their presence in nature is irrefutable. Take a look at the drawing of the human arm in Figure 1.7. If the length of the hand is 1.0, the forearm is 1.618 the hand.

Known as Phi (rhymes with *fly*, and is also the 21st letter of the Greek alphabet), the number 1.618 has fascinated humankind for eons. Jennifer Elam in her handsome book *Geometry of Design: Studies in Proportion and Composition* posits that mathematics and design are inextricably linked by analyzing the underlying structure of everything from brook trout to Da Vinci and from Braun blenders to the Volkswagen Beetle.

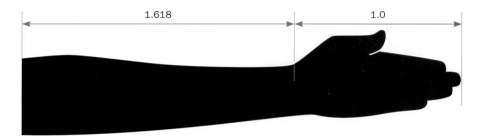

Figure 1.7 Look no further than nature itself to see the ubiquity of the Divine Proportion. In this drawing of the human arm, the forearm is 1.618 the length of the hand.

This 1:1.618 ratio is known as the *Golden Section* or *Golden Mean*. For centuries, artists have relied on this ratio to provide balance and structure to their work. In Figure 1.8, Leonardo's monumental fresco *The Last Supper* is neatly divided into nine quadrants, each of which represents the Golden Section, or what was described during the Renaissance as the *Divine Proportion*. Looking further, we see that the most important characters in the painting—Pontius Pilate, and Judas—are placed at the lower-third intersections of the quadrants. Notice too how the 35° angle of the diagonal lines extending through those quadrants are echoed in the lean of the other characters at the table, and their intersection forms a perfect trapezoid framing the ill-fated Christ.

What I find fascinating about *The Last Supper* is how I never feel the structure of the grid driving or constraining the composition. In fact, for years I never knew that artists even used grids to provide visual structure. Now that I do, my enjoyment of great art is enhanced.

Figure 1.8 Leonardo Da Vinci's *The Last Supper* stands as a convincing argument to the way in which artists use mathematics to provide structure to their work.

Starting Your Design

When beginning any design project, the designer needs to spend a few moments thinking about not only where to begin but how to begin. For some this means doodling on a napkin or scrap of paper. Although my method of work is usually just to sit down at the computer and dive right in, for many the best approach is to draw rough thumbnails first. Regardless of which method suits you best, at some point you'll have to choose which Adobe Creative Suite 3 component to use—Illustrator, Photoshop, InDesign, Dreamweaver, or Flash. Assuming your piece is intended for print, not screen, you can eliminate Flash and Dreamweaver. Still, that leaves us with three ledges from which to jump.

Acrobat's Role in the Design Workflow

Not to be overlooked in the design process is the importance of Adobe Acrobat 8 Professional, the Swiss Army knife of Creative Suite 3. Over the years Acrobat has far outgrown its humble PDF beginnings and has matured into a powerful program that deserves a place in every designer's toolbox. Here's a quick list of some of Acrobat's many uses:

- Reviewing, annotating, and marking up documents
- Combining dissimilar documents into a universal PDF
- Collecting and distributing form data
- Assigning digital rights and managing permissions
- Applying complex preflighting rules and assuring document integrity
- Creating sophisticated interactive presentations that incorporate a range of popular audio and video formats

Like a wallflower at the high-school cotillion, Acrobat is rarely asked for the first dance. Still, its importance to designers should not be overlooked, which is why we'll revisit this versatile Creative Suite component throughout this book.

Choosing the Right Tool for the Job

Sometimes the decision of which application to use is made for you. If you know how to use only Photoshop, then you start with Photoshop. If Illustrator is your forte, then Illustrator it is. Fortunately, today each of the big three Creative Suite 3 components has broadened its toolset so that, although Photoshop is ostensibly a pixel-editing tool, it can also easily edit vectors.

To help those who remain confused about what to use when, see Table 1.1. As the table shows, sometimes the choice is clear. When it comes to editing pixels, Photoshop is king. Producing a book? InDesign is the ticket. Ninety-nine percent of all product packaging (toothpaste or cereal boxes, for example) is done in Illustrator. Get the idea?

But what about designing ads? Or book jackets? Here the choice gets murky. As the table shows, any one of these Creative Suite 3 components could handle the job. So, which one is right? Where do you begin?

Unfortunately, there's no simple answer here. The fact is that most design projects benefit from what all three programs have to offer. Yes, I could design a book jacket in Photoshop, but what about when it comes time to set the flap copy? Although type handling in Photoshop has come a long way in recent versions, it's still largely no match for InDesign (with a couple of exceptions that we'll see later).

Table 1.1 When to use what application

PROJECT	PHOTOSHOP	ILLUSTRATOR	INDESIGN
Photo retouching or image editing	Best		
Color correction	Best		
Contact sheets	Good		Best
Advertisements	Good	Good	Good
Books			Best
Magazines/Newspapers			Best
Catalogs			Best
Book jackets	Good	Good	Good
Product packaging		Best	
CD packaging		Good	Good
Corporate identity		Best	Good

On the other hand, a lot of complex image compositing that would have been performed in the past with Photoshop can now be handled faster and more efficiently in InDesign CS3. This change in workflow is the happy result of InDesign's new effects.

As in life, choosing the right Creative Suite 3 component for the job can be its own job. But have heart; how you get there is less important than getting there. Over time, experience will help dictate what to use when. Also, keep in mind that it's OK to start over in another component even though you're halfway down the road. This has happened to me many times. Each time it happens, I scratch my head a few times, wondering why I chose one program instead of another, and then I take a hard left to another program. The beauty of digital design is that, other than the loss of time, my errors cost me nothing in paint, ink, paper, or clay.

As you'll see in the coming chapters, I like to traipse lightly across many of the Creative Suite 3 components, cherry-picking the best features of each to assemble my finished piece. Working this way not only makes sense, but it's also fun. And ultimately, isn't it all about the fun?

NOTE: Effects are one of the most powerful new features in InDesign CS3. Unlike in previous versions where simple transparency was limited to entire frames, Creative Suite 3 allows a broad range of Photoshop-like effects (Inner Glow, Outer Glow, Bevel and Emboss, for example), each of which can be applied to the object, fill, stroke, or text. For more about effects, see Chapter 9, "Making Your Workflow Work."

Organizing Your Work with Adobe Bridge

The world is largely separated into two groups: those who are organized and those who aren't. If you're among the not so organized (that is, disorganized), you seem to be in the majority. Quick, take a look at your computer desktop. Are there icons scattered hither and yon? Do you vigorously defend your lack of tidiness by claiming, "But I know exactly where everything is"? If so, you're like most of the world it seems—less Felix and more Oscar.

Although I can't really knock anyone's method of work because ultimately the end is more important than the means, I can't help think that if the path to that end were better organized, the means of getting there would be more enjoyable and less stressful. Apparently Adobe concurs, so on that note let's now turn to Bridge, the Felix Unger of Creative Suite components.

Welcome to Adobe Bridge

Those familiar with the initial version of Bridge—a hyperspawn of the Photoshop 7 File Browser that debuted in Creative Suite 2—will be pleasantly surprised by its improved speed, performance, and features in Creative Suite 3. If you used Bridge in Creative Suite 2 but gave up, you're in for a treat. Not only is Bridge CS3 fast and fun (thanks to its Flash-based interface), but it looks great too. On top of all this, the new Bridge also includes direct links to a wide choice of free Creative Suite 3 video tutorials.

Bridge Basics

Bridge is organized by default into three columns (Figure 1.9). In the top-left corner are the Folders and Favorites panels. The Folders panel allows access to any file normally available via the Finder (Mac OS) or Explorer (Windows) tools. The Favorites panel is just that—a customizable list of files and folders you use frequently. By default, the Bridge Favorites panel also includes links to Adobe Stock Photos and the Adobe Photographer Directory, as well as a link called Start Meeting, which allows you to initiate an Acrobat Connect session from within Bridge. (For more on Acrobat Connect, see Chapter 4, "Newsletters and Forms.")

Beneath Favorites and Folders is one of Bridge's killer functions, the Filters panel. To see how filters work, open a folder of images. If you've downloaded the files for this book, you can use them; otherwise, another good folder to try might be the Samples folder that comes in the Photoshop CS3 folder, which is located in /Applications/Adobe Photoshop CS3/Samples (Mac OS) or in Program Files\Adobe\Adobe Photoshop CS3\Samples (Windows). In this view (Figure 1.10), I've opened the Samples folder and selected the **Fish.psd** and

NOTE: Although not a stock library per se, Adobe Stock Photos allows one-stop searching for royalty-free stock images and illustrations from more than 23 well-known agencies such as Getty, Corbis, Stockbyte, and Comstock. Searches are stored on your hard drive for later reference as are watermark-free comps.

The Preview panel is resizable.

From the Bridge Home, roll over these icons to choose the application you'd like to explore.

The Metadata panel is editable as is the Keywords panel behind.

Hyperlink to lynda.com video tutorials.

The Filter panel allows the user to sort content based on criteria such as rating, labels, file type, creation date, and other variables.

Figure 1.9 The default layout of Bridge CS3, showing three columns.

TIP: Pressing the Tab key toggles between Bridge's default three-column view and its one-column content-only view.

Figure 1.10 The normal three-column view of the Photoshop Samples folder shows the Fish.psd and Flower.psd files selected and on display in the Preview panel, along with two enclosed folders, Merge to HDR and Photomerge.

Figure 1.11 Click the Flatten View button (circled) to display the contents of the Samples folder and Merge to HDR and Photomerge subfolders in the Content window. Click the Flatten Folder button again to reconstitute the original folder structure.

Flowers.psd files in the Content window, both of which appear in the right column's Preview panel.

NOTE: Visit www.peachpit.com/ prodesignCS3 to access sample image files for practice using the Filters panel.

But what if you also want to see the images inside the Merge to HDR and Photomerge folders while seeing the existing Samples images? For this you click the Flatten View button in the upper-left corner of the Filter panel (Figure 1.11). Notice how Bridge lets you see a folder and any subfolders in the same view. This simple but useful function is typical of the kind of thought that went into Bridge this time around (Figure 1.12)

Viewing Additional File Information

Metadata, or data about data, is additional information that can be stored with a file such as author name, resolution, color space, copyright, and any keywords applied to it. Most digital cameras also use metadata to attach basic information to an image, such as height, width, file format, and when the image was

Figure 1.12 The Filters panel lets you apply various criteria to limit the Content view. The button in the lower-right corner removes all filtering, while the pushpin icon in the lower-left corner remembers filter choices when browsing.

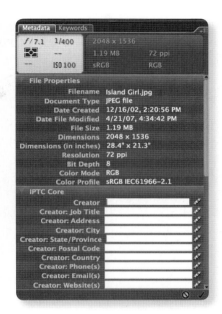

Figure 1.13 Metadata can be used for more advanced searches. Here we see the kind of information that can be included such as IPTC data.

taken. Metadata is based on the Extensible Metadata Platform (XMP) standard and is compatible with Adobe Bridge, Illustrator, InDesign, and Photoshop. Adobe Camera Raw changes are also stored as XMP metadata. Because XMP is based on Extensible Markup Language (XML), the information stored with the file can be repurposed in many ways and is particularly useful for storing and archiving images. Figure 1.13 shows Bridge's Metadata panel. Although the entire panel isn't visible, we see part of the International Press Telecommunications Council (IPTC) Core fields, which allow specific information such as title, author, and copyright information to be written to the file. To view IPTC information in Photoshop, choose File > File Info.

Other Useful Bridge Features

Now that we've covered the primary function of Bridge, it's time to look at what else it can do. Here's a short list of other Bridge features:

Slideshow viewing   Select a range of images or an entire folder, and choose View > Slideshow. Bridge will enter full-screen mode and run a slideshow according to the settings found in View > Slideshow Options.

Batch Rename feature   You've got a folder full of images from a recent shoot, and they're all named something like DSCF0001.JPG, DSCF0002.JPG, and DSCF0003.JPG. Wouldn't it be nice to be able to rename the entire folder in one easy mouse click? Use Bridge's nifty Batch Rename feature found in the Tools menu.

Contact sheets   Improved since the previous version, Bridge can run a built-in script to create beautiful contact sheets in InDesign. To find this feature, choose Tools > InDesign > Create InDesign Contact Sheet. Don't like the stock contact sheets? Make and save your own template, and use that instead.

Stacks   Have you ever wanted to organize a bunch of images into a group instead of having to create a new folder? Well, now you can with stacks. To create a stack, select as many images as you want to include (hold Shift if they are contiguous or press Command [Mac OS] or Ctrl [Windows] if they are noncontiguous), and choose Stacks > Group as Stack (Command+G [Mac OS] or Ctrl+G [Windows]). All the images in the stack will appear in the Preview panel. Clicking the stack while pressing Option (Mac OS) or Alt (Windows) will toggle Preview and show only the topmost image in your stack. To open the stack, simply click the number that appears in the upper-left corner of each stack.

Start-up scripts   When you install Creative Suite 3, a number of free scripts are automatically loaded with Bridge. To enable these scripts, choose Preferences > Startup Scripts. If performance becomes an issue, Adobe recommends turning off any scripts you're not using.

File > Place command   Another convenience of Bridge is that you can use it to place multiple files at once in InDesign and Illustrator. First select the files you'd like to place from inside Bridge, and then choose File > Place > InDesign.

Camera Raw processing   For serious photographers, Camera Raw has become the undisputed file format of choice. Comparable in concept to a digital negative, raw files allow photographers to process images themselves, instead of leaving this critical step to one's camera. If you use Camera Raw or want to learn more about it, pick up a copy of Bruce Fraser and Jeff Schewe's *Real World Camera Raw with Photoshop CS3* (Peachpit Press, 2008).

With Bridge CS3, Camera Raw 4 takes another step forward as a creative digital photo-editing tool. Among many new features is the ability to now process both JPG and TIFF formats via the powerful Camera Raw dialog. If a Camera Raw workflow is for you, I suggest clicking the General preference panel and choosing the Behavior preference (Preferences > General > Behavior) that automatically launches Photo Downloader when a camera is connected. While you're there, I also recommend turning on the other preference that launches Camera Raw inside Bridge when double-clicking an image.

Synchronizing Color Settings I always tell students if you use Bridge for nothing else, at least do yourself a favor and take advantage of its ability to synchronize color settings across the Creative Suite. In Bridge CS3, this feature is accessed in the Advanced panel shown in Figure 1.14. What does this setting mean in the real world? Back in the old days, the same image in Photoshop, Illustrator, InDesign, and Acrobat might not look the same, because each application might be applying different color settings. Even up to Creative Suite 2, synchronizing color in Bridge had no effect on settings in Acrobat. With Creative Suite 3, this problem has been resolved, so enabling color management applies to all applications. To see what color settings are being used by Creative Suite 3, choose Edit > Creative Suite Color Settings.

In the Suite Color Settings dialog (Figure 1.15), you're presented with a short list of possible settings. By checking Show Expanded List of Color Settings Files,

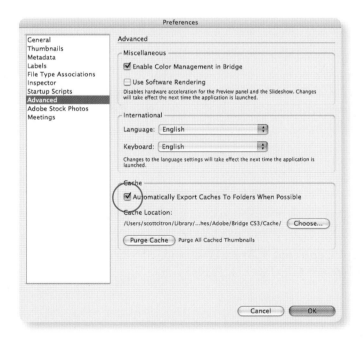

Figure 1.14 In the Advanced panel, select the Enable Color Management in Bridge check box. I also recommend selecting the Auto Export Cache check box (circled).

Figure 1.15 The Suite Color Settings dialog that's accessed by choosing Edit > Creative Suite Color Settings.

we can choose from a list of nineteen settings instead of the default four. If you don't know much about color management (and who among us really does?), stick with the North America General Purpose 2 default setting shown here.

Before leaving the Advanced panel of Preferences, be sure to select Automatically Export Caches to Folders When Possible from the Cache options (circled in Figure 1.14). For those familiar with the Use Distributed Cache feature in the previous version of Bridge, this check box does the same thing. That is, cache files (bits of information such as metadata, labels, and ratings) are saved into the folder being viewed. This means Bridge doesn't have to build these files each time we revisit a particular folder, which ultimately means faster file previews.

Creative Suite 3 Preferences

The last major step before actually starting any project is to make sure to properly set all application preferences for each component you plan to use in Creative Suite. Given that many of the default preferences across Creative Suite are what I would consider less than optimal, I'm forever amazed by the number of designers who never touch their preferences. These are often the same designers who moan and groan that they're not getting the results they expect yet do little to find out why.

The following sections, for the benefit of all who either know nothing about setting Creative Suite 3 preferences or are confused by what to set them to, are an overview of what I consider to be the most mission-critical Creative Suite 3 preference settings. If a particular preference panel is *not* shown, that means I leave it set to its component's default.

Photoshop CS3 Preferences

I use most of Photoshop's default preferences, but for the few I change, refer to Figures 1.16a–c. In Figure 1.16a, you'll do yourself a favor by choosing the Automatically Launch Bridge check box. Also, zooming is easy if you use the scroll wheel of your mouse. What, no scroll wheel? If you're stuck in the past, hanging on to the Zen beauty of Apple's original one-button mouse, it's time to join the 21st century. With scroll support built into all Creative Suite 3 components and other right-clickable context menus sprinkled throughout Mac OS X, you're working too hard with a one-button mouse.

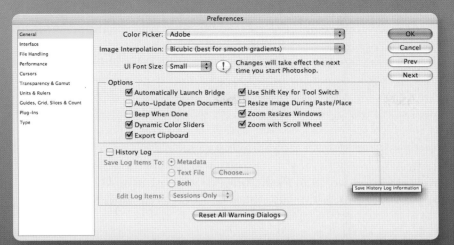

Figure 1.16a I like Automatically Launch Bridge and Zoom with Scroll Wheel. Still using a one-button mouse? What?!

Figure 1.16b I'd rather not be asked every time about file compatibility, so I set Maximize PSD and PSB to Never.

Figure 1.16c If you have another attached drive, then allow Photoshop to use it as a scratch disk.

TIP: If you're a Mac user, I highly recommend Apple's Mighty Mouse. Not only does it feel good in the hand, but the software that comes with it has one important timesaving feature: the ability to set the scroll button to trigger the Mac OS Application Switcher when pressed. Once you've experienced computing where a simple click on the scroll wheel/nub brings up a list of active applications, you'll never again have to visit the Dock to change apps.

In Figure 1.16b, set the Maximize PSD and PSB File Compatibility preference to Never. If you need to make a file that's backward compatible, you can always do it later. Meanwhile, you'll reap the benefit of smaller files by turning this choice off. Figure 1.16c allows you to use your external drive as a scratch disk. This means Photoshop can offload disk-intensive tasks to another drive, which pays off in greater speed. If you don't have an external disk attached, the question is why not? How do you back up every day? If the answer is "I don't," then don't be surprised when something goes wrong with your computer. As the saying goes, it's not a question of *if* your hard drive will fail, but when. Besides, if you're among the very lucky and go through life without hard drive failure, you'll still sleep better knowing that you can always revert to yesterday's work. All thanks to the $150 you spent on another drive.

Illustrator CS3 Preferences

A number of new preferences are now found in Illustrator CS3. One is in the General panel (Figure 1.17a) that, via double clicking, allows editing in Isolation Mode. Isolation Mode is a nifty feature that arrived half-baked in Illustrator CS2, but deserves full attention in Creative Suite 3.

For example, let's say you have an illustration of a bowl of fruit (Figure 1.18). Each fruit is its own group, as is the bowl and shadow. You want to edit only the apple without disturbing the other groups. Previously you'd have to do so with either the Direct Selection or Group Selection tool. Now with Isolation

Figure 1.18 Left: Here the apple group is selected. After double-clicking, the window changes to Isolation Mode. Right: In this mode only the items in the apple group are editable, with all other page items dimmed. After editing, another double click returns you to normal view.

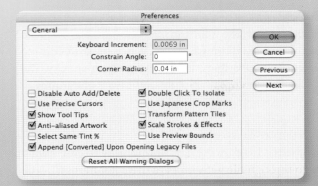

Figure 1.17a The big preferences here are Double Click to Isolate and Scale Stokes & Effects.

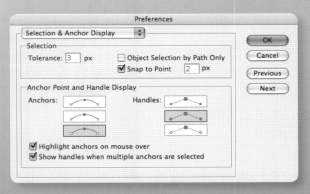

Figure 1.17b Illustrator CS3 finally improved anchor points and handles. Use these preferences to get the most out of these new features.

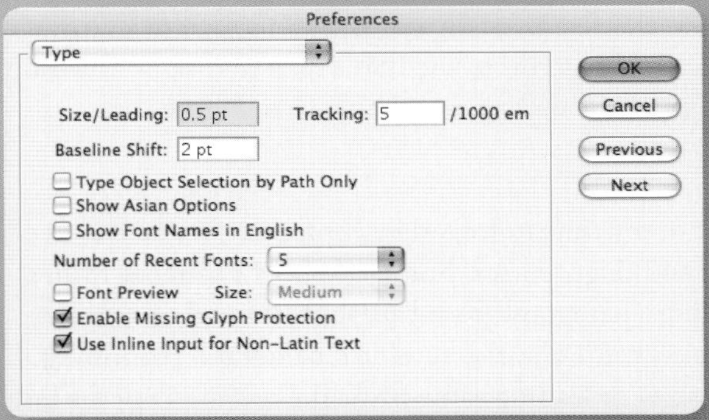

Figure 1.17c I'll talk more about these preferences with InDesign, but for now do yourself a favor and set Size/Leading to .5pt and Tracking (and Kerning, by extension) to 5/1000 em.

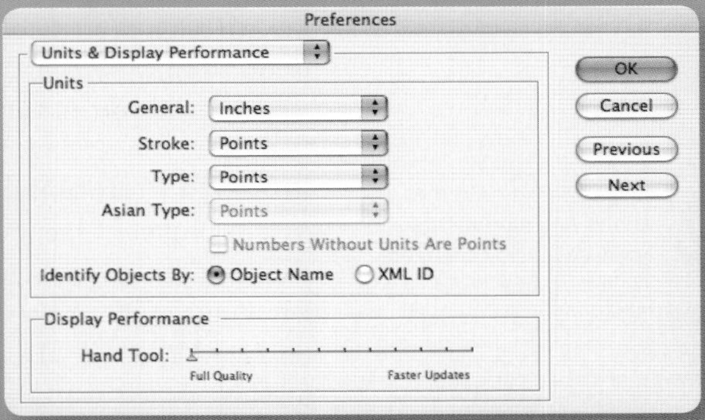

Figure 1.17d Illustrator CS3 uses points as its default measurement unit. I recommend either inches, picas, or millimeters.

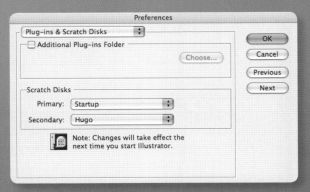

Figure 1.17e Like with Photoshop, if you have another attached drive, always assign it as your scratch disk for better performance.

Mode, you double-click the apple group, and a separate window opens in which only the apple and its grouped objects (the stem and leaf) are editable. To make editing even easier, all other objects are dimmed as well. When finished editing, double-click again to return to the original layout and group hierarchy. The same principle also works for editing compound paths and Live Paint groups. Try it; once you get the hang of this feature, you'll love it.

Another new Illustrator CS3 feature has to do with selecting the handles and anchor points of Illustrator paths. Gone are the days of squinting to grab hold of the little buggers, but only if you set your preferences as in Figure 1.17b.

If you work with type, you'll be much happier by following the preferences in Figure 1.17c, which gives you greater control over type sizing and kerning. For more in-depth information about typography in Illustrator, see the next section on InDesign preferences, since they are basically the same. Finally, just like in Photoshop, if you have an external hard drive, use it as a scratch disk in Illustrator. To make Illustrator recognize the disk, it must be set as in Figure 1.17e.

InDesign Preferences

Maybe because I spend most of my time in InDesign, for me its preferences need the most attention. Starting with Figure 1.19a, I prefer Apply Leading to Entire Paragraphs. This makes leading a paragraph-based attribute instead of a character-based attribute. This means that if one character in a paragraph (including invisibles, such as spaces) has a 13 pt leading value while the rest use 12 pt leading, the entire paragraph will be set at 13 pt. Why is this better? Well, at least all the lines in my paragraph are the same distance apart. This is preferable to having one line farther away from the rest because of the invisible with 13 pts of leading. Another nice by-product of this setting is that I can adjust paragraph leading by inserting my cursor anywhere in my paragraphs and pressing Option+Up Arrow (Mac OS) or Alt+Up Arrow (Windows)—or the reverse, Option+Down Arrow (Mac OS) or Alt+Down Arrow (Windows). Following the default setting in InDesign, the entire paragraph must be highlighted to do the same.

Most North American designers I know younger than 40 use inches for their system of measurement. Although I understand why inches prevail in the United States, they're probably the worst unit of measure you can use. Any other system—picas, points, millimeters, or even agates (new to Creative Suite 3)—has smaller increments than inches. Although InDesign will accept any measurement system or combination of systems, the problem arises when trying to nudge elements such as drop shadows or blurs. Since inches are divided into eighths, each tap of the cursor key moves your shadow or blur 1/16 of an inch at a time (a somewhat chunky amount). Picas, on the other hand,

TIP: Don't forget that units and increments can be quickly changed in InDesign without opening Preferences. To do so, Control-click (Mac OS) or right-click (Windows), and then click your rulers. When the context menu appears, choose the measurement system to which you'd like to switch. New in Creative Suite 3: Command-clicking (Mac OS) or Ctrl-clicking (Windows) the zero point (the intersection of both rulers in the upper left of any window) allows you to change both horizontal and vertical measurement units at the same time.

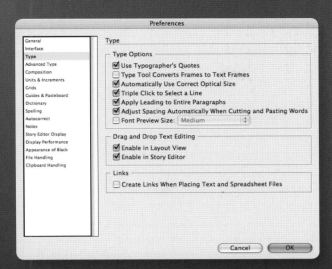

Figure 1.19a I like Apply Leading to Entire Paragraphs and Enable in Layout View (Drag and Drop Text Editing). Font Preview is off.

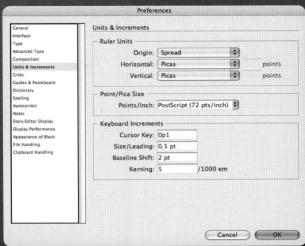

Figure 1.19b I like picas, but most don't. If you must use inches, choose Inches Decimal. Kerning must be 5/1000 for maximum control.

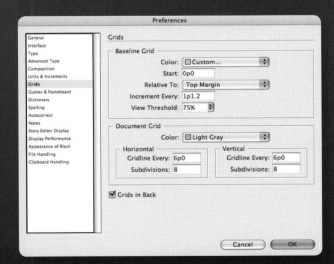

Figure 1.19c I hate seeing grids or guides when designing, so I create custom colors that are very faint.

Figure 1.19d To reduce visual clutter, I change Margin and Column to faint tints of their default pinks and purples. I also like a darker Gray Preview Background setting.

NOTE: Although InDesign can place just about any file format, certain formats are preferable. Fortunately, there are only four, all of which are easy to remember. They are .psd, .pdf, .ai, and .indd. Other formats such as .jpg or .eps lack transparency. The .tif format supports transparency but layer visibility in InDesign can't be controlled. If live transparency support is integral to your creative concept, use the four Adobe native file formats listed whenever possible.

nudge values 1 point at a time, a much smaller and more predictable increment (Figure 1.19b). Regardless of which system you end up using, my advice is to set Size/Leading increments to 0.5 and set Kerning to 5/1000 of an em space. Doing so will give you much appreciated control when changing type size or leading from the keyboard.

In Figures 1.19c and 1.19d I've changed colors for grids and guides to be less intrusive on screen. This change has nothing to do with anything other than my own obsession about lessening visual clutter while I work. If the appearance of grids and guides doesn't bother you when working, then skip to the next preference setting.

The Display Preference settings in InDesign work fine by default, but they also benefit from some tweaking. For those with a speedy machine, changing the Vector Graphics slider (Figure 1.19e) to Higher Quality means all vector-based .ai or .eps files will crisply display in full resolution. Setting Greek Type Below to 0 pt means you'll no longer have to look at gray lines instead of real text when working at lower magnifications.

Figure 1.19f shows two new Creative Suite 3 preferences dealing with snippet import position and how relinked images are displayed. Neither choice will change your life, but both just might make things easier.

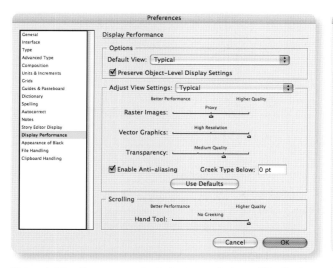

Figure 1.19e If your computer is fast enough, try setting Vector Graphics to Higher Quality. I also change Greek Type Below to 0 pt.

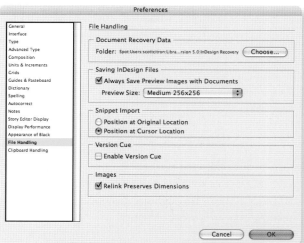

Figure 1.19f The Snippet Import and Images preferences are new in Creative Suite 3. These are my choices.

Acrobat 8 Professional Preferences

Acrobat 8 has many preferences from which to choose. At this point I'm concerned only with those found in the Page Display panel (Figure 1.20). Among the most important here is the choice to turn off local fonts. When left enabled, Acrobat ceases to be a useful preflighting tool, since any missing fonts will be covered by local fonts. If you're interested in seeing any font matching discrepancies for yourself, try toggling this preference on and off. Although your page may not look so nice with local fonts disabled, at least you'll be warned of potential font embedding problems before they occur.

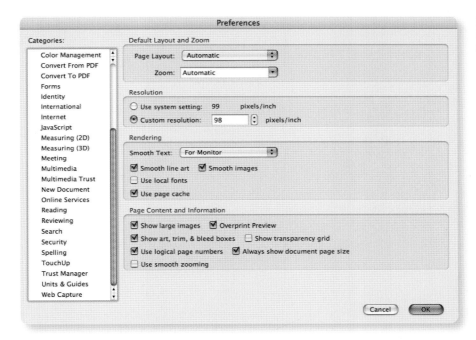

Figure 1.20 Follow these Page Display settings if you use Acrobat as a forensic preflighting tool.

In Conclusion

I realize that this chapter touched on a lot of tough topics, many of which might have sailed over your head. If this is the case, don't despair. I'll revisit many of these concepts throughout this book, so if things seem foggy now, they'll become clearer as you continue.

In the next chapter, you'll dive in to your first full project, an elegant gallery invitation that will begin in Illustrator, move to Photoshop, and then complete its journey in InDesign. Along the way, you'll explore the beauty of fine typography and learn how to use Creative Suite 3 to get the best-looking type possible.

Chapter 2 | Creating Effective Typography

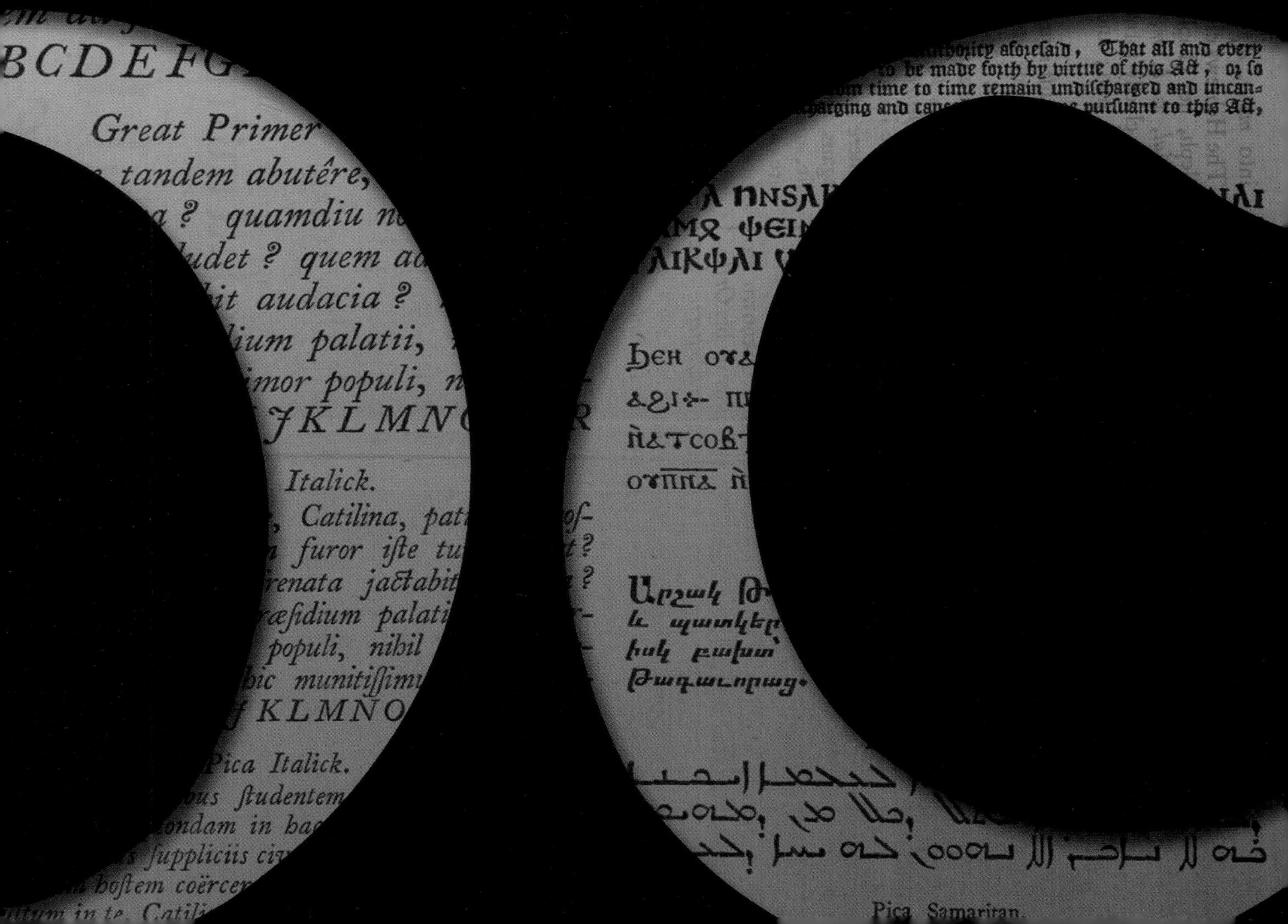

"SIMPLICITY IS NOT THE GOAL. IT IS THE BY-PRODUCT OF A GOOD IDEA AND MODEST EXPECTATIONS." — Paul Rand

These days if you own a computer, you're a typesetter whether you like it or not. Not long ago, if designers needed type for a layout, they marked up copy by hand to indicate typeface, size, leading, kerning, tracking, and length of line, and then they gave the markup to the typesetter. From these specifications, the typesetter took hours or days to produce the type. With luck, the type that came back confirmed that the designer chose the right font, size, leading, and so forth, and showed no mistakes or typos added by the typesetter. The better designers became at specifying, or *specing*, type, the faster the process went. But in the end, they could rest assured that the type always looked its best.

Introduction to Using Type

As a designer who broke his teeth by learning to spec type the hard way, I'm thrilled those days are gone. It's great to be able to shave days off a project by setting my own type. Today, with a small collection of quality fonts, now anyone can set professional-looking type, right? Not necessarily. Creating professional-looking type means adhering to established design principles and knowing how to coax a computer and sophisticated software into producing the best results.

Figure 2.1 The project for this chapter is a three-panel invitation.

In this chapter, you'll try your hand at setting professional-looking type in Adobe InDesign CS3 by creating a simple three-panel invitation for a gallery exhibition. The first half of the chapter is devoted to creating the panel artwork that opens to reveal the type. In the process, you'll also learn how to create patterns and work with color in Adobe Illustrator CS3, and you'll create displacement maps to convincingly bend objects in Adobe Photoshop CS3. Then you'll set the type. Don't be fooled that it's only a dozen lines or so. You're about to see how good design choices have major impact.

 For a look at the invitation, open the file named **NWNY_Invite.indd** in the Chapter 2 folder at www.peachpit.com/prodesignCS3 (Figure 2.1).

Creating the Pattern Art

The first step in designing the invitation is creating the lemon pattern that makes up the outer panels of the invitation. If your artwork balances the typography you use, it will have a greater impact when communicating your ideas.

Here are the first steps to creating the pattern in Illustrator:

1. Start by drawing an oval with the Ellipse tool to get the general shape and fill the oval with yellow (Figure 2.2, left).

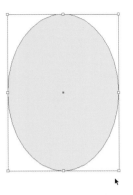
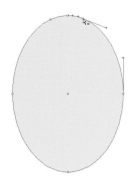

Figure 2.2 (Left) A simple yellow ellipse. (Center) Points are added using the Pen tool. (Right) The Direct Selection tool is used to move the new points.

Figure 2.3 Create an inner pulp for the lemon by dragging inward.

2. Use the Pen tool to add two more anchor points on both ends that will be manipulated to make the ends of the lemon (Figure 2.2, center).

3. Switching to the Direct Selection tool, drag the added points inward, thereby creating the protruding ends. Then drag the side anchors somewhat so that the shape looks less symmetric and more organic (Figure 2.2, right).

4. Copy the lemon (Edit > Copy), and paste the copy in front (Edit > Paste in Front). Switch to the Selection tool. While holding down Shift to constrain the copy's proportions and holding down Option (Mac OS) or Alt (Windows) drag inward. Doing so causes the copy to scale down from the center, giving the effect of the lemon's inner pulp (Figure 2.3).

5. Fill the inner pulp with a different shade of yellow.

The last touch is to add the seeds:

1. Draw the basic shape of a seed with the Ellipse tool and fill with black.

2. Use the Convert Direction Point tool to convert the top rounded end point into a corner point.

3. Finish the job by again relying on the Direct Selection tool to distort the shape just enough to make it look less perfect (Figure 2.4).

4. Place the seed toward the middle of the lemon to prepare for rotating four similar copies.

Because precision is neither important nor desired in this case, I could simply press Option (Mac OS) or Alt (Windows) and drag copies of the seed to a circle manually. Instead, I've chosen to use a handy technique for achieving almost the same effect with much less effort:

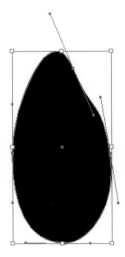

Figure 2.4 Here again points are manipulated with the Direct Selection tool to create a new shape for the lemon's seeds.

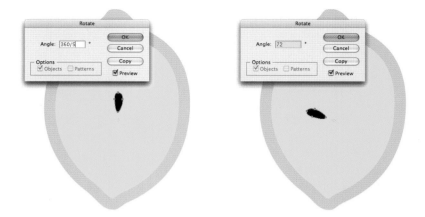

1. Select the seed, and choose the Rotate tool.
2. With the Rotate tool, Option-click (Mac OS) or Alt-click (Windows) below the seed to set the center of your upcoming rotation.
3. In the Rotate dialog, type **360/5** in the Angle field, with 5 representing the number of seeds you'll rotate for your lemon (Figure 2.5).
4. Press Tab to return 72° as the value of your rotation. Because you want to rotate a copy of the seed, not the original, click Copy to exit the dialog.
5. To add more rotated copies of your seed, simply press Command+D (Mac OS) or Ctrl+D (Windows) three more times.
6. To finish this piece of the pattern tile, surround the lemon shape with a solid rectangle, and send it to the back.

The next step is to group the elements so they can be easily assembled into a pattern tile of four mirrored blocks:

Figure 2.6 After copying the block of tiles, use the Reflect tool to rotate the axis vertically.

1. Create a copy of the original grouped tile, and rotate it 180°.
2. Select both groups, then use the Align panel and set Distribute Space to 0. This places the rotated copy precisely next to the original.
3. Group the two blocks together (Object > Group).
4. Select the group and double click the Reflect tool in the tool box to open the Reflect dialog (Figure 2.6). Select Vertical and then click copy to apply the transformation and create two flipped clones.
5. In the Align panel, again set Distribute Space to 0 to ensure that all four tiles touch perfectly at their sides.
6. Using the Direct Selection tool, select the opposing tiles, and then recolor them so that the overall pattern tile looks like that in Figure 2.7.

To complete the pattern, select all four tile groups, and drag them into the Swatches panel.

Editing Your Pattern

Now that you've finished your pattern, how does it look? With the Rectangle tool, draw a large rectangle that fills the page. With the rectangle still selected, click the pattern swatch in the Swatches panel to fill the rectangle with the new pattern. Are the pattern tiles too big or too small? What about the colors you chose? Assuming you'd like to experiment a bit with the pattern before going to the next step in this project, Illustrator has some convenient tools for modifying existing patterns.

For the curtain artwork, you can opt (or not) to scale down your pattern tiles; it's easy enough to do. Simply select the pattern, and double-click the Scale tool in the Tools panel. In the Scale Options dialog, select Patterns and deselect Objects. Select the Preview box to see the pattern scale dynamically according to the value entered in the Scale field of the Uniform area of the dialog.

Here's another, perhaps more intuitive, method to scale patterns without opening the Scale dialog. Select the pattern, and then choose the Scale tool in the Tools panel. Press and hold the Shift key to constrain the pattern's proportions, and then drag in or out from the object's center along a 45° angle while also holding down the tilde key (~). When you release the mouse button, the pattern, not the object containing the pattern, updates automatically. This technique is also useful for rotating patterns and can be done exactly the same way when using the Rotate tool.

Recoloring Your Pattern with Live Color

Before Illustrator CS3, recoloring a pattern was a many-step process that involved editing the original pattern tile and then creating and applying the new tile. With the release of Creative Suite 3, Adobe has provided designers with an amazing and powerful new feature for achieving color bliss: Live Color. By using Live Color, designers can easily remap a pattern's existing group of colors to other hues, without losing the relationship of the original colors. Relationship, you wonder? Yes. Look at any color wheel. On one side is red. On the opposite side is green. Those colors have what is known as a *complementary* relationship (Figure 2.8a). Yellow and blue form another complementary relationship. Colors that are close together in a particular area of the wheel have an *analogous* relationship (Figure 2.8b). There are many other kinds of color relationships, or *harmonies*, and Live Color is a great tool for experimenting with color in Illustrator. For now, though, you'll use Live Color to play with the colors of your pattern.

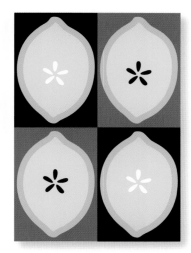

Figure 2.7 Here is the completed pattern tile, which you can then drag and drop on the Swatches palette.

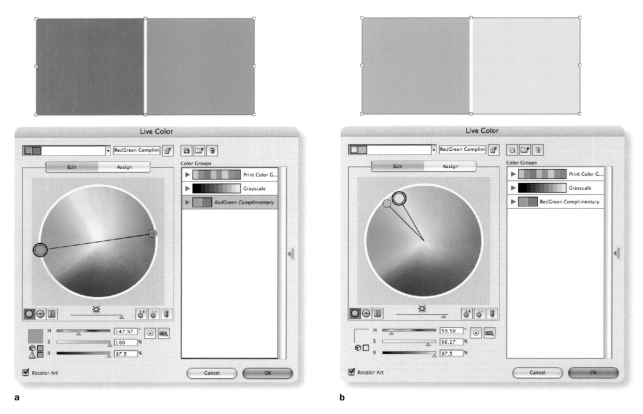

Figure 2.8 (a) Complementary colors are shown here as red and green. (b) Yellow and green have an analogous relationship.

Figure 2.9 Click the Recolor button in Illustrator's Control panel.

1. Select the patterned rectangle, and choose the Recolor button in the Control panel (Figure 2.9) to open the Live Color dialog.
2. In the Live Color dialog, choose Edit.
3. In the Edit window, select the Link Harmony button to maintain the relationship between current colors.
4. Click the Harmony Rules pop-up menu to experiment with a different color relationship (such as Analogous).
5. To keep the existing color relationship but remap those colors to new values, simply drag any of the color paddles around on the wheel. Dragging the paddles toward the center decreases color saturation; dragging the paddles out from the center increases color saturation (Figure 2.10).
6. When you've finished experimenting, click OK to accept your changes, or click Cancel to exit with no change.
7. Save and close your document.

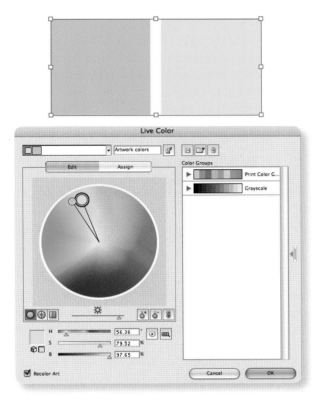

NOTE: For an alternative to Live Color in Illustrator, I highly recommend taking a look at the Phantasm plug-in from Astute Graphics (www.phantasmcs.com). For less than $40, Phantasm CS gives users Photoshop-like control (options for level, curves, hue, and saturation, and so on) over images in Illustrator CS2 and CS3. Because the plug-in runs as an effect and not a filter, all changes are nondestructive and can be edited by double-clicking the effect name in the Illustrator Appearance panel.

Figure 2.10 Dragging the color paddles changes your color saturation.

Adding Dimension and Lighting in Photoshop

The pattern we've just created is attractive enough, but it's flat. Unless you're comfortable using a dedicated 3D program, adding realistic lighting and texture can be a challenge. Although you might try by using the Warp feature in Photoshop (Edit > Transform > Warp), you'll quickly see that using this feature isn't nearly as effective as employing a displacement map, which is what you're about to learn. You'll also learn how to leverage two new features in Photoshop CS3 that allow making changes to the curtain that uses the pattern you created in the previous section, even after you've saved and closed your file.

Working Smart with Smart Objects

Years ago, Adobe GoLive (then the Adobe flagship web-authoring tool) introduced a new feature called Smart Objects. It worked like this: from inside GoLive, a designer would place native Photoshop, Illustrator, or Acrobat files.

Doing so would trigger a new window to open where the file would be optimized and saved for the Web and then placed on the GoLive page. In the event that the designer later wanted to alter the file in some way, a simple double click opened the original source document. Back in the original, changes would be made (to the scale, rotation, color, and so on), and the file would be resaved. Finally, those parent changes would then be reflected in GoLive via the linked Smart Object. Neat!

Today, Smart Objects have found their way into Illustrator and Photoshop. In the latter they can be created in several ways: by using the File > Open As Smart Object command, by using the Edit > Paste command to place a file, or by converting a layer to a Smart Object (Layer > Smart Objects > Convert to Smart Object). In this project, you'll open your Illustrator pattern file in Photoshop as a Smart Object.

To get a handle on Smart Objects, it's helpful to think of a Smart Object as not the placed art itself but more like a placeholder or proxy of the original art. This means that each time you transform the art by scaling or rotating, for example, Photoshop points to the original for fresh information instead of working on art that has already been rasterized into pixels. Doing so means that image degradation, which usually results from multiple transformations, doesn't occur. Transformations such as this are considered nondestructive and are always preferable to destructive editing. It might also be helpful to understand that once an object has been rasterized, there exists no way to *unrasterize* the object. Yet with a Smart Object, designers can simply point to the original file to try different effects or transformations.

Once the conversion to a Smart Object is complete, a layer's status as a Smart Object is indicated by the small layer icon shown in Figure 2.11. In Photoshop, open the pattern you made for the curtains and then follow these steps:

1. Start by double-clicking the layer and renaming it *curtain*.
2. Add a new layer above the curtain Smart Object layer.
3. On this new layer, drag out several vertical rules that will act as guides for the thick, black lines you'll paint.
4. Selecting the Airbrush tool, set its diameter to about 400 pixels, and set the flow to 50%. Remember to click once above the actual image and then Shift-click again below the image to draw straight vertical lines from edge to edge (Figure 2.12).
5. Once the lines are drawn, choose Edit > Select All, and then choose Edit > Copy to copy this layer to the clipboard.

Figure 2.11 The small icon in the lower-right corner of the layer icon indicates that this icon is a Smart Object.

Creating and Applying the Displacement Map

The first time I heard the term *displacement map,* I ran for cover. Fortunately, somewhere down the road I learned about displacement maps from the incomparable Bert Monroy and have never been the same. In theory, a displacement map is a file whose pixel brightness or darkness at any position is used to shift or displace existing pixels of another file. The actual process is handled via the Displace filter in Photoshop. The amount of displacement can vary from 0 (the maximum negative shift) to 255 (the maximum positive shift). A value of 128 produces no shift.

Here are the steps to creating the displacement map:

1. In Photoshop, choose File> New. In the New dialog, choose Preset > Clipboard. This creates a new, blank document the same size as the layer just copied.
2. Choose Edit > Paste. Then save your document in the Photoshop native format, and name it **curtain_map.psd**.
3. Back in the curtain document, in the Layers palette click the visibility icon to hide the layer with the black lines, and then click the curtain layer.

4. Choose Filter > Distort > Displace. Depending on the size and resolution of your curtain artwork, the default scaling settings of 10 pixels horizontal and 10 pixels vertical may create enough distortion for your taste. For now, click OK to accept the defaults.

5. Once the distortion has been applied, in the Layers palette click the painted lines layer to make it visible. The black airbrushed stripes should line up with your displaced layer underneath, helping to sell the undulating curtain effect (Figure 2.13). Change the blending mode from Normal to Multiply, and try adjusting the layer's opacity if the stripes are too dark. Feel free to use the Gaussian Blur filter to soften the stripes if they feel too heavy.

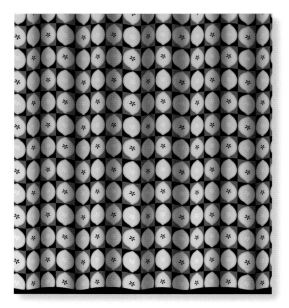

Figure 2.14 New in Photoshop CS3 are Smart Filters and the ability to change blending modes for those filters.

Figure 2.13 With a few tricks in Photoshop, you can create realistic-looking curtains like these.

If, on the other hand, the distortion itself is too subtle, you're in luck. Now thanks to Smart Filters, the fix is easy. Just like Smart Objects, Smart Filters maintain a link to the original source file so that any filter can be reapplied or deleted at any time throughout the design process. This is huge! Better still, when Smart Filters are created, they include not only an empty layer mask but the ability to apply a separate blending mode and opacity level for all effects. This added functionality means that if you want the Smart Filter to affect only part of a layer, you can hide the part you want to protect by painting on the layer mask. Try adding a black-to-white gradient to the empty layer mask to see what I mean. Once you've finished experimenting with the layer mask, double-click the Displace filter options icon, and play with the different blending modes (Figure 2.14). Then choose File > Save, and save the curtain as **stage_curtain.psd**.

Creating the Stage Background and Lighting Effect

Before you leave Photoshop, you need to create the inside middle panel for the invitation. This panel is designed to look as if five spotlights were shining down on the actual invitation itself, which will be assembled in InDesign. To build this element, follow these steps:

1. In Photoshop, choose File > New, and create an RGB document that's 6.25 inches wide by 4.25 inches high at a resolution of 300 pixels per inch. The dimensions represent the center panel of the invitation, plus an .125-inch bleed on all four sides.
2. Fill the background layer with the color you'd like for the center panel (here a pale tan).
3. Convert the layer for Smart Filters by choosing Filter > Convert for Smart Filters.
4. Choose Filter > Render > Lighting Effects. In the Lighting Effects dialog, choose Five Lights Down from the Style pop-up menu. Move the five individual lights by dragging the white target dots to the top, and space them as best you can by eye (Figure 2.15). Click OK to close the dialog and apply the effect.

 NOTE: Most times when creating original art, you'll want to start with an RGB document rather than a CMYK document. This is because many of the Photoshop filters are not supported in CMYK. An example is the Render Lighting Effects filter that's used in this part of the project.

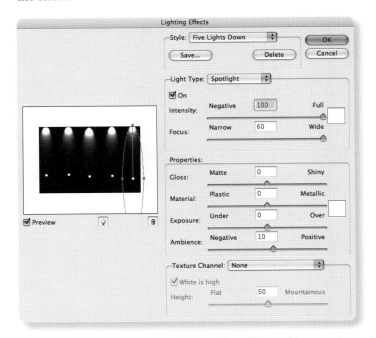

Figure 2.15 Photoshop's Lighting Effects filter offers a wide array of presets for producing convincing lighting effects.

At this point your page should be light gray with areas of white that indicate the lights. If you decide you want to alter anything about your lights, just double-click the Lighting Effects icon in the Layers palette to display the Lighting Effects dialog again. To move a light, drag the white target dot, not the light itself.

Next you'll add two layer styles to the same layer:

1. In the Layers palette, double-click the right side of Layer 0 to display the Layer Styles dialog.
2. In the styles list in the left column, select the Color Overlay check box. Instantly the page will be flooded with red, but not to worry.
3. Click the small color swatch to the right of the Blend Mode pop-up menu to open the Photoshop color picker. Choose the color you'd like for the background of the invitation panel (Figure 2.16). Click OK to apply the color you chose. At this point, your lighting effect will seem to disappear.
4. To show the lighting effect, change the blend mode of the color overlay from Normal to Screen. Also try playing with the opacity of the color.
5. Before exiting the Color Overlay area of the dialog, try also experimenting with the Pattern Overlay features. Adding a pattern here gives the pages a little more "tooth" or texture. Set the Pattern blending mode to Screen so

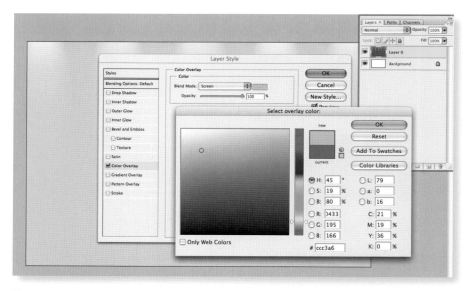

Figure 2.16 Choose a color from the color picker. You can also play with opacity and the blend mode in the Layer Style dialog.

the lights remain visible, and feel free to experiment again with the Scale and Opacity sliders before clicking OK.

6. When you're satisfied with the effect, save the layered file as **invite_bg.psd**, and exit Photoshop.

Putting It Together in InDesign

Now that you have all the elements for this project, let's head over to InDesign where you'll create the layout, set the type, and composite the final invitation.

Setting Up the InDesign Mechanical

In graphic design, the word *mechanical* refers to the actual layout that goes to the printer. A mechanical can be either a physical object with type and images attached or, more often today, a digital file made up of similar elements. Today, InDesign is the leading page layout tool for creating digital mechanicals.

You'll begin by setting the dimensions of the layout and then create guides to indicate the folding panels:

1. Choose File > New > Document. The unfolded trim size is 12 inches wide by 4 inches high. Since you need a front and a back, type **2** for Number of Pages. Margins are set to 0 all around with a bleed of 0.125 inches on all sides. You need to add fold marks, so add a top and bottom slug value of 1 inch for this purpose. Finally, deselect Facing Pages, and then click OK (Figure 2.17).

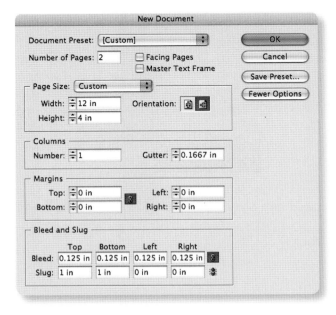

Figure 2.17 A 1-inch slug is added on top and bottom to allow room for fold marks.

2. You'll need guides on both pages, so double-click the A-Master page, where you'll apply your guides.

   Although each outside panel is 3 inches wide, making them that wide may cause the panels to touch and prevent the invitation from closing. To allow the panels to close, you'll make each panel slightly less than 3 inches wide.

3. Drag a vertical ruler guide from outside the page area to 2.9375 inches. Dragging from outside the page area makes the guide span both the page and the pasteboard.

4. Drag another guide that snaps to the right side of the page at 12 inches. Make sure the guide at 12 inches is still selected, and then place your insertion point in the X Location field directly after *in*. Type **–2.9375**, and press Return or Enter (Figure 2.18). This action will relocate your guide now at 9.0625 inches.

   Because these guides indicate folds, now is a good time to draw your fold marks.

5. Using the Line tool (\) and following the ruler guides, Shift-click to drag a 90° line from just inside the bleed area to just beyond the slug area. Typically folds are indicated with dashed lines, so in the Stroke panel, choose Dashed Line from the Type menu. If the default 12-pt dash is too long, change the length to 3 pts in the far-left field at the bottom of the panel (Figure 2.19).

Figure 2.18 Relocate your guide by changing the numerical value in the X Location field.

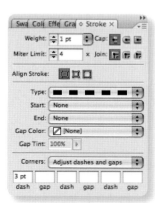

Figure 2.19 You can easily change the length of a dash.

6. Duplicate this line with the Selection tool by holding down Shift+Option (Mac OS) or Shift+Alt (Windows) and dragging the line into place so it snaps to the other guide at 9.0625 inches. With two top fold lines now in place, select both and duplicate once again by dragging copies to the bottom of the page (Figure 2.20).

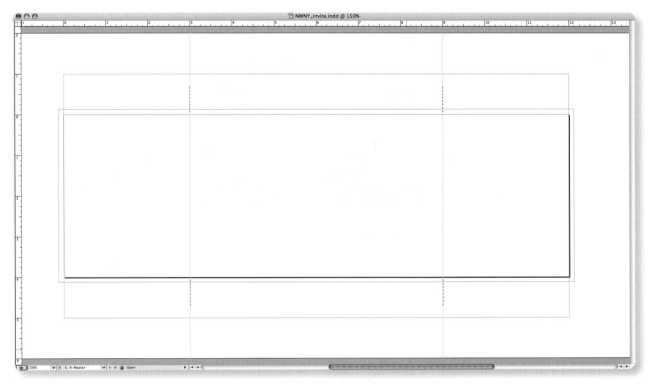

Figure 2.20 Master pages are used to place all marks or artwork that repeats within the document. Here, I've placed ruler guides and dashed marks within the prescribed slug area to indicate where the panels fold.

Placing Your Artwork

Now you're ready to begin building the actual layout, starting with the outside panels:

1. In the Pages panel, double-click document page 1 to select it. Notice how the fold marks you created on the A-Master page are locked by default on the document page. This behavior prevents you from accidentally moving master elements.

   Page 1 represents the outside of the invitation, so you'll begin here by placing the curtain artwork for the side panels.

2. Choose File > Place, and navigate to the file named **stage_curtain.psd**. Resize and rescale as needed until the curtain looks like it does in Figure 2.20.

3. When you're satisfied, Option-drag (Mac OS) or Alt-drag (Windows) a copy of the curtain to the opposite side of the stage until it snaps into the far-right panel. With the center point of the frame selected in the Transform proxy in the Control panel (Figure 2.21), apply the Flip Horizontal command to create a mirrored curtain.

Figure 2.21 The Transform proxy represents the nine anchor points on all bounding boxes. By clicking a point (the center, in this case), you tell InDesign where the center is for any transformation (scale, flip, flop, rotate, and so on).

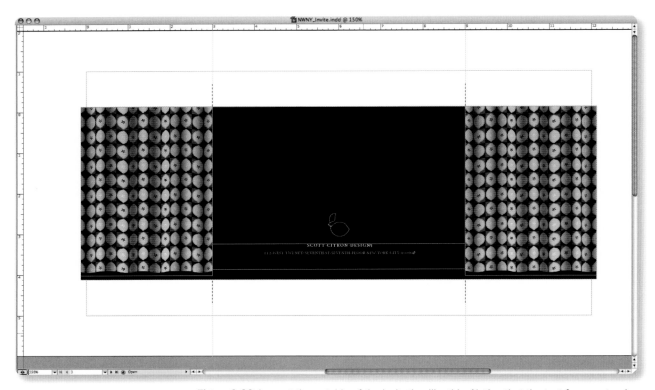

Figure 2.22 Lay out the outside of the invitation like this. Notice that the text frame extends to both edges of the middle panel, insuring that the text is centered, even though the text does not.

Black vs. Rich Black

The remaining outside center panel is filled with only black. Here I want the black to look deep and rich. To achieve this effect, I create a *rich* black, that is, a black that incorporates percentages of all four process colors instead of using only black ink. Don't expect to see a difference on the screen when using rich black. In print, though, the payoff will be pronounced. Compared to 100 percent or plain black, rich black is truly rich and luxurious, like some dark, Arthurian pond. But care must be taken when using it, because the precise registration of its four component colors becomes critical.

To create a rich black swatch, in the Swatches panel, choose New Color Swatch from the panel menu. Deselect the Name With Color Value check box, and name your swatch Rich Black. Although the formula for Rich Black varies depending on whom you ask, a safe bet is to set the CMYK sliders to 60/40/40/100. Add the logo, company name, and address, as shown in Figure 2.22. This completes the layout for the outside of the invitation.

Laying Out the Inside Panels

Whereas the outside panels were relatively type-free, the inside is where it all counts. Place the art for the two inside side panels exactly as you did for the outside. Once that task is completed, it's time to turn your attention to the important center panel, the guts of the invite.

Start by placing the file called **invite_bg.psd**:

1. To help organize your content, create a new layer for any type elements by choosing New Layer from the Layers panel menu and naming it Text.
2. Select the Text layer. Now either type your copy—typically, you'd either type this short copy or paste it from the body of an email—or place the text provided (**02_invite-text.txt** in the Chapter 2 project folder).
3. If you decide to place the text instead of type it, choose File > Place, and navigate to the **02_invite-text.txt** file. Select the file, and click Open to return to the InDesign document with your now-loaded text icon. Drag from the left edge of the center panel across and down to the right edge. Your pointer should snap to the ruler guides that you drew for the fold marks, creating a single text frame and placing your text inside (Figure 2.23).

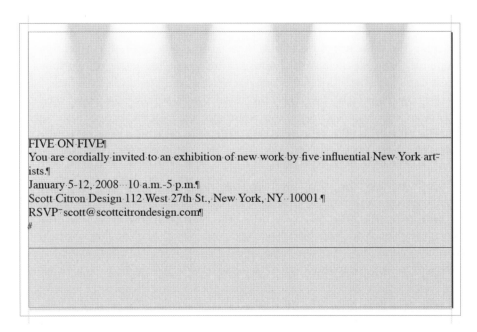

Figure 2.23 Raw text often looks like this example (or worse). If you look closely, you should spot multiple spaces, hyphens for en dashes, and unnecessary punctuation.

Even though your text won't span the entire width of the panel when it's anchored to the ruler guide, don't assume the frame should be narrower. This is a common mistake made by legions of designers who were never taught any better. When text frames float without being anchored to a guide or an edge, designers expose themselves to two possible problems: either text must then be aligned visually (not a good idea) or more guides must be drawn to help align text (again, not a good idea). Anchoring text frames on both edges simplifies the job of aligning text to your page or area. To center text, all you need do is click the Align Center button in the Paragraph panel or press Shift+Command+C (Mac) or Shift+Ctrl+C (Windows).

Further, when a text frame is anchored, it reduces the chances of the frame moving by accident. If the frame *does* move, the designer also has a better chance of noticing the shift because the frame will no longer snap to the guides. Keep in mind that good design relies on precision and repeatability, even if the design itself looks random and appears to lack formal structure.

Formatting Your Text

Now the fun begins. Formatting text is the process of choosing a typeface or typefaces and applying attributes such as size, leading, alignment, kerning, and tracking. For those not familiar with these terms, *size* refers to the size of type in points. Typically there are 72 points per inch, provided you're talking about more common PostScript inches and not the less common traditional inch (72.27 points per inch). *Leading* is the distance between the baselines of type measured in points. *Kerning* is the amount of space in points between pairs of letters or glyphs, and *tracking* is the space in points between a range of letters or glyphs.

When discussing type, it's clearly helpful to understand the nomenclature used to describe the various parts of a letter. To this end, see Figure 2.24, which highlights those parts.

Just like people, dogs, and handwriting, type has personality. Choosing the right typeface is thus about matching the personality of a font with its use. In some ways, this process is easy. If I'm sending out a death announcement, I probably should steer clear of using a font that's too fun and frothy. Likewise, if I'm inviting friends to a Fourth of July backyard barbecue, a fancy wedding script would not be my first choice.

Figure 2.24 This figure should help clarify many of the terms commonly used to describe letter forms.

Yet somewhere in the middle of these two extremes lies the bulk of the typesetting you will do. Most type you'll set will be for things such as a business letter, an advertisement, a newsletter, or an annual report. So, where do we begin?

Choosing the Right Typeface

As with cooking, starting with the best ingredients improves your likelihood of producing a good meal. Designing with type is much the same concept. If you choose typefaces that are proven classics, you'll decrease the possibility of setting a bad-looking page. Notice I said *decrease*, not eliminate. Just as you can shop at the specialty grocery store and buy only the most expensive ingredients, that alone won't prevent you from baking a lousy cake. But it can't hurt either.

Major Type Classifications

When talking about type, it helps to understand the major classifications beyond just serif, san serif, and script. Without getting too technical here, most experts tend to classify type into seven major groups: roman, italic, san serif, slab serif, blackletter, script, and display.

Roman faces are usually subdivided into more specific categories according to historical traits like serif style and stress emphasis, roughly broken down in Table 2.1.

Table 2.1 Roman Type Styles

ROMAN SUBCATEGORY	REPRESENTATIVE FACE	CHARACTERISTICS
Humanist	Arno Pro, Stemple Schneidler, Centaur, Italia, ITC Berkeley	Strong, bracketed serifs; wide and heavy color; bar in lower case *e* slants up
Garalde (Old Style)	Garamond, Goudy Old Style, Bembo, Plantin	Rounded serifs with moderate stroke contrast, stress angle less pronounced than Humanist style
Transitional	Times New Roman, Lucida, Baskerville	Curved letters more balanced than Garalde; stress angle nearly vertical
Didone (Modern)	Bodoni, Walbaum, Americana, Didot	Strong vertical emphasis and contrast; thin, straight serifs

HUMANIST
(Centaur)

GARALDE
(Bembo)

TRANSITIONAL
(Baskerville)

DIDONE (MODERN)
(Didot)

When speaking of type, the word *roman* is also used to describe characters that stand upright, the opposite of italic. Table 2.2 shows other examples of major type classifications.

Table 2.2 Major Type Classifications

Th	Th	**Th**
ITALIC *(Bookman)*	SAN SERIF *(Helvetica)*	SLAB SERIF *(Clarendon Bold)*
𝔗𝔥	*Th*	T H
BLACKLETTER *(Fette Fraktur)*	SCRIPT *(Bickham Script)*	DISPLAY *(Mythos)*

Choosing Compatible Type

Now that you know a little bit about type, how do you go about using it? Better yet, how do you know what goes with what?

All in the Family

Like I always say, when in doubt, keep it simple. The same goes for type. Begin by choosing a typeface that has been tested over time: Garamond, Jenson, Caslon, Bodoni, and Centaur are good places to start. Using any of these classic fonts is a mark of good type breeding and will rarely identify you as a type newbie. Of course, before using any of these fonts, you have to ask yourself, "What am I trying to say, and does this face convey it?" Usually the answers will be obvious. In the middle of August, do you wear a down parka or shorts and a T-shirt? Choosing the right font is the same idea. Also, just because you have 17,000 fonts on your computer doesn't mean you have to use them all, does it? That's like the fledging painter who is suddenly handed an enormous box of paints. Sure, it's tempting to use every cool font you have, but unless you're a genius, do yourself a favor and keep it simple.

The simplest tack to typesetting is to stay within a particular type family. Take Minion Pro, for example. The complete family of Minion Pro offers more than 60 styles, everything from Condensed to Bold Italic Subhead. The Adobe Kepler typeface encompasses more than 70 type styles. Still too many choices? How about Garamond? Depending on which Garamond you choose, you're guaranteed at least four styles (regular, italic, bold, and bold italic), which, for most jobs, should be more than enough.

As your command of typography improves, you may want to spread your wings and try new typefaces for fun. I encourage you to experiment freely, because doing so costs nothing other than time and the price of the fonts. Eventually if you decide to settle down with a handful of friendly fonts, don't despair. There's nothing wrong with returning to the same typefaces again and again.

Mixing Serifs with San Serifs

One of the safest gambits when mixing fonts is to choose faces that are as different as possible. Garamond Premier Pro (serif) looks great when paired with ITC Franklin Gothic Std (san serif). The page you're reading is a testament to this winning combo. What makes it work is the contrast between the classic elegance of Garamond Premier Pro Regular and the sturdy reliability of ITC Franklin Gothic Std Demi.

Sometimes combining contrasting fonts does not work, however. In this sentence, note how I've set the words Franklin Gothic in Franklin Gothic. The problem is related to the x-height of the two faces. Notice how Franklin Gothic has an x-height that's about 70 percent of the cap height (see Figure 2.24 for more on x-height and cap height). The x-height of Garamond, on the other hand, is perhaps 60 percent its cap height. This isn't a problem when Franklin Gothic is used as a separate subhead, as I've done in this book. But when a word is formatted with Franklin Gothic inside a paragraph that uses all Garamond, the x-height discrepancy sticks out (Figure 2.25).

Figure 2.25 Like most Humanist typefaces, Garamond Premiere Pro (left) has a small x-height. Note the difference with that of ITC Franklin Gothic (right), which, even at the same point size, has a much larger x-height.

The other problem that occurs when mixing a san serif font inline with a serif font is how the san serif appears to float above the baseline when compared to the well-grounded serif. This is because san serifs terminate with nice, clean straight bottoms, whereas serifs sit on bracketed feet. In the case of Garamond Premier Pro, notice how the brackets are arched slightly, too, giving the font a balance and needed stability. Compare this feature with a more modern serif font like Bodoni, whose serif is straight, not arched (Figure 2.26).

Figure 2.26 Garamond Premier Pro (left pair) and Bodoni (right pair). Note how the Bodoni characters feel lighter than the Garamond. This quality is due more to the shape of bottom serifs than the actual thickness of the letter forms.

Once again, when the two faces are placed next to each other, the Bodoni appears to float above the Garamond, making this pair incompatible in the same line. (Frankly I'd say these two are generally incompatible just because they're too much alike, despite their differences.)

Type and Color

When type nuts talk about color, chances are they're not discussing the merits of black or blue ink, but rather *typographic color*. Try looking at a page of type while squinting. Does the type look smooth overall, does it spread evenly across the page, or do you see holes of white or clumps of black? If so, your type lacks consistent color, a clear sign of poor typesetting.

In Figure 2.27, I've set two columns of text from the first chapter of *The War of the Worlds* by H.G. Wells. The typeface is Arno Pro, a new OpenType font (designed by Robert Slimbach of Adobe) that's installed by default with Creative Suite 3. Notice how the column on the left shows even, consistent color, making the text easy on the eyes and soothing to read. In the column on the right, just for comparison's sake, I've peppered the same paragraph with Century Gothic, a wide san serif with a large x-height. Even though both fonts are the same size (9.5 pt), notice how the color of the right column is uneven, making the text hard to read.

The surest way to advertise one's lack of typographic skill is to either combine type that's not compatible or use too many typefaces. Remember, unless there's a good reason to switch fonts, stay within one or two families for the best results. Like most things in design, when in doubt, keep it simple.

Figure 2.27 Watch for speed bumps? Although this example is oversimplified, it does make the point about the importance of type color and consistency.

No one would have believed in the last years of the nineteenth century that this world was being watched keenly and closely by intelligences greater than man's and yet as mortal as his own; that as men busied themselves about their various concerns they were scrutinised and studied, perhaps almost as narrowly as a man with a microscope might scrutinise the transient creatures that swarm and multiply in a drop of water. With infinite complacency men went to and fro over this globe about their little affairs, serene in their assurance of their empire over matter. It is possible that the infusoria under the microscope do the same.

No one would have believed in the last years of the nineteenth century that this world was being watched keenly and closely by intelligences greater than man's and yet as mortal as his own; that as men busied themselves about their various concerns they were scrutinised and studied, perhaps almost as narrowly as a man with a microscope might scrutinise the transient creatures that swarm and multiply in a drop of water. With infinite complacency men went to and fro over this globe about their little affairs, serene in their assurance of their empire over matter. It is possible that the infusoria under the microscope do the same.

Monospaced vs. Proportional Type   Other factors affect type color. In the days before digital typography, characters typed on a typewriter typically took up an equal amount of space when placed on the page. This means that even though the letter *i* is narrower than the letter *w*, the space for each character was the same. As a result, consistent type color was impossible to maintain throughout a document because the *i* had more space on either side (or *sidebearing*) than the *w*. Type whose characters occupy equal spacing is known as *monospaced*. Examples of monospaced fonts are Courier, Letter Gothic, and Andale, all of which are still used today (Figure 2.28).

Figure 2.28 Use monospaced font examples such as these when equal spacing between characters is important.

```
Courier: The quick brown fox jumped over the lazy dog.
Letter Gothic: The quick brown fox jumped over the lazy dog.
Andale: The quick brown fox jumped over the lazy dog.
```

With the advent of computer-based typesetting, type foundries developed fonts with differing amounts of space on either side, called *proportional* fonts. No longer would the letter *i* use the same value as the letter *w*. An important feature of proportional type is kerning tables, which are numerical values that assign a distance from each other to pairs of letters. These parameters, or *metrics*, instruct the letter *i* how to behave when placed next to the letter *w*, for example. With proportional fonts typesetting took a significant leap forward.

Preparing Text for Formatting

I often receive text in the body of an email, as is the case here. When placing small amounts of text like this, the easiest method of import into InDesign is copy and paste (Figure 2.29).

FIVE·ON·FIVE¶
¶
    »   You·are·cordially·invited·to·an·exhibition·of·new·work·by·5·influ⁼
ential·New·York·artists.·Saturday,·January·12-17,·2008.·¶
¶
Scott·Citron·Design·¶
112·West·27th·St.,·New·York,·NY··10001·¶
RSVP:·scott@scottcitrondesign.com⁂

Figure 2.29 Look familiar? God bless writers. Where would we be without them? Now if they could only learn that "formatting" their copy with extra returns, tabs, and spaces only makes extra work for designers.

Copy like this is usually either unformatted or (most of the time) badly formatted. To see what's going on with your text "under the hood," it's essential that you turn on the visibility of all hidden characters. In InDesign, you can find this feature under Type > Show Hidden Characters. Make sure you're not in Preview mode when working with type (View > Screen Mode); otherwise, your hidden characters will remain hidden. With hidden characters turned on, it's easy to spot the things writers use to "help" designers, such as tabs, multiple returns, double dashes, and extra spaces that eventually must be removed (Figure 2.30). Go ahead and zap these typographic gremlins with your Delete or Backspace key before continuing.

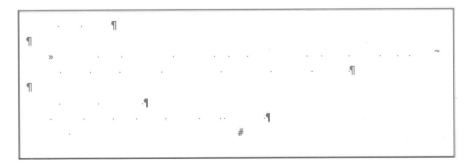

Figure 2.30 Many of the characters need to be deleted before you can work with the text.

Also avoid hyphenation in elements such as invitations or headlines. For cleaning text that's more than a few sentences, use the powerful InDesign Find/Change feature (Edit > Find/Change) to make short work of this task. The Creative Suite 3 release included a major overhaul of Find/Change, and now even the prickliest job can be handled without breaking a sweat.

In the case of this short invitation, manually cleaning the text will take only a minute. Often out of respect for the copywriter (or because they just don't know any better), inexperienced designers will neglect to remove things like a period after an abbreviation like "St." or a comma between "New York, NY." If you fall into this camp, understand that designing with type is not the same as typing a letter. Whereas rules of style exist for good reason when writing a report, those same rules are often ignored when type is set for an ad or invitation.

Organizing Typographic Content

Among the principles of design covered in Chapter 1, "Getting Started," is the importance of unity. The law of unity says that like objects attract and unlike objects repel. The same holds true with type. This principle is also known as *proximity*. As designers, it's our job to take raw text and give it shape so that like information goes together, regardless of whether it was provided that way.

Let's analyze the copy for our invitation. Looking it over I see that the text consists of four main components: the name of the event, the description of the event, the time and location of the event, and response information for the event. Breaking down the copy like this now makes my job of formatting the text much easier. It gives me a kind of structure I'll use to create that all-important concept I recite over and over throughout this book: *hierarchy*.

Establishing Typographic Hierarchy

Imagine trying to navigate in a foreign country with a road map where every city, big or small, is listed in 8-pt Times Regular. And all superhighways are indicated with the same 1-pt black rule as the tiniest country road. Get the picture? If so, then you understand the importance of design hierarchy.

Likewise, type can also convey hierarchy. Typically large, black type has the most importance on a page, and small, white type has the least. Of course, with every rule there are exceptions, and it's no secret that a whisper can often silence a room faster than a yell. Once again, when setting type, having a clear grasp on the message goes a long way toward informing designers' choices.

Final Formatting and Adjustments

For the invitation shown in Figure 2.31, I've elected to use Arno Pro, a new OpenType font that comes preinstalled by default with Creative Suite 3. Arno Pro comes with special characters called *opticals* (as discussed in "Choosing Compatible Type"). Here, I've used opticals for the "FiveOnFive" headline (Figure 2.31, item 1), which is set in Arno Pro Display. Considerably more delicate than the Regular style, Arno Pro Display is designed to be used at larger sizes.

Using Special Characters

Line 3 (Figure 2.31) uses an ornament found in Arno Pro, which is available in the Glyphs panel (Type > Glyphs). In Line 4 the date and time uses en dashes instead of normal hyphens. Notice how the en dash is a bit longer than a hyphen, but not as long as the em dash. To insert an en dash, choose Type > Insert Special Character > Hyphens and Dashes > En Dash. In line 5, I've set the type in all lowercase and then applied All Small Caps from the Character panel's OpenType menu (Figure 2.32). Likewise, I also used All Small Caps and Arno Pro Caption in Line 6, another optical, to help make the smallish RSVP line more readable.

Figure 2.31 Type specs in order are: 1) Arno Pro Display, 21.5/25.8 pts; 2) Arno Pro Italic, 10.5/12.9 pts; 3) and 4) Arno Pro Regular, 11.5/12.9 pts; 5) Arno Pro Semibold and Arno Pro Regular 9.5/12.9 pts; and 6) Arno Pro Caption 7/12.9 pts.

Figure 2.32 The Character panel's menu displays a wealth of choices, particularly when using OpenType. Here the All Small Caps feature is chosen, which often works nicely when setting small, formal type.

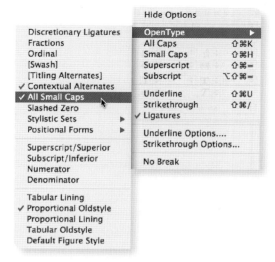

Kerning and Tracking

Kerning and tracking are the final and most important text attributes for setting professional type. Used correctly, artful kerning and tracking clearly separates a pro from a not-so pro. In theory, these features' objectives are simple: to ensure evenly spaced letter pairs (kerning) and words (tracking). In practice, achieving uniformity of type color is not always so easy.

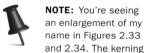

NOTE: You're seeing an enlargement of my name in Figures 2.33 and 2.34. The kerning choices I made were based on type that originally was set at 36 pts. If I were setting real type at the size shown here (about 180 pts), I'd use different kerning and tracking values, specifically, values that would be much tighter than what you see.

Unlike other page layout software, InDesign offers two kerning methods, metric and optical. Simply put, metric kerning relies on the default values (or *metrics*) built into a font by the type designer. These values control the distance a letter sits from its neighbor. In Figure 2.33, I've set my first name three times in Garamond Premier Pro and placed each instance directly on top of one another in a stack. The black type on top was set using Optical kerning. The red middle layer was set using Metric kerning. The bottom green type was set with zero kerning. Whereas the topmost black type with Optical kerning looks the best of its group, the kerning is not perfect. As a result, a bit of manual kerning was needed to really do the job right, which is what we see with the lavender type beneath the stack (Figure 2.34). Here, each pair of letters was carefully adjusted to achieve a better balance of spacing.

So, what does this mean in the real world? Here are some tips:

- Don't necessarily trust anything or anyone to kern your type. For the best-looking type, you *must* roll up your sleeves and kern type manually.
- Body type (9–12 pts, give or take) will generally not need manual kerning or tracking except in all but the fussiest of cases. Often, large runs of body

Scott

Figure 2.33 Three kerning settings are represented. Green = No Kerning; Red = Metric Kerning; Black = Optical Kerning.

Scott

Figure 2.34 Beginning with Optical kerning, here's how my name looks after manual kerning, which was needed to set the type just right.

type (a book, for example) can be set by experimenting with your software's overall tracking, hyphenation, and justification controls. InDesign provides all the requisite tools to do just that.

- When setting small runs of type for ads or invitations, most of the type will benefit from a bit of manual tweaking. Once you become familiar with the tools for kerning and tracking, the process shouldn't take too long.

Setting Type Preferences in InDesign

Now that you've learned some important rules for setting type, I'll address one final component to get the best-looking type you can in both InDesign and Illustrator. You learned how to set preferences for units and increments for InDesign and Illustrator in Chapter 1, "Getting Started," but this point bears repeating here.

By default, both InDesign and Illustrator use 20/1000 of an em because of their kerning increment. An em is the width of type at any particular point size. For example, if I'm working with 24-pt type, an em is 24 pts wide (an en is half that width or 12 pts). This means that each click of the kerning increment's Up or Down Arrow (Figure 2.35) moves my type 20/1000 of an em space. The same

Figure 2.35 InDesign's default increment of 20/1000 of an inch is too coarse when trying to finely kern type.

Figure 2.36 5/1000 em is the recommended setting here. Even lower values can be used for the super finicky.

thing occurs when using the keyboard shortcut of Option+right/left Arrow (Mac) or Alt+right/left Arrow (Windows). Unfortunately, 20/1000 of an em is a rather coarse increment when working with type. To remedy this problem, try using 5/1000 for your default preference setting. Choose InDesign > Preferences > Units and Increments (Mac OS) or Edit > Preferences > Units and Increments (Windows), as shown in Figure 2.36. Doing so will reward you with much greater control when trying to fine-tune your type.

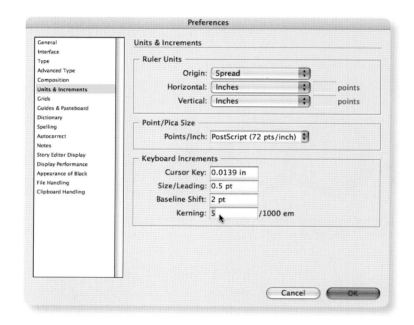

Typesetting with Adobe Illustrator

Although nine times out of ten I'll recommend InDesign for all your typesetting needs, sometimes Illustrator really shines. Yes, you can use Illustrator to create linked columns of text that even wraps around objects just like in InDesign, but why? InDesign does it so much easier. Yet when you're looking for just that special typographic touch you can't find in InDesign, Illustrator may be your answer.

Whereas InDesign excels at setting multiple page documents while barely breaking a sweat, Illustrator is often the tool of choice for single-page or relatively short documents such as brochures or flyers. Just ask anyone in the packaging industry. Many an ad agency has also turned to Illustrator when creating one-off pieces that don't involve long, complex typesetting. Recently Illustrator has taken a cue or two from InDesign, and it too now sports many familiar features. Among its strengths are the following:

- Point type (that is, no need to create a text frame)
- Adobe Every-line and Single-line Composers
- Paragraph Style and Character Style sheets
- Vertical type setting
- True roman hanging punctuation
- The Fit Headline feature
- Complete OpenType support
- Unicode support
- Type warping and enveloping effects

There are few knocks against Illustrator when it comes to setting type, as long as you're not planning to use it for creating long documents. A couple of years ago a publisher hired me to take over a 320-page book from a designer who was well behind his deadline. The reason, I discovered, was because he was using Illustrator not only without style sheets but (of course) with each page as its own separate file! Assuming you stick to using Illustrator for what it was intended, you'll find a few checks in the minus column. These include no multipage support, uneditable text wrap paths, and no backward compatibility with text set in Illustrator 10 or earlier.

Without going into too much detail, allow me to say that typesetting in Photoshop has also come a long way over the last few years. Beginning with the first version of Creative Suite, Photoshop has also shared the same typesetting engine as Illustrator. Once again, I can't recommend Photoshop for typesetting a phone book or other long document, but for smaller projects such as book jackets, posters, or some packaging, Photoshop is a legitimate possibility.

Project Wrap-Up

This chapter covered a lot of ground. Aside from using features such as Smart Objects, displacement maps, Illustrator patterns, and Live Color, the real meat of this project was learning about type. Although the project used type sparingly, the principles of typesetting are the same as for longer documents. The fact is that whereas type is less "noticed" in a longer document even though there's more of it, using type well in an invitation or a full-page ad exposes it to greater scrutiny. Just ask anyone who works in advertising.

Probably the biggest mistake beginners make with type is to use too many typefaces. By limiting yourself to only a handful of classic fonts, you'll find that your projects will look better with far less effort. Before long, what once appeared limiting will suddenly feel liberating. Trust me. I have more than 12,000 fonts and probably use fewer than 10 with any regularity!

NOTE: Although few would argue that text handling in Illustrator is better now than ever, fewer still would suggest that features such as Unicode, OpenType support, and optical kerning haven't come at a price. That price, specifically, is the loss of backward compatibility with text set with Illustrator 10 or earlier. Because the issue of legacy text is a heated topic worthy of its own discussion, I'll avoid the gory details other than pointing out that if working with type in Creative Suite and pre-Creative Suite versions is an area in which you often travel, please do yourself a favor and read up on how to handle this ornery beast before plowing blindly ahead. For more on this subject (and on Illustrator in general), I highly recommend my friend and colleague Mordy Golding's excellent *Real World Adobe Illustrator CS3* (Peachpit Press, 2007).

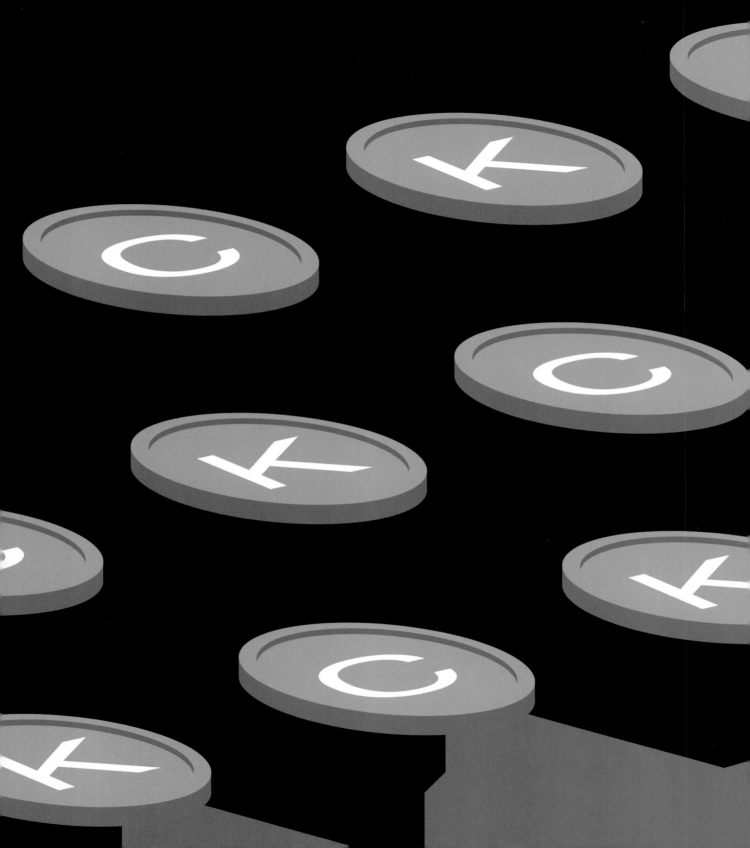

Chapter 3 | Designing a Corporate Identity System

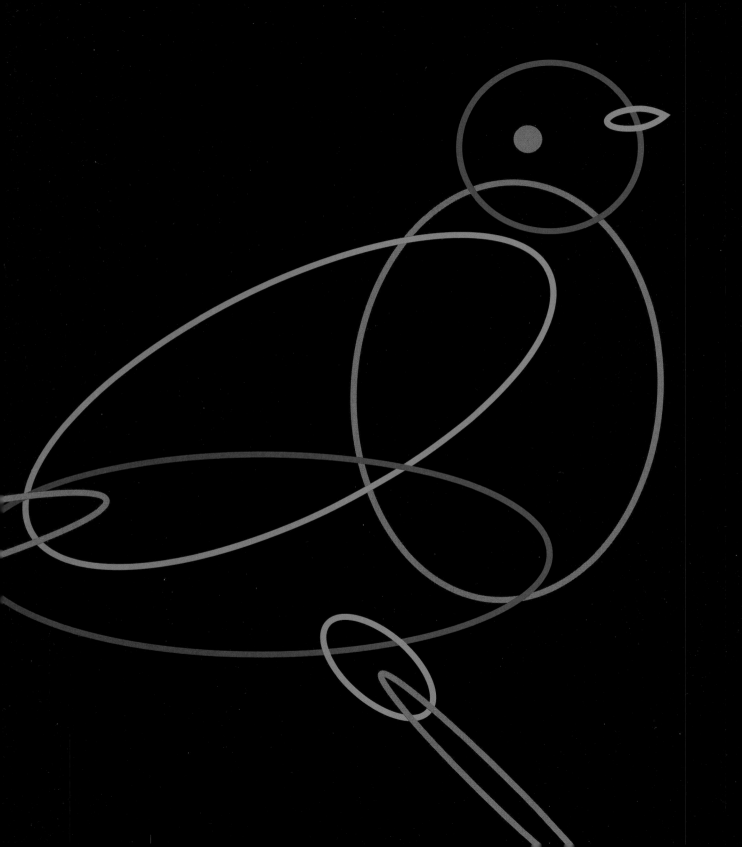

"The least touchable object in the world is the eye."
— Rudolf Arnheim

mong the best jobs a designer can land is to create a corporate identity. Even if the logo isn't for a corporation, building an identity system for a client, big or small, involves the purest form of graphic design. Whereas a book or magazine designer has pages to develop themes and concepts, the logo designer works in a kind of shorthand. Described and contained in only a few gestures, the designer must encapsulate the meaning of an entire company, enterprise, or organization. Not only must the logo be simple and direct, but it needs to be nimble enough to work as effectively on billboards as on mobile phones. And, given the increasing number of products all vying for the same morsel of consumer attention, a logo must shout "Buy me!" without looking desperate.

Not only must the logo represent the physical company, but it also does double duty expressing many intangible qualities about the enterprise. Corporate values such as social responsibility, honesty, trustworthiness, commitment to excellence, and so forth, are all part of the message conveyed by the logo. Imagine a logo for a huge bank set in Grunge type, and you'll get the picture. Or, how much faith would you have in a plastic surgeon whose logo features a bloody ax?

But developing the logo is only part of the job. Once the logo is created, the designer must then use the logo to create business cards, letterhead, envelopes, labels, and other parts of what's known as an *identity system*. Each piece of the identity system is part of what's known as *business collateral* or just plain *collateral*. Creating a compelling logo and developing related collateral is what this chapter is all about.

What Is a Logo?

Here's a quick test. In the table below you'll find seven logos. Across from the logos is a randomly ordered list of the companies they represent. How long does it take you to correctly identify each logo with its company or organization?

LOGO	COMPANY NAME
●	Apple
✚	Playboy
⸧⸧⸧	Adidas
🐰	Nike
adidas	CBS
✓	Olympics
🍎	Red Cross

Unless you've been living in a cultural cave, chances are you'll have no trouble scoring 100% on this exam. This simple quiz attests to the power of a strong logo. When a company has a strong logo, just the sight of it can elicit emotions and powerful associations for the viewer. Before getting into the nuts and bolts of creating a logo, let's take a look at how logos developed and why they are important.

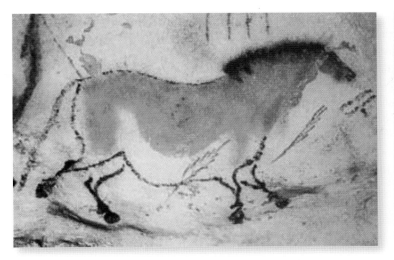

Figure 3.1 These pictographs express meaning without words.

Figure 3.2 Hieroglyphics are another form of expressing a visual meaning.

From Cave Paintings to Coats of Arms

At its core, a logo is a mark. Long before man codified a written language, marks were used as a tool to communicate visually. Figure 3.1 shows cave paintings found in Lascaux, in southwestern France. Discovered by four teenagers in 1940, these paintings are considered to date back to about 13,000 to 15,000 BC. Although these paintings aren't considered logos in the modern sense, still they express ideas or thoughts without words. Egyptian hieroglyphics, shown in Figure 3.2, are another form of ancient logos.

Thousands of years later when Europe was ruled by monarchs, kings and noblemen used coats of arms to identify themselves or their families. These emblems or blazons were also precursors to the logos of today. Nowadays logos are often classified as being one of three types, described in the following sections.

Wordmarks   Sometimes described as a logotype, a *wordmark* is a logo that simply uses the name of the company or organization, usually with some slight variation to its letters. For example, the Mobil logo, designed by the legendary firm of Chermayeff & Geismar, is little more than the word Mobil set in a variation of Helvetica bold (Figure 3.3). What makes it unique are the blue letters and the red *o*. Crate & Barrel is another great example of a successful wordmark (Figure 3.4). Coincidentally, it too uses Helvetica bold. So, what then makes the words *Crate & Barrel* into a logo? Do you see it? If not, look again. Notice how there's no space on either side of the ampersand? By running the word *Crate* into the ampersand the ampersand into the word *Barrel*, a memorable logo is born.

Mobil

Figure 3.3 The simple wordmark for Mobil is little more than good use of a bold font.

Crate&Barrel

Figure 3.4 The Crate & Barrel logo is distinguished by the lack of space on either side of the ampersand.

Figure 3.5 In order for this connection between clothing and crocodile to be made, Lacoste includes its company name with the logo.

Figure 3.6 This monogram for the United Postal Service has become so pervasive that the company is now simply known by its abbreviation.

Figure 3.7 An unfortunate design for the 2012 Olympic games.

Symbols   Symbols are marks or icons that do their job without the need for type. Take the seven logos shown at the beginning of this chapter, for example. Granted, these symbols represent their brands because they belong to successful companies that have ingrained themselves into society. Just about everybody knows the Nike swoosh. Yet the strength of the symbol logo is also its weakness. Although it seems almost inconceivable that one might not recognize the green crocodile as the symbol of Lacoste (Figure 3.5), the symbol logo relies on a connection at some point to the wordmark. Symbols that are not as recognizable must always be paired with their wordmark to be understood, and as the strength of the company declines, so too does the strength of the symbol alone.

Monograms   Just like on a shirt pocket or bathroom towel, a monogram is a logo made from letters that represent a product, company, or service. Often monograms act as a shorthand for a longer company name. Not only does consolidating a long name make it easier to say, but, more important, such an abbreviation is easier to remember. In the case of United Parcel Service, its monogram became so well accepted and pervasive that the company is now simply known as UPS (Figure 3.6).

What Makes a Good Logo?

Flip through the yellow pages of any phone directory, and you'll be assaulted by pages of bad logos. Recently the city of London caused a flap when it unveiled its logo for the 2012 Olympic games (Figure 3.7).

A year in the making and at a cost of about $835,000, the logo has been described as everything from a monkey relieving himself on a toilet to two people making a love connection.

Although creating a bad logo may seem easy, creating a good logo can be hard. But what makes a good logo? A successful logo has all of the following attributes:

- Easy to describe
- Representative of the personality of the company or organization
- Memorable
- Consistent in size and presentation
- As effective in black and white as in color
- Recognizable regardless of size
- Equally recognizable when used in print or on the Web
- Recognizable over time without dating itself too quickly

Now apply these definitions to the companies mentioned earlier in the chapter such as Apple or CBS. What about other great logos? Do they meet the requirements? Now apply these rules to the London 2012 Olympics logo and see how it fares. If nothing else, no one can accuse it of not being memorable.

How to Develop a Logo: A Quick Case Study

Like many creative projects, logos are rarely developed in a vacuum. Instead, logos tend to grow out of a long series of creative ping-pong between the designer and client. The process usually begins with an initial concept meeting where the client and designer discuss the company and its philosophy in the hope that the designer, by gaining a deeper understanding of the client, will use this information to guide the design process. Typically, the designer develops at least three or four directions, or *comps*, in an effort to give the client a choice. Once the direction is chosen, the designer and client work closely together to hone the logo further. This process can be done informally by a small group of people, spouses, or friends or through a more formalized procedure such as a focus group. Fortunately for those involved, time (or the eventual lack thereof) forces the client and designer to make a choice. It is at this point that the final logo is decreed, and stylebooks are created that strictly outline how and where the logo can be used.

Recently I was contacted by a small business owner in Minneapolis who engaged me to develop a logo for his new home-organizing company called Smart Closet. Steve Furey, the owner, had a clear idea of how he wanted his logo to look, and even went so far as to send me a rough mock-up of the design including type (Figure 3.8). After I'd spent some time with the mock-up, Steve and I spoke by phone about the logo. In the course of our brief conversation, he expressed his fondness for clean, simple design, which was evident by his mock-up. What he envisioned was a cleaned-up version of his original.

Like many clients, Steve had a clear vision of how he saw his own logo, but his vision wasn't clear to others. My job as the designer was to translate what Steve saw in his head into something that would be clear to anyone.

Figure 3.8 The initial mockup of the logo for Smart Closet helped me see the client's vision.

After taking a quick and unsuccessful whack at Smart Closet á la Steve, I set about to design what I thought Steve was trying to say. Working directly in Adobe Illustrator CS3, I drew some simple boxes with pulls to represent a neat stack of drawers. Over the boxes I drew a solid triangle to represent the roof of a house. In less than 30 minutes I had the essence of the logo (Figure 3.9). Ping.

Steve liked the logo, but explained his company was called Smart Closet, not Smart Drawers. My reply was that a closet is hard to distill into an easily recognized icon, a requirement for any successful logo. Besides, much of what makes Smart Closet smart is its system of neat rows of tidy drawers and dividers for things such as socks, shoes, jewelry, and underwear.

While Steve chewed on the design, I continued to noodle with it too. One of his concerns was that it didn't look enough like a house, even though he knew it was a house. To that I took out two rows of drawers. His other concern was that the black logo might feel too masculine, especially to women who he saw as his core market. On that point we agreed, and I changed the color to orange after sending Steve a page of 12 different-colored logos from which to choose (Figure 3.10).

After a brief period experimenting with placing the mark to the left of the company name instead of centered above (Figure 3.11), I changed the tag line to 60 percent black. With Steve's approval I moved on to creating the final business cards, followed by the letterhead, envelopes, and labels (Figure 3.12).

Figure 3.10 Providing color choices for the client.

Figure 3.11 Playing with the type until the right look is achieved.

Figure 3.12 Once the design for the logo is completed, the company's business collateral is created.

Choosing the Right Design Tool

When designing a logo, there's really only one choice of software: Illustrator. The reason is simple. Illustrator is vector-based design software. Vector graphics are made from a series of points that are joined by paths whose locations on the page are expressed mathematically. This means when vector objects are moved, scaled, flipped, or flopped, Illustrator generates a new set of instructions to rebuild the object. As a result, vector objects are considered *resolution-independent,* which simply means they can be infinitely redrawn and rescaled without a loss of sharpness (Figure 3.13).

Pixel- or raster-based software, of which Adobe Photoshop is king, works quite differently than vector-based graphics software. Raster images are composed of a fixed number of tiny colored squares much like a mosaic. The number of tiles, or *pixels* (short for *pic*ture *el*ements), in the mosaic determines its resolution. The more tiles in a given space, the higher the resolution. The fewer, the lower the resolution. Whereas pixels excel at displaying more photographic-like images, their weakness is their resolution dependence. This means if you take an image with 144 pixels in a 1-inch by 1-inch space and scale it four times in size, those same 144 pixels will no longer provide their original sharpness (Figure 3.14).

But what about using Adobe InDesign to create logos? Doesn't it also have many of the same drawing tools as Illustrator? The answer here is yes, InDesign could be used to create logos, and, yes, it does share some tools in common with Illustrator. And if you were on a desert island with only InDesign and Photoshop, InDesign would be the way to go. Yet baring such a scenario, Illustrator still has an impressive array of drawing tools that run laps around any other software, Adobe or otherwise.

Sadly, today Illustrator seems to be used (and taught) less and less. But when it comes to logo (and packaging) design, Illustrator can't be beat. I therefore encourage all young designers to become fluent in Illustrator as soon as possible.

Creating Your Logo in Illustrator

As you saw from the Smart Closet case study, creating a logo is an iterative process. This means developing the design generally involves multiple *iterations*, or revisions, of a concept. If you're not used to working like this, chances are you're not sufficiently self-critical to produce good work. This is not to say that it's impossible to create something good or even great the first time out of the gate. With Smart Closet, the first version was very close to the final logo. Typically,

Figure 3.13 The icon in this example is resolution independent, and will retain its sharpness regardless of size.

Figure 3.14 Here, that same icon suffers when resized, resulting in a *pixelated* look.

though, creating a logo takes a lot of work and a lot of rework until a final product emerges. To paraphrase an old saying about writing, logos aren't so much designed as redesigned.

In the following sections, you'll learn how to set up your document in Illustrator, begin work on the logo, and then refine it for placement into letterhead, business cards, and envelopes. The logo you'll create will be for a fictitious gallery named The Painted Bird. The gallery specializes in finely made objects and gifts, handcrafted by artists specializing in textiles, pottery, woodworking, and

Figure 3.15 The project for this chapter is a logo and corporate identity for The Painted Bird gallery.

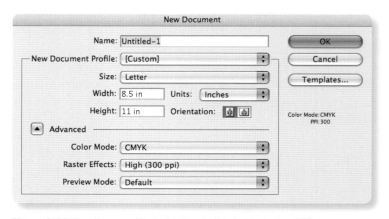

NOTE: In previous versions of Adobe Illustrator, a document's raster effects settings were tucked away in the Effects menu, which often led to designers forgetting (myself included) to choose the correct setting for elements such as drop shadows or gradient meshes. Now, with these settings moved into the New Document dialog, leaving raster effects resolution at 72 ppi (suitable only for on-screen art) when they should be 300 ppi (the standard for offset, commercially printed, art) is less likely.

glass. For the logo, the owners need something simple and elegant to reflect the quality of artwork they carry. Also in the works is a Web site, where buyers can browse and purchase works of art (Figure 3.15).

Setting Up Your Document

You'll start by creating a new document in Illustrator CS3. To make the process easier, begin by taking advantage of the new Welcome Screen in Illustrator:

1. If the Welcome Screen is hidden, redisplay it by choosing Help > Welcome Screen.
2. Choose Create New > Print Document. In the New Document dialog, accept the default settings, and click OK (Figure 3.16).

TIP: Press and hold Option (Mac OS) or Alt (Windows) when choosing Create New > Print Document to bypass the New Document dialog.

Figure 3.16 Use these settings for the design in Illustrator CS3.

Beginning the Design

Everyone is different. Some designers doodle on a napkin, scan their doodle, and then redraw it in Illustrator. Others doodle and then redraw their doodle in Illustrator. Whereas I occasionally work one of these two ways, most of the time I prefer to just start drawing right in Illustrator. I like a looser drawing style and find that when I try to trace a sketch or photo, I tend to follow it too closely. But when I draw freehand in Illustrator, my drawing has a less strict, more organic style, which I prefer.

After looking at a few photos of some birds, I chose one to follow loosely. Again, because of my style, I broke the drawing into primitive shapes, using almost only ovals and circles to produce the bird (Figure 3.17). The only exceptions were the beak and the foot. To make the beak, I clicked an end point of the ellipse with the Convert Direction Point tool. This created a sharp point. For the foot, I overlapped one ellipse with another, selected both, and clicked Minus Front in the Pathfinder panel.

Coloring the Design

Since the gallery is called The Painted Bird, it's logical that the logo be something more than black, white, and gray. Fortunately, Illustrator CS3 has a couple of invaluable tools for experimenting with color. The first, Live Color, was introduced in the "Recoloring Your Pattern with Live Color" section of Chapter 2, "Creating Effective Typography." This time, you'll turn again to Live Color, but you'll limit your palette to three Pantone solid colors.

Figure 3.17 Here's an example of how a group of simple shapes drawn in Illustrator can be used to create an elegant graphic.

Figure 3.18 A pattern of halftone dots appear when colors are combined.

Why limit a logo to two or three Pantone colors instead of working with an almost infinite number of process combinations? The answer, quite simply, is dots—halftone dots (Figure 3.18). Process colors are created by layers of cyan, magenta, yellow, and black dots, printed during separate passes through the printer with each dot applied at a different angle. By varying the size (traditional halftone screen) or density of the dots (stochastic or frequency modulated screen), the printed piece gives the illusion of lighter or darker colors. Although the dots are small and don't appear as dots from a distance, close examination of any halftoned image will reveal this pattern.

Conversely, Pantone solid colors are exactly that: solid. In other words, a light blue ink prints using 100 percent light blue ink, not 10 percent of a dark blue ink. Of course, Pantone solids can be screened back, but that somewhat defeats their purpose. By printing as 100 percent solids, Pantone inks cover better and look better on the page than process inks. It's for this reason that most professional logos are designed with solid inks in mind.

Live Color   To start experimenting with Live Color and create Pantone color groups, follow these simple steps:

1. Open the Color Guide panel, and click the small button in the lower-left corner of the panel to choose a particular color library (Figure 3.19).

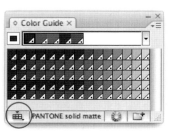

Figure 3.19 Click the button in the lower-left corner of the panel to limit the Color Guide to a specific library of color.

2. Choose Color Books > PANTONE solid matte.
3. Click the Edit Colors button just to the right to open the Live Color dialog (Figure 3.20).
4. Click the Display Color Bars button (Figure 3.20, left), and explore different color harmonies and combinations.
5. Try the Randomly Change Color or Randomly Change Brightness buttons for more variations (Figure 3.20, middle).
6. As you create pleasing groups, click the Save Group button at the top (Figure 3.20, upper-right).
7. Click OK once you've created a few Pantone color groups to try.

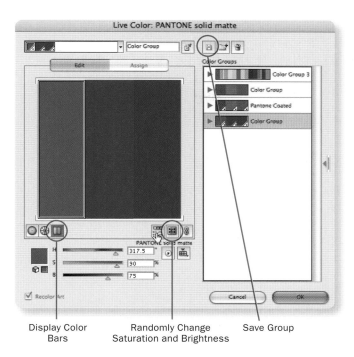

Figure 3.20 The Live Color dialog contains many options for recoloring your artwork.

Display Color Bars

Randomly Change Saturation and Brightness

Save Group

As you've probably discovered, the beauty of Live Color is that it allows you to specify a library of colors from which to work. Once you've chosen the library, every color you choose will be from within that library. This is great in a situation like a business identity where you need to stick to only Pantone solids.

Live Paint   Now that you have a Pantone color group or two from which to work, you'll turn to Illustrator's next great tool: Live Paint. To use Live Paint, you must first create what's called a Live Paint *group*:

1. With the Selection tool, drag to select the entire drawing.
2. With the artwork selected, click the Live Paint Bucket button in the Tools panel to open the Live Paint tool (Figure 3.21).
3. Hover your Live Paint Bucket tool over the artwork. Illustrator will display the instructions Click To Make A Live Paint Group (Figure 3.22).
4. Click once more to create the Live Paint group.
    Now that you've created a Live Paint group, it's time to start painting.
5. Click to select a Pantone color group in your Swatches palette.
6. With the Live Paint Bucket tool selected, you'll see your three colors in the painting pointer. In the center is the color you'll paint when you click. To the left and right are the two other colors from your group (Figure 3.23).
    Live Paint can paint the strokes of your artwork, too. By default this option is turned off.

Figure 3.21 Click the Live Paint Bucket button in the Tools panel to use Live Paint.

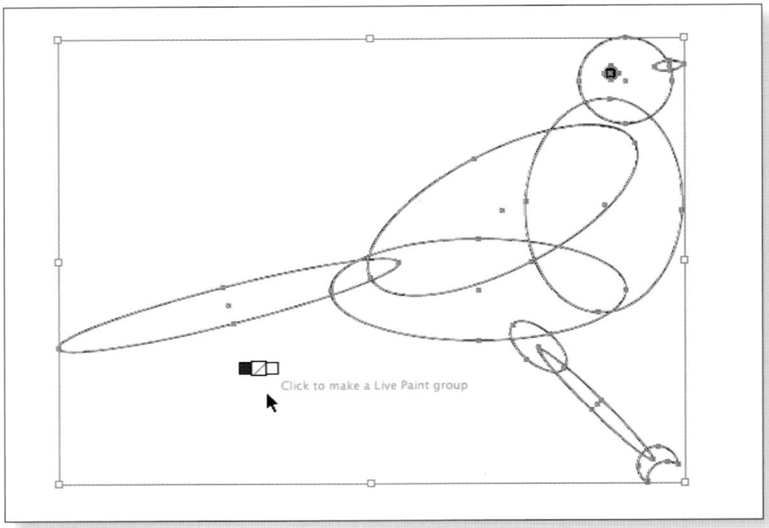

Figure 3.22 Just follow the instructions.

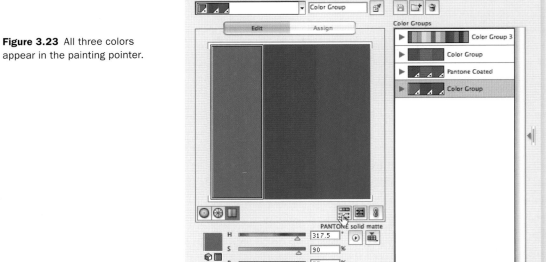

Figure 3.23 All three colors appear in the painting pointer.

7. To enable Live Paint to paint strokes, double-click the Live Paint Bucket tool in the Tools panel, and select the Paint Strokes box in the Live Paint Bucket Options dialog (Figure 3.24). I chose to paint only the strokes and not to fill the shapes; this is your call.

8. When you're done with Live Paint, choose File > Save to save your work in Illustrator.

The next step will be to bring your artwork in to Adobe InDesign CS3.

 NOTE: New in Illustrator CS3, the Cursor Swatch Preview (Figure 3.22) allows you not only to see which color you're painting but to also toggle between any swatch in your Swatches panel simply by pressing the Up Arrow, Down Arrow, Left Arrow, or Right Arrow keys on your keyboard.

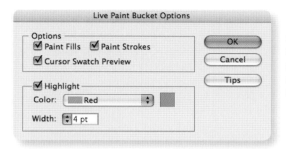

Figure 3.24 The Live Paint Bucket Options dialog is where you set options for the Live Paint Bucket. Click Tips for information on how to use Live Paint.

Laying Out Business Cards in InDesign

Once my logo is approved, I usually start by creating the business card. The rule of business identity systems is that the logo must appear at the same size throughout every piece so as to establish brand consistency. Since the business card is the smallest collateral component, it makes sense to design it first, thereby establishing the largest size at which the logo can be used elsewhere. For laying out the business cards, you'll turn to InDesign CS3:

1. Choose File > New Document, and create a letter-size document. Turn off Facing Pages, and click OK.

2. Using the Rectangle tool, click anywhere on the page.

3. Type the card's dimensions in the Rectangle dialog (Figure 3.25).

4. Click OK.
    By default the Rectangle tool creates shapes with no fill and a 1 pt black stroke. Eventually you'll remove the black stroke, but for now it'll help you see what you're doing.

5. Select the frame, choose File > Place, and navigate to your Illustrator logo.

6. Click Open (Mac OS) or OK (Windows) to place the artwork.

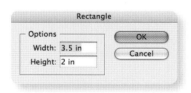

Figure 3.25 Clicking the Rectangle tool anywhere on the page brings up this dialog.

Once the logo is placed, the job turns to sizing the artwork and adding the necessary text.

Business Cards: What Size?

In the old days people would place business cards in binders or rotary files designed to accommodate the standard 3½-inch by 2-inch format. God forbid if your card didn't fit! Perish the thought! Nowadays, business cards come in all shapes and sizes. Some are one-sided, some are two-sided, some fold, some are clear, and so forth. Recently I received a handsome card from a graphic designer that was round, with scalloped edges like a doily or fussy beer coaster. It was beautiful!

The rule here is there is only one rule: business cards exist to generate business. Let convention dictate: if it's important the card fit in a standard wallet, keep that in mind when designing, but business cards don't have to adhere to only one size or format.

Composing the Card Elements

Once you've placed your logo into your card, the next challenge is creating a pleasing composition within such a confined space. To create my composition, I often think of the card as a tiny picture frame or stage that holds a prescribed set of information. Unlike a more free-form design project where it's up to you to choose what or what not to place on the canvas, the business card by definition dictates that it must include a logo, company name, physical address, Web address, one or more phone numbers, and the name and email address of the person whose card it is. Although you can view the strictness of the format as limiting, I prefer to see it as freeing. Yes, it's a lot of information to pack into a small area, but therein lies the fun as the designer.

So, what exactly makes a good business card? If I had to choose one quality above all, it would memorability. A card that's memorable has a better chance of making a positive impression than one that's bland. And positive impressions tend to generate further business for their owners than do boring, unattractive cards printed on flimsy stock. Think about it. Without knowing anything about either job candidate, who would you hire: the woman with the strong, clearly designed card that's printed on thick, high-quality paper or the man with the drab card that's poorly designed with goofy fonts and printed on el-cheap-o paper?

Designing a good-looking business card is easier than you might think:

1. In InDesign, start by double-clicking your card with the Selection tool. Doing so converts the tool into the Direct Selection tool, which allows moving and resizing the bird logo within the card space.
2. Take a few minutes to move the logo around to different positions within your card.
3. Try scaling the logo up or down. See how it looks very large and very small. Most important, be aware of how each time you move or resize the logo within the card it creates a different compositional *feeling*.

One of the most common traps of inexperienced designers is what I call the *box effect*. This occurs when the designer feels obliged to place all the design elements inside the box, and in the case of a 3½-inch by 2-inch space, it can be very limiting. But who says everything has to fit *inside* the box? Although certain, more formal, compositions work better when all the elements are inside the box (a wedding invitation, for example), other designs are more interesting when they push beyond their four walls, like the logo shown in Figure 3.26.

Figure 3.26 What makes this logo work is the way in which it forces itself beyond the four walls of its box. Being slightly cryptic doesn't hurt either, so long as it's not too hard to figure out.

To test this theory, take another few minutes to scale the logo art up so it's no longer contained within the box. Try making it really large. Reposition the logo a few times at its current size. Notice how that feels? Notice how the logo no longer seems constrained by the box?

Another way to think of this phenomenon is the difference between watching a play or a movie. When you watch a play, the action is contained within the proscenium. The actors move; the stage doesn't. In a movie, both the actors and the stage can move. Does this mean movies are better at communicating thoughts, feelings, or ideas than theater? Not at all. Both can be equally thrilling or boring, but as the director/designer, it's your job to choose which format works best for you and your design.

Adding Type to the Card

Your first job is to pick a typeface for the name of the business, The Painted Bird. Here, as always, font choice is critical, because the type style must work harmoniously with the logo.

Even if you can't come up with a clever logo or mark, you'll never go wrong by using classic typefaces, such as Caslon, Garamond, Bodoni, Minion, Baskerville, or Bembo set tastefully on your tiny stage. Prefer a san serif font for your card? Avenir, Helvetica, Gill Sans, Trade Gothic, Benton, Franklin Gothic, and Univers are all beautiful choices.

Beware of script typefaces. Scripts can be hard to read and tend to be fussy in attitude. Yes, I suppose if I were designing a card for a bridal gown company, script type would be appropriate. But I would limit the script to the business name only, setting the rest of the information in something else like Copperplate.

Because I rarely know which typeface I want to use at this stage, I favor the following method for previewing fonts:

1. Use the Type tool to draw a text frame. In the frame, type **THE PAINTED BIRD**.
2. Press the Escape key to toggle from the text insertion cursor to the Direct Selection tool. Notice that the frame is now selected.
3. Select the Type tool again in the Tools panel, or simply type **T** to open the Character and Paragraph formatting side of the Control panel.
4. Click to place an insertion point in the Font name field of the Character formatting panel (Figure 3.27).
5. Press the Up or Down Arrow key on your keyboard to cycle through all currently loaded fonts on your computer.

NOTE: Typically a good logo should maintain consistency in size and presentation. This rule, like all rules, can sometimes be bent or broken. The trick is knowing when and where to take a bit of creative license. In the case of our business card for The Painted Bird, I've chosen to bend the rules by allowing part of the logo to extend beyond the bottom of the card. I've done this because I like the feel of this composition better. It's more dynamic and more active, which I think better suits the design and the client.

Figure 3.27 Click to place your text insertion cursor after the word Times and then press the Up or Down Arrows keys to cycle through all loaded fonts.

Managing Your Fonts

Most font managers such as Suitcase Fusion, FontAgent Pro, or Linotype Font Explorer X allow you to type custom text and then click fonts (active or inactive) to preview the text. Even Apple's built-in Font Book allows users to preview installed fonts. Figure 3.28 shows the Font Player feature in FontAgent Pro, which allows you to not only preview fonts but also to place those you like in a special set for further review.

Figure 3.28 Fonts can be previewed easily in your font manager.

For the store name I've chosen Giza SevenSeven, a sturdy slab-serif that complements the delicacy of the logo drawing. I've also used the InDesign Mixed Ink Swatch feature to create a new color for the name by combining 18 percent of PANTONE Warm Gray 11 with 23 percent of PANTONE Violet (Figure 3.29).

Other type elements use Minion Pro Regular, an OpenType font that's installed by default along with Creative Suite 3. In this case, you'll use Minion Pro to take advantage of its true small caps. Highlight your type, and choose OpenType > All Small Caps in the Character panel menu.

One last note about setting white type on a dark color, as I've done here: be sure to use a typeface that's not too delicate, such as Minion Pro. Otherwise, it's likely that fine features such as delicate serifs or terminals will close up because of dot gain when printing on uncoated stock.

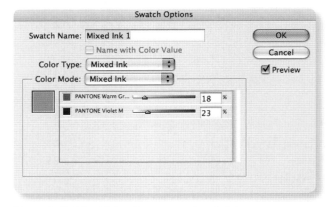

Figure 3.29 Mixed inks allow you to, uh, mix inks.

Using Mixed Inks

By combining two inks, we effectively create another color without the expense of adding another plate. You should experiment with not only mixed inks but also mixed ink groups in InDesign. This is a powerful feature not available in Illustrator or Photoshop, which is why we're using InDesign to composite our logo and text. To create mixed inks, click to reveal the Mixed Ink Options dialog, which appears in the Swatches panel menu (Figure 3.30).

Be careful, though, when it comes to using mixed inks for small type (8 points and smaller) where color registration is crucial. I'm not saying it won't work, but I advise you to consult your printer first before using this technique on anything other than larger text.

Figure 3.30 The Mixed Ink Options dialog.

Getting Ready to Print

Once you have the design for the card finished, it's time to lay out a page of cards for your printer. Typically business cards are printed several at a time on one sheet. For example, eight cards placed on one page is known as printing *eight up*. That's what you'll do here. Mind you, how you lay out our cards may not be the way your printer wants you to deliver your file. Some printers prefer business cards laid out as one up, two up, or four up. As always, it pays to talk to your printer in advance.

Adding Crops and Bleeds   Before cards can be arranged eight up, the printer needs to know how they should be trimmed. For this you'll create crop marks using a handy free script that comes preinstalled with InDesign CS3:

1. With the Selection tool, select only the outside frame of your business card (Figure 3.31).
2. Choose Window > Automation > Scripts. In the Scripts panel, choose Application > JavaScript. In the list, double-click the **CropMarks.jsx** script.
3. Follow the settings in the Crop Marks dialog shown in Figure 3.32. Then click OK.

Figure 3.31 Select the outside frame of the card.

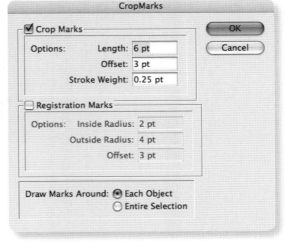

Figure 3.32 The Crop Marks script is handy when you want to apply marks to a page of business cards.

Nice, huh? Notice how the crops were added to their own layer called myCropMarks in your Layers panel. But what happens if the printer is slightly off the mark when trimming your cards? To avoid leaving a white edge, you'll now increase the size of the black background frame, thereby creating a safety or bleed:

1. With the black frame selected, click the center of the Transform proxy to display a black dot. If the dot appears elsewhere in the proxy or not at all, click the center of the proxy (Figure 3.33).
2. In the Control panel, check that the Width and Height fields are locked together. Click to nudge the width of the frame larger, thus increasing the height at the same time. A couple of clicks should provide enough bleed for the cards when trimmed.

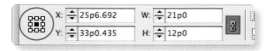

Figure 3.33 A black dot should appear in the center of the Transform proxy. The Width and Height fields should be locked together.

Laying Out the Page   Next you'll take your one business card with crops and duplicate it to make eight up for the printer:

1. Select everything (Edit > Select All), and choose Object > Group.
2. Drag the card, and crop to the upper-left corner of your page.
3. Press and hold down Option + Shift (Mac OS) or Alt + Shift (Windows), and drag to create another card to the right.
4. Select both groups, and choose Edit > Step And Repeat.
5. Set the same options as shown in Figure 3.34 in the Step And Repeat dialog. If your card is a different size from that shown here, then use your own settings for Step And Repeat. Be sure to turn on the preview, a new and much appreciated addition to the Step And Repeat dialog. When everything fits neatly on the page, click OK.

Figure 3.34 The new Preview check box is a welcome addition in CS3.

As I mentioned, not all printers want business cards eight up as shown here. Some may ask for cards to be laid out without white gutters in between, or *kiss fit*. Others may ask for only one card per page, with the document page size the same as the card itself. Although I'm in danger of sounding like a broken record (note: records are those big, flat, black vinyl things your parents used in the old days for listening to music), talking to your printer before you start any project is the best insurance against unwanted problems later.

A Handy Script for Business Cards

f you lay out a lot of business cards, you'll want to take a look at the BusinessCards CE JavaScript by Stephen Carlsen (Figure 3.35). To use the script, you lay out just one card and select the sheet size of your document, and the script does the rest. To download this script, visit http://carlsenenterprises.com.

BusinessCards CE

Your card is 252.000pt wide by 144.000pt high.

OK

Cancel

Margins: Top: 4p6   Left: 3p0
          Bottom: 4p6   Right: 3p0

Number of Cards Across: 2
Number of Cards Down: 4
Horizontal Spacing Between Cards: 3p0
Vertical Spacing Between Cards: 3p0

☑ Printer Marks
  ☑ Crop Marks
    Crop Mark Length: 15 pt
    Crop Mark Outset: 5 pt
    Mark Stroke Weight: 1 pt
    ☑ Inner Marks
  ☑ Color Bars
    Cell Size: 12 pt
    Outline Weight: 1 pt
  ☑ Page Information
    Text Point Size: 5 pt

  ☑ Registration Marks
    Inside Radius: 3 pt
    Outside Radius: 5 pt
    Out Length: 6 pt
    Along Length: 6 pt

Get the latest version of BusinessCards CE at products.carlsenenterprises.com.
Send any feedback to stephen@carlsenenterprises.com.

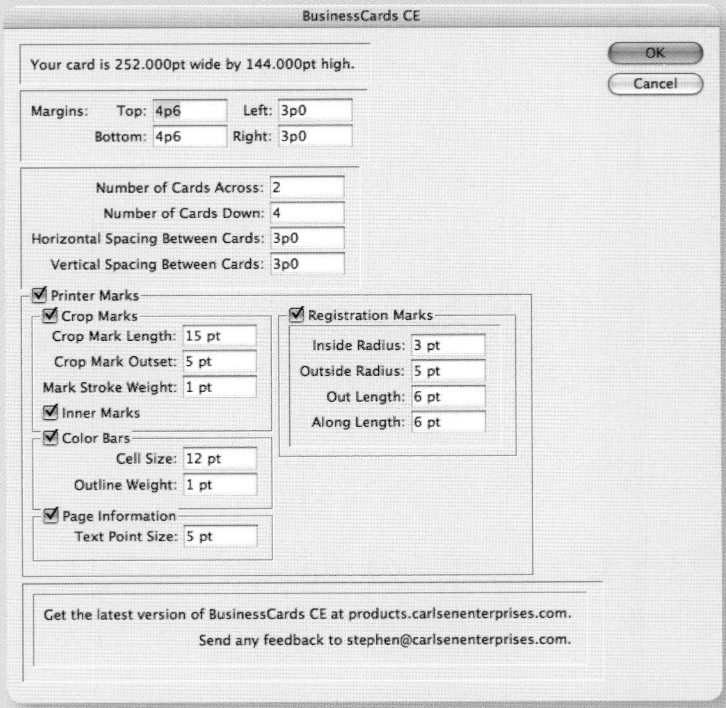

Figure 3.35 If you design business cards and hate having to lay out multiples on one page, you'll bow towards Seattle every time you run this amazing script.

Automatically Updating Business Cards in InDesign

Because The Painted Bird is a small shop with a handful of employees and only one location, adding names to a half dozen business cards is not much work. But what about companies with hundreds of employees, each with different phone numbers, email addresses, and locations? Suddenly what represents a few minutes work for The Painted Bird becomes an ungainly task at the corporate level.

Fortunately, if you find yourself having to create stacks of individual cards, each with different names and contact information, you're in luck. In fact, you're in luck twice, because InDesign offers at least two ready-built solutions to handle this kind of need.

Automating the Process of Adding Data to Business Cards   If you know that XML means Extensible Markup Language and you are comfortable using it, I encourage you to move forth down this powerful path. Short of scripting, XML is the most industrial-strength automation tool in the InDesign tool belt, but using it is not for wimps (like me).

Data Merge, on the other hand, is fairly easy to grasp, is quick to set up, and provides plenty of control for automatically inserting a long list of names and email addresses into your existing business card template.

In Figure 3.36 I've changed the card from a black to a white background. Using white or any light color allows a company to print what are called *shells*, which are cards with only basic information. The idea is that as new cards are needed for new employees, only the employee name and other specific information such as an email address is added by overprinting just the new copy onto the existing shell.

NOTE: One drawback to printing cards with dark backgrounds is that all text must "knock out" from its background. This means it's impossible to create shells of empty cards to which names can be quickly and economically added as needed. Does this mean you should never design a card with a dark background color or image? Hardly, but such a practice is rarely done in large corporate environments. In other words, save this design approach for smaller companies that are more interested in how things look than what they cost.

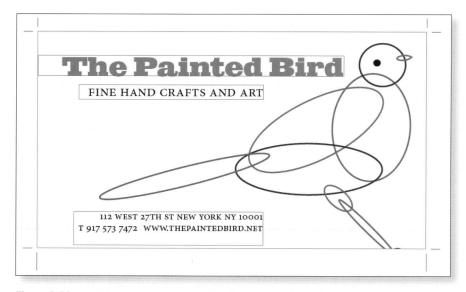

Figure 3.36 Use a light color background for the company's shells.

Formatting Business Card Data   Before data can be merged, it has to be created. Microsoft Excel is the perfect tool for creating business card information, requiring little, if any, knowledge of the application. If you don't have Excel, a number of other common programs let you save data in the comma-separated value (CSV) or tab-delimited text (TXT) format, including the free Google Docs & Spreadsheets Web site. Figure 3.37 shows a simple spreadsheet that I created in Excel. The top line is filled with the field data names, in this case Name and Email. The columns below list the names of the employees and their respective email addresses. Save this file in the CSV or TXT format.

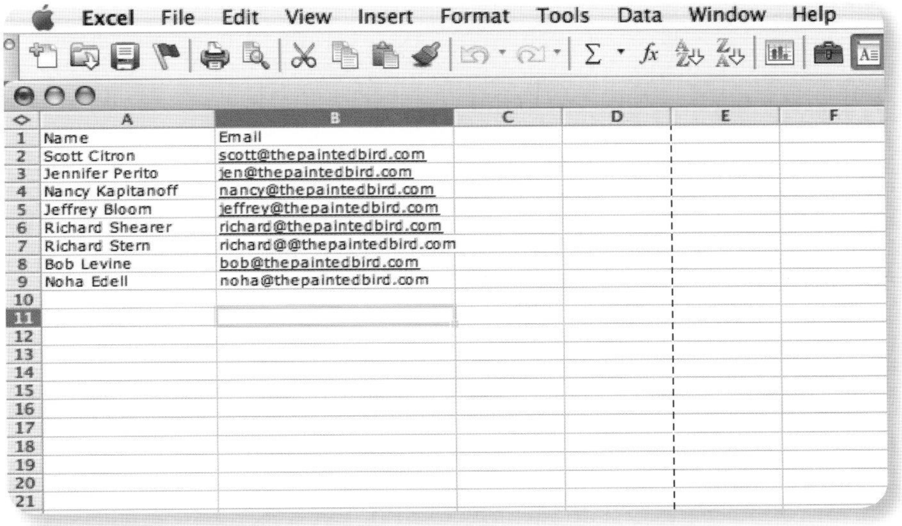

Figure 3.37 To create a data merge you must first collect the data to merge. This can be easily done in Excel or by creating any tab or comma delimited file.

Now that you have your data, it's time to bring it into InDesign:

1. In InDesign, create a text frame (preferably preformatted for font and size) for the incoming name and email address data.
2. Choose Window > Automation > Data Merge.
3. Click to display the Data Merge panel menu, and choose Select Data Source.
4. Navigate to your spreadsheet data file with the .csv or .txt file extension, and click Open. The Data Merge panel will display the name of your document and a list of the two data fields you'll use to populate the cards, Name and Email.
5. Double-click each data field name to insert it into your text frame. You can also drag and drop data from the panel into the text frame (Figure 3.38).

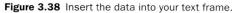

Figure 3.39 Select this button to open the Create Merged Document dialog.

Figure 3.38 Insert the data into your text frame.

6. At the lower left of the Data Merge panel, select the Preview box to preview your first name and email address. To preview the entire list, click the Next or Previous buttons at the bottom right of the panel.

7. Once everything looks good, choose Create Merged Document from the panel menu, or click the Merged Document button at the bottom of the panel (Figure 3.39).

8. In the Create Merged Document dialog, match your settings to those in Figure 3.40. Click Preview Multiple Record Layout to make sure the names and email addresses look as they should.

9. If no problems are visible, click OK to create a new, merged data document.

What's great about the Data Merge solution is that updating the layout is as easy as editing the original data file and then choosing Update Data Source from the panel menu. For more robust data automation, XML is the way to go but regrettably beyond the scope of this book (and author).

Creating Letterhead and Envelopes

Years ago it would be unthinkable for a business not to print letterhead and envelopes. In today's digital world, not every business really needs the standard collateral of the past. In my own business, I have physical business cards but no envelopes. My letterhead exists as an InDesign template into which I compose correspondence or invoices, which are ultimately converted to PDF and sent as an email attachment. If I need to physically send something by mail, I use Avery labels printed on my Epson ink-jet printer.

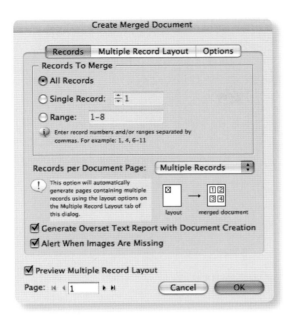

Figure 3.40 Use these data merge settings when you're looking to place multiple records (different business cards, for example) on one page.

If your needs or those of your client are less tree-friendly than mine, then you'll need to design standard letterhead and business envelopes. Because the hard work of designing the logo is now done, repurposing the mark to the rest of the collateral pieces is fairly quick and painless. In the following sections, you'll see how this is easily done using The Painted Bird logo and type treatment established in the business card.

The Art of Letterhead Design

Bookstores are filled with books featuring wonderful examples of letterhead and business card design. If you've never seen these books, I encourage you to go look at them. You'll be amazed and no doubt inspired by what can be done within this particular corner of graphic design.

Whether your letterhead is ever actually printed, chances are you'll need something for sending invoices or correspondence that requires more than just a simple email. Once again, you'll use Adobe InDesign CS3 as you create the letterhead:

1. Choose File > New Document > Letter.
2. Deselect Facing Pages, and click More Options > Bleed to add a small bleed value of 0.125 inches or 0p9.
3. Click OK, and save the file as **Painted_Bird_ltrhd.indd**.

4. Open the **Painted Bird White Shell.indd** business card file. Select one entire card, and choose Edit > Copy.
5. Return to the letterhead document, and choose Edit > Paste.
6. Because you cropped the bird logo on the business card, you need to drag open its frame with the Selection tool (Figure 3.41).

Figure 3.41 Drag open the frame with the Selection tool to work on the image for the letterhead.

TIP: New in InDesign CS3 is the ability to double-click a frame's handle to automatically expand the frame to show its complete contents. In the case of the **Painted Bird White Shell.indd** business card, try double-clicking the lower-right corner handle to see what I mean. Earth-shattering? No, but it's just another small example of how the InDesign user interface engineers cleverly look for ways to make the mundane easier.

Place the artwork with the logotype and "Fine Hand Crafts and Art" text in the upper-right corner. It seems to work naturally here, since the bird appears to looking down to us and toward the left. The address, though, needs its own place on the sheet and should be resized up a few points.

As you can see in Figure 3.42, I've decided to break the address onto four separate lines and right-align the frame with the *d* of *Bird* in the logotype. I've raised the type size from 7 to 8.5 points and added 13 points of leading between lines, giving the type a more elegant and refined feeling.

Adding the Watermark

Traditionally a watermark is a symbol or graphic that's actually woven into a sheet of paper. First seen in Italy in the late 13th century, watermarks were used by papermakers to identify their products. Today, watermarks are still used on fine papers but can also be seen more commonly on postage stamps or government documents or currency to discourage counterfeiting.

Although this letterhead could work as is, you'll use the logo art to create a watermark effect. Here the watermark won't be part of the paper but instead will be lightly printed to give a similar effect. The purpose of this watermark is to help fill the large, white void of the empty sheet and to reinforce the brand mark. This technique of repetition is often employed to reinforce an identity and, if used cleverly, can add much to your design.

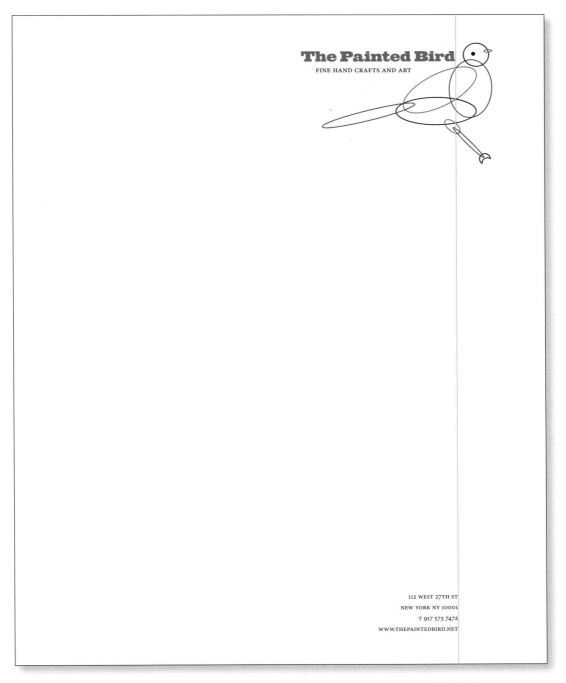

The Painted Bird

FINE HAND CRAFTS AND ART

112 WEST 27TH ST
NEW YORK NY 10001
T 917 573 7472
WWW.THEPAINTEDBIRD.NET

Figure 3.42 The address moves to the bottom of the page and is right-aligned with the "d" in the logotype.

Copy and Paste vs. Placing Art in InDesign   Most of the time, artwork, whether images or graphics, is placed into InDesign as a link. Links appear in, and are modified from, the Links panel. Sometimes, though, you'll want to modify your artwork within InDesign, instead of doing so in its parent application, so you can see the change in context of the overall design. A note of caution: usually a logo is sacrosanct and should never be modified for the sake of brand consistency. Here you'll do it only for the sake of the watermark effect. Otherwise, hands off.

1. In Illustrator, select the logo art, and choose Edit > Copy (grouping the various pieces of the logo is unnecessary).
2. In InDesign, choose Edit > Paste. As you see, the artwork appears with a dashed line around it (Figure 3.43), indicating that the pieces have been grouped.

Figure 3.43 The artwork is grouped, indicated by the dashed line that surrounds it.

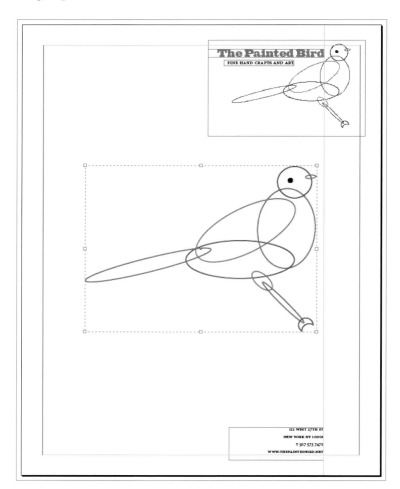

Linked vs. Embedded Files

It's important to understand the difference between linked files and embedded files in InDesign. When files are linked, they can exist independently anywhere on your computer or any other computer as long as InDesign can "see" them. Linked files can be selected and transformed in many ways (scaled, rotated, flipped, sheared, and so on), but the individual components of the file are not themselves editable. To edit components of a linked file, you must return to the file's parent application, such as Photoshop or Illustrator.

Embedded files are copied into InDesign at their full resolution, which increases the size of your InDesign document by the size of the embedded link. Embedded files also appear in the Links panel with a small icon as in Figure 3.44 to indicate the file is embedded.

Embedded files can be unembedded by selecting the link and choosing Unembed from the Links panel menu. When files are unembedded, InDesign asks where you'd like it to unembed the file, either to its original location or to a new location.

Figure 3.44 The small icon indicates the file is embedded.

3. Choose Object > Ungroup.
4. Try selecting any of the oval pieces with either the Selection or Direct Selection tool. Notice how the shapes are fully editable, as if they were originally created in InDesign. Also notice in the Links panel that not one of these elements is listed, further indicating that they are neither linked nor embedded but, instead, now part of your InDesign document.

Creating Tint Swatches For this watermark, I've set the stroke weight very thin; 0.25 to 0.5 is enough. Remember, you don't want the watermark to intrude on what's typed on the page. I also suggest you create tint swatches of your three Pantone colors because, again, you don't want the watermark to be too strong, and printing the inks at 100 percent (even at such a narrow stroke weight) will overpower the page. Here's how to create tint swatches of your Pantone colors:

1. In InDesign, in the Swatches panel, select a Pantone swatch, and choose Create New Tint Swatch from the panel menu.
2. In the Swatch Options dialog, set the tint to 40 percent, and click OK.
3. Repeat steps 1 and 2 to create the other two tint swatches.
      Now you're ready to color the artwork components and regroup them:
4. With the individual logo components still ungrouped, change the 100 percent Pantone colors to their various tints.

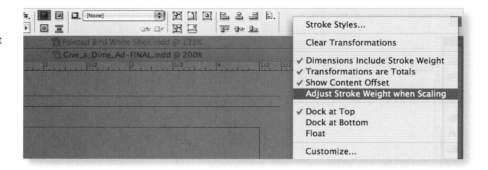

Figure 3.45 Failing to adjust the stroke weight of the watermark once you've scaled it up will result in a mark that's much too heavy here. Turning this attribute on will allow you to adjust stroke weights once you've finished scaling the artwork.

5. When done, group all the components back together.

6. Make sure that Adjust Stroke Weight When Scaling is deselected (Figure 3.45). Doing so will allow you to scale your watermark up or down in size without affecting its stroke weight.

Composing the Watermark Design   Take some time to play with your watermark. Make it bigger or smaller, flip it, flop it, rotate it, or shear it. Reposition it on the page. To help visualize how it will eventually look, set your screen mode to Preview (by choosing View > Screen Mode > Preview or typing **W**). Now try making it the same size as it is in the logo.

If you're not happy with the watermark being the same size as the logo, then you've just witnessed a key concept of repetition. The reason the watermark looks weird now is that it's *repetitive*. Repetition need not be repetitive; in fact, it's better when it's not. For repetition to add to a composition, it needs to be *reflective* of the overall design. That is, by changing the watermark just enough (making it bigger or flipping it, for example), we add visual interest while maintaining design unity without redundancy.

Polishing Your Letterhead

If money is less of an object, consider a few other options that can add further levels of polish to your letterhead. Such add-ons might include higher-quality paper, printing on the back of the sheet, foil stamping, embossing or debossing, or letterpressing. A favorite technique of mine when budget allows is to add a watermark not with ink but with a spot varnish. Depending on the watermark, seeing the varnished mark on an otherwise dull sheet adds a handsome touch to the right job. To add the watermark as a varnish, follow these steps:

1. Click any existing swatch other than None or Registration in the Illustrator Swatches panel.

2. Display the Swatches panel menu, and choose New Swatch.

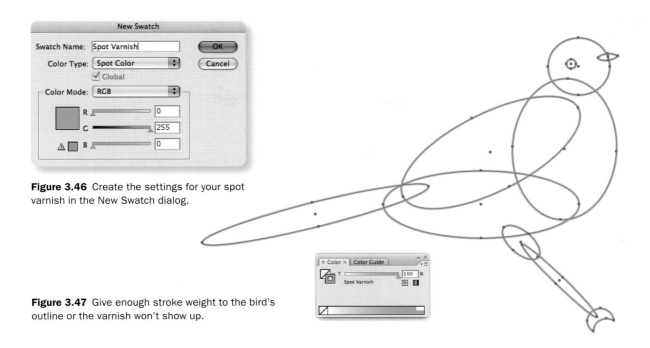

Figure 3.46 Create the settings for your spot varnish in the New Swatch dialog.

Figure 3.47 Give enough stroke weight to the bird's outline or the varnish won't show up.

3. Name the swatch Spot Varnish, set the color type to Spot Color, and set the color mode to RGB, as in Figure 3.46.

4. Click OK to close the dialog.

5. Apply the Spot Varnish color to the artwork, making sure the stroke weight of the ellipses are at least 2 pts; otherwise, the varnish will be barely visible (Figure 3.47).

6. Either save the file and name it something like Watermark Varnish or simply copy (Edit > Copy) in Illustrator and paste (Edit > Paste) in InDesign. Either way, the new Spot Varnish color will appear in the InDesign Swatches panel.

For clients with deep pockets or for those who want to appear as having deep pockets, paper companies are only too happy to manufacture paper with a real watermark woven in. But as you can see from this brief exercise, it's easy to embed one yourself.

Laying Out Envelopes and Labels

Envelopes are a dying breed, at least in my office. Assuming you or your client need envelopes, then read on as I show you how to lay out an envelope and label using our The Painted Bird logo.

Printing or Converting Envelopes?

When considering printing envelopes, designers must choose whether to print on prebuilt envelope stock or on unfolded envelopes and have them converted afterward. For best results, converting die-cut stock to envelopes after printing is the way to go. Regardless, many a handsome envelope has been licked whose life began as a prebuilt item. For our envelope for The Painted Bird gallery, we'll opt for printing on a simple, preassembled #10 envelope. The steps are as follows:

TIP: The U.S. Post Office is very fussy about where you can and cannot place graphics on items sent through the mail. Don't disregard these rules; otherwise, you'll be the one paying to reprint your client's unusable envelopes. For complete information on mail-piece design, look for USPS instructions at http://www.usps.com/business/mailingshippingguidelines/.

1. Start by opening a new InDesign document (File > New) using the settings in Figure 3.48. Save the document, and name it **Painted_Bird_#10envel.indd**.
2. From the document named **Painted_Bird_ltrhd.indd**, select only the logo, the logotype, and the subhead, and then choose Edit > Copy.

Figure 3.48 Use these settings when designing for a prebuilt #10 envelope.

3. In the envelope document, select Edit > Paste.
4. Return to the letterhead, and repeat steps 2 and 3 for the watermark art and the address text. If InDesign refuses to paste objects that are too large for the pasteboard (such as the watermark), resize those objects first before choosing Edit > Copy. Close the letterhead document without saving.
5. Continue to choose Edit > Paste so that all the design elements are now in the envelope document.

Figure 3.49 Arrange objects that make sense for your particular project.

6. Arrange the envelope objects as in Figure 3.49 or to your liking. Here you'll let the watermark artwork bleed off the bottom edge. I've also aligned the right side of the "Fine Hand Crafts and Art" subhead with the right edge of the address.

If your client wants an even flashier envelope, consider printing on the backside of an unfolded sheet. A solid color, metallic, or simple pattern is a nice touch, making for a very nice effect when opening the finished envelope.

Laying Out Labels

Even if you or your client never needs business envelopes, chances are that at one time or another a mailing label will be needed. Depending on budget (there's that word again), labels can be commercially printed if used frequently, or simply done using precut Avery label templates and a good laser or ink-jet printer. It's also possible to combine the two methods and ask your commercial printer to print labels using prebought Avery templates, although generally you'll find they'd prefer to make their own. Using this approach also means you're stuck with thin Avery template stock, which isn't the most exciting when it comes to paper.

Whichever method you choose, what's important is maintaining design consistency with the other collateral pieces. Since the method for laying out labels is

 NOTE: Some printers may balk when they see artwork such as the watermark bleeding off the bottom of the envelope. In a perfect world (that is, one with a bigger budget), this kind of design treatment should be done on a flat sheet and then assembled afterward into an envelope for best results. The fact is, I've printed bleeding artwork on preassembled envelopes before with great success. As with many things in life, let money be your guide.

basically the same as setting up our other collateral pieces, I'll bypass the individual steps but add a caveat. If you decide to print on precut Avery labels, take care to set up your document precisely to the dimensions of the template. The easiest way to do this is to download a template for your label from the Avery website. These templates are saved as tables in Microsoft Word and can be easily placed into InDesign. For my labels I'm using the Avery 5524 template.

1. Choose File > Place. Don't worry about where on the page the template goes.
2. With the Selection tool, draw the table's frame so it's slightly larger than the table.
3. Choose Type > Show Hidden Characters, and look for the end-of-story character (the number sign).
4. Once you've located the end-of-story character, make sure the character is just to the right of the last table cell in the lower-right corner. If the mark is below the bottom-left cell, press Delete (Mac OS) or Backspace (Windows) to bring it up one line.
5. Choose Object > Fitting > Fit Frame to Content.
6. Select the table, and choose Edit > Cut.
7. Choose View > Fit Page in Window.
8. Choose Edit > Paste.
9. Save your page, and name it **Avery_5524.indd**.

The template is now pasted perfectly in the center of the page because the page is perfectly centered in the window. You might also prefer to perform this whole operation on your master page instead of the document page, but it really doesn't matter much.

If you're a neat freak like me, you'll now want to set your margins to match the outside edges of the table (Layout > Margins and Columns) as in Figure 3.50. If not, simply drag ruler guides that align precisely with the table cells. At this point you're free to delete the Word table, because you no longer need it.

Now we're ready to lay out one label and then place it six times to fill up the Avery template. This time you'll take advantage of a great new feature in InDesign CS3—the ability to place an InDesign document in another InDesign document. Just like with a Photoshop Smart Object, placing an InDesign document inside another InDesign document means that by modifying or updating the original document file, all instances of the file will be updated inside the new document.

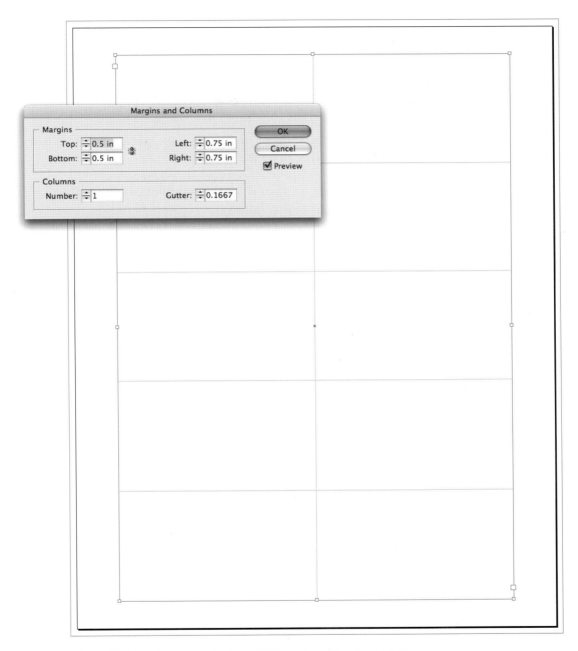

Figure 3.50 Match your margins to match the outer edges of the table.

1. Create a new InDesign document that's the same size as one cell in your table. Using Avery 5524, the cells are 4 by 3.333 inches or 24 by 20 points. Save and name the document **Painted_Bird_Avery_5524.indd**.

2. From the envelope layout, copy and paste all elements into the layout.

3. Arrange the elements as you choose or as shown in Figure 3.51. Notice how the two text frames are aligned to their right edges.

4. Either delete the watermark or arrange it on the label. If you use the watermark, consider where it falls in on the page, but don't feel beholden to its position in the previous collateral components.

5. Choose File > Save when done, and close the document.

6. Return to the **Avery_5524.indd** document with the six-up template, and use the Rectangle Frame tool to draw one frame for the first label. Your frame should snap to the guides we placed earlier.

7. Choose File > Place, and place the InDesign label document named **Painted_Bird_Avery_5524.indd** in the frame. Double-click with the Selection tool to reposition the label art if needed.

8. Hold down Option (Mac) or Alt (Windows), and drag to copy the label; repeat to fill up the page (Figure 3.52).

Figure 3.51 The text frames right-align, which is a little more visually pleasing.

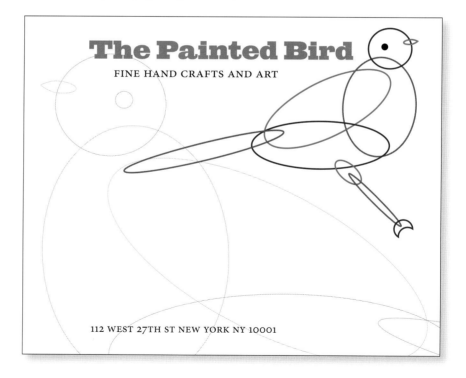

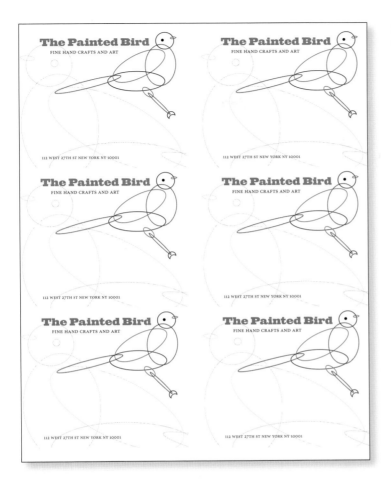

Figure 3.52 Copy the label and you're done!

Project Wrap-Up

If you survived this chapter lesson, you deserve a break considering all the ground we covered. As I hope you've learned by now, the key to creating business collateral is consistency without rigidity. Look to apply the concepts of repetition and unity, but above all else, keep in mind that a good logo reflects the personality of the company it represents. If you can capture a company's personality with its logo, you're halfway home to creating a successful identity.

I also hope that the lesson on using Data Merge was helpful. It's unlikely you'll need this feature often, but when you do, you'll be glad to know how to use it. Whether you use it or not, automation, whether it's Data Merge or style sheets, is fundamental to becoming an efficient and productive professional designer.

"The designer is not an artist, yet he can be one."
— Walter Gropius

Until a few years ago, the word *newsletter* was a synonym in my personal dictionary for *junk mail*. Like many graphic artists, for me the job of designing a newsletter ranked up (or down) there with creating flyers for the church bake sale. Only later in life did I discover that the problem with newsletters wasn't the newsletters themselves, but the way most were designed. In place of arresting images and dynamic graphics, bold fonts, and handsome colors, most newsletters were drab and dreary salutes to crummy clip art and Times Roman.

Yet despite the preponderance of pathetic publications, some newsletters are so engaging, so vibrant, so breathtakingly beautiful that readers can't wait to tear into them. Newsletters that would make even Picasso proud.

In this chapter, you'll learn how to take the drabbest newsletter and make it dramatic. You'll see how to work with inexpensive images and graphics and make them look like a million bucks. And you'll discover how to use type to effectively convey meaning to your newsletter. Along the way, you'll also learn about creating interactive newsletters, setting up flexible baseline grids, designing eye-popping charts and tables, and converting Adobe InDesign documents into Adobe Acrobat forms.

What Makes a Good Newsletter?

Before the age of the Internet, the need to design and distribute printed news-letters was unquestioned. Businesses had information to get out on a timely basis to clients and constituents, and newsletters provided just the low-overhead vehicle for such information. Most newsletters were eight to twelve pages, rarely bound, and printed in one or two colors. At the end of the process were untrained secretaries or assistants conscripted to design newsletters using Micro-soft Word or Corel WordPerfect.

Today the need to push through corporate information is just as strong; in fact, it's stronger. With more information competing for your attention than ever before, cutting through the daily dross is more of a challenge for those trying to be heard. Fortunately for designers, the modern world is starting to realize that design does matter. Thanks in part to people such as Steve Jobs and others who recognize that form and function need not be mutually exclusive, design is enjoying a renaissance. In a world of sensory overload, once again society is turning to design as a way to distinguish ideas and products from the mosh pit of daily information.

Who Needs Newsletters When You've Got the Web?

Since the emergence of the Internet as more than a sandbox for nerds, legions of progressive social critics have proclaimed the end of print. Granted, sales of books, newspapers, and magazines are at all-time lows, with many publishers and media giants looking to consolidate or divest their holdings rather than expand. Yet despite this dreary financial forecast, the death of print is greatly exaggerated. At least for now.

No doubt the day will come when ink-stained fingers are a thing of the past. But at the moment, a good newsletter can be a great way to communicate with friends, customers, colleagues, and clients. Portable, light, cheap, unbreakable, and decidedly low-tech, the newsletter continues as a viable means to communi-cate on a small scale.

Newsletter Varieties

Although newsletters are traditionally defined as a few sheets of paper saddle-stitched together, it's good to take stock of other formats or variations on the theme:

- *Electronic*: Typically a Web-based HTML page might start life as an email; recipients receive the newsletter in their inbox and click a hyperlink that takes them to a page in their Web browser.

- *Interactive*: This kind of newsletter might also be HTML- or PDF-based. PDF newsletters can either be sent as email attachments (less likely these days because of security concerns surrounding attachments, even though PDF is a secure format) or downloaded via a link in the email. Often these kinds of links are password-protected so that only subscribers, members, or trusted recipients can download the PDF.
- *Hybrid*: The hybrid newsletter crosses over both the paper and electronic world. Again, PDF is the current vehicle of choice for this kind of newsletter because of the format's ability to embed interactive material such as sound, video, or active form data. Although embedding audio or video elements greatly increases file size, PDFs can also simply link to off-site multimedia content. This content is then pushed down to the recipient from a Web server when a particular page or object is accessed. Often the PDF is set up for easy printing so users can access the content in an offline environment.

Paper Newsletter Preproduction Checklist

When planning a newsletter, it's essential to think through what kind best suits the needs of your client. A newsletter for a nonprofit environmental organization will have a different look and constituency than a newsletter serving Catholic charities. Likewise, newsletters designed to reach the health and medical professions will vary from those aimed at higher education.

To help clarify the choices, here's a checklist of items you should consider before diving in:

- [ ] Number of pages
- [ ] Process or spot colors (if spot, how many)
- [ ] Trim size
- [ ] Format (portrait or landscape)
- [ ] Paper quality
- [ ] Binding
- [ ] Envelope or self-mailer
- [ ] Publication frequency
- [ ] Who is responsible for supplying content
- [ ] Photography or illustrations
- [ ] Print run (quantity)
- [ ] Inserts or special printing needs

Developing the Newsletter

Once you've resolved issues of trim size, page count, ink type, and so on, it's time to dig in. Although the old saying "You can't tell a book by its cover" applies to newsletters, too, you'd never know it by the amount of energy that's invested in designing the front page. And rightly so. If the front page is humdrum, overly busy, or just plain unattractive, what's the incentive to turn the page? Why bother?

But if the front is clear, dynamic, and well organized, then readers will rush to the second page, which is just what you want. And it's just what they want, too. Readers (like any audience) want a good experience. They want to like what they see, because liking is fun; not liking is a drag. So, your job as a graphic designer is to set them up to like what's about to come. And if your readers like what they see on the first page, they're predisposed to like what comes after it. So, how do you make your audience like your modest newsletter?

It Starts with the Nameplate

Often mistakenly called the masthead, the *nameplate* is the big type (usually) at the top (usually) of most newsletters, newspapers, or magazines. You'll notice the *usually*. When you study really great newsletters, you'll discover that not all follow this standard formula. Alternate locations for nameplates include running vertically up the left side, horizontally across the bottom, through the middle, or practically anywhere else you can imagine (Figure 4.1). The point is that wherever you decide to place your nameplate, it's important that you treat your nameplate, like your logo, consistently. Occasional variations in color and size are two exceptions to this rule, but otherwise vigilantly protect your identity from different interpretations or usages.

Figure 4.1 Many well-designed newsletters run the nameplate in an untraditional location.

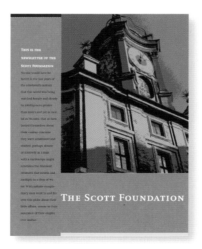

Figure 4.2 The project for this chapter is a neighborhood association's newsletter, which you'll piece together in InDesign.

In this chapter's project, you'll create the nameplate for your fictitious neighborhood block association in Adobe Illustrator CS3 and place it in InDesign CS3, where you will construct the newsletter (Figure 4.2). You could create this particular nameplate directly in InDesign, but instead you'll work in Illustrator because you can then easily place or repurpose the final file into any other program, as you'll see.

Creating the Nameplate in Illustrator

Like many design projects, most of the battle when creating a nameplate is figuring out what your design is and how it will look. Once you've surpassed that hurdle, building the nameplate is easy, as you'll see here. To begin, start Illustrator CS3, making sure you've activated the font Aachen Std Bold. If you don't have Aachen Std Bold, use any other bold font such as Rockwell or Myriad Black.

1. Choose File > New. In the dialog, set New Document Profile to Print, and set Size to Letter. Click the Advanced button, set Color Mode to CMYK, and set Raster Effects to High (Figure 4.3). Now click OK.
2. With the Type tool, click anywhere in the blank document, and type 100.
3. Select the number 100, and apply the Aachen Std Bold font.
4. Set the point size of the number 100 to 200 pts, and notice the uneven letter spacing between the *1* and the middle *o* as well as between the middle *o* and the rightmost *o* (Figure 4.4).
5. With the number selected, in the Character panel, choose Optical from the kerning field. Notice how optical kerning improves the letter spacing, but not perfectly.

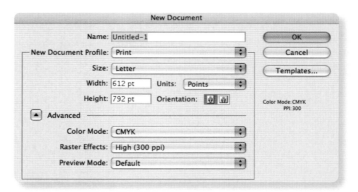

Figure 4.3 Set up your document with these settings.

Figure 4.4 You can fix the uneven spacing with a series of simple steps.

6. Put the insertion point between the *1* and the middle *o*, and apply negative kerning either by using the Character panel or by using the keyboard shortcut of Option+Left Arrow (Mac OS) or Alt+Left Arrow (Windows). I suggest using −64 as your kerning value so that the spacing looks even across the three numbers.

7. Making sure that your rulers are visible (View > Rulers), drag a ruler guide on both sides of the three-character block. Be precise, ensuring that the guides touch just the left and right edges of the two outside digits, not the overall bounding box, which is wider.

8. Beneath the previous line, click with the Type tool to start a new line. Type **STREET**. Apply optical kerning, and then kern manually as needed.

9. Using the Selection tool, position the left edge of the *S* of *STREET* until it snaps to the left ruler guide. Hold down Shift, and drag the lower-right corner of the bounding box until the right edge of the second *T* aligns with the right ruler guide (Figure 4.5)

10. Repeat step 9 for the word *NEWS*.

11. Repeat step 9 for the phrase *A MONUMENTAL BLOCK*, making it slightly wider than the other three words above it so that the quotes hang just a bit outside.

12. Fill all the type with 100 percent black.

13. Save the file in Illustrator CS3, and name it 100_Nameplate.ai.

Figure 4.5 Here's why auto kerning can't be trusted, especially with large type.

At this point, you can use the nameplate exactly as it is, but for this project let's take it one step further. Launch Photoshop CS3, choose File > Open, and open the **100_Nameplate.ai** file. In the Import PDF dialog, accept the defaults, being sure to set the resolution to 300 pixels per inch. Follow these steps to complete the nameplate:

1. In Photoshop CS3, choose File > Place, and navigate to the file named **Trees. jpg** in the Chapter 4 Links folder. Click OK to place the file as a Smart Object in a new layer above the 100 STREET NEWS layer.

2. Scale the tree image up to cover the words *100 STREET NEWS*, leaving the lower tag line uncovered. Press Return (Mac OS) or Enter (Return) to accept the scaling.

3. Place your pointer on the black line separating the two layers, hold down Option (Mac OS) or Alt (Windows), and click to clip the image to the text (Figure 4.6).

4. Double-click the text layer, and add a slight drop shadow in the Layer Style dialog. Use the settings as shown in Figure 4.7

5. Save the file as a Photoshop (.psd format) file.

Now that you have your nameplate, you're ready to start building the newsletter in InDesign CS3.

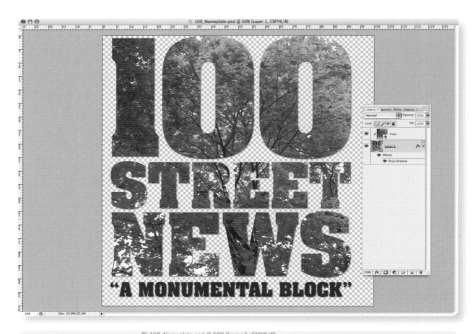

Figure 4.6 Clip your image to the text to add drama to your text.

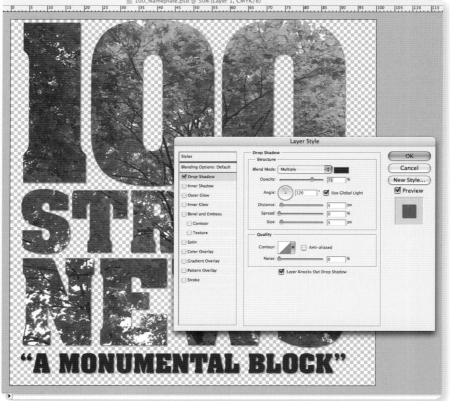

Figure 4.7 From the Layer Styles dialog, apply a slight drop shadow to help lift the text off the page.

Laying Out Master Page Items

Here you'll create the basic newsletter document and structure the master pages. Once this is complete, you'll be set to begin the design process.

1. In InDesign, choose File > New. Choose Letter from the Page Size pop-up menu. Use the settings as shown in Figure 4.8, and click OK when you've finished.

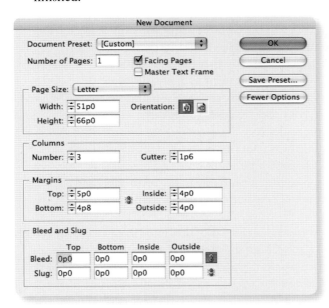

Figure 4.8 Use the following settings to set up your new document, which will give you the structure needed for the master pages.

Understanding Picas and Points

All dimensions for this project are expressed in picas and points. Each pica consists of 12 points, and 6 picas equal an inch. Therefore, 72-pt type is nominally 1 inch in height—nominally because some fonts are inherently larger or smaller than others because of how type is measured from descender to ascender. Also, *x-height*, the distance from a font's baseline to the top of the lowercase characters, varies from face to face. Some fonts have large x-heights, which tend to make them appear optically larger than fonts with smaller x-heights. For more about type, see Chapter 2, "Creating Effective Typography."

What's more important about working with picas is knowing how to express various measurements. Just as if you're working in inches in InDesign, 5 means 5 picas, which can also be written 5p. On the flip side, 5 points can be expressed as either p5 or 0p5. One-half pica can be written as either .5, p6, or 0p6.

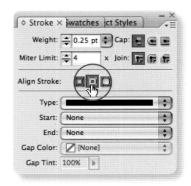

Figure 4.9 Click this button to align the stroke to the inside.

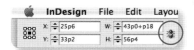

Figure 4.10 Enlarge the frame by using the Width and Height fields in the Control panel.

NOTE: If you're wondering why you typed +p18 to increase the frame 9 pts all around, remember that p9 + p9 = p18, which equals 1p6, which equals the width of your column gutters. By adding 9 pts all around, you moved the frame half the gutter width outside the live area.

Figure 4.11 Drag a horizontal guide outside the page area.

2. In the Pages panel, double-click the words *A-Master* to center the master pages in your view. Draw a 0.25-point black frame that snaps to your four margins of your left master (known as the *verso*). For greatest accuracy, make sure the Align Stroke setting in the Stroke panel is set to Align Stroke To Inside (Figure 4.9).

   The idea is that you want to enlarge this frame p9 outside the margins or what's called the *live* area. The easiest and most accurate way to enlarge the frame is by using the Width and Height fields in the Control panel.

3. With the frame selected, go to the Control panel, and unlock the button that's used to constrain Width and Height proportions (Figure 4.10).

4. In the Width field, type **+p18** directly after the 43p width that's displayed. Press Return (Mac OS) or Enter (Return) to apply the value.

5. In the Height field, type **+p18** directly after the 56p4 height that's displayed. Press Return (Mac OS) or Enter (Return) to apply the value.

6. Click outside the frame to deselect.

7. Repeat steps 4 and 5 for the 0.25-pt frame on the right-hand master page (known as the *recto*). Or, press Shift+Option-drag (Mac OS) or Shift+Ctrl–drag (Windows) to copy of the verso frame to the recto page, and click the Align Horizontal Center to Page button in the Control panel.

As you can see, you've now increased the size of the frame in equal amounts both vertically and horizontally, all without drawing ruler guides *and* with none of the measuring that usually goes along with placing such guides. Remember this trick of combining an existing value with an added amount, because it's very handy in many other situations. Not only can you add new values, but you can also subtract, multiply, or divide values by using the − (minus), * (times), or / (divide by) keys.

In the next steps, you'll add a guide that stretches across both masters. Before drawing the guide, use the Measure tool to check the distance from either side of the existing 0.25-pt frame to the outside of the page. The distance, found in the Info panel, should be about 3p4. With this in mind, drag a horizontal guide outside the page area from the top ruler until its *y* coordinate reads 3p4 in the Control panel (Figure 4.11).

1. Using the Selection tool, drag the top of the 0 .25-pt master frame up so that it snaps to the 3p4 rule.

2. Click in the verso frame with the Type tool to place the insertion point.

3. Type the header information using Aachen Std Bold 7.5 pt (or whatever font you chose for the nameplate): **100 STREET NEWS • AUGUST 2007**.

4. Center your text horizontally by clicking the Align Center button in the Paragraph panel.

5. Choose Object > Text Frame Options, and add a 6-pt top inset to the frame.

6. Select Paragraph Rules from either the Paragraph panel menu or the Control panel menu to create the 0.25-pt rule with an offset of 0p4 (Figure 4.12).

7. Repeat steps 1 through 6 for the recto master frame.

TIP: By default guides are always page-specific. To drag a guide across a spread, either drag from outside the page area or hold down Command (Mac OS) or Ctrl (Windows) while dragging across a single page. Pressing the Shift key while dragging helps position guides because it forces the guide to snap to the tick marks on your ruler.

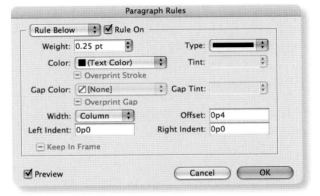

Figure 4.12 Set the offset to 0p4 in the Paragraph Rules dialog.

Before you've finished with the A-Masters, you need to add a 0.25-pt black rule that's perfectly centered in the two column gutters. Although you could probably eyeball the position of the rule and get away with it, here's a simple way to add the rule and ensure that it's dead-center in the gutter every time:

NOTE: If you're unable to insert your pointer in the frame, choose Preferences > Type, and select Type Tool Converts Frames To Text Frames.

1. With the Line tool (or Pen tool; either works fine), hold down the Shift key, and draw a line anywhere on your page that snaps from the top margin to the bottom margin.

2. Using the Rectangle tool, draw a ½-inch wide (approximately) rectangle that also snaps from the top margin down to the bottom margin.

3. Select both objects, and click the Align Horizontal Centers button in the Align panel.

4. Choose Object > Group.

5. Move the grouped objects to the proper gutter, and adjust the frame so that it snaps to the gutter's width. Notice how the center rule remains centered, regardless of how tall or wide the gutter.

6. Copy the object, and drag to the other three gutters. Then choose File > Save. Save the file as 100_**Newsletter.indd**.

Designing the Front Page

Now the fun begins. The front page of a newsletter is the most important page. The success of your newsletter lives or dies based on the strength of its front page, so it has to be great. The front page has to make you want to pick it up and read it.

No matter what's inside, if your front page is dull and lifeless, then chances are few will want to turn the page. Even if they do, their opinion of your newsletter will be tainted by their reaction to its front page. Remember, first impressions in design are like first impressions elsewhere in life: they're everything.

Placing Key Elements

You'll begin by placing the nameplate file across the first two columns on page 1. Then you'll flow in your text. The files you'll use are located in the Links folder of the Chapter 4 folder. If you haven't already done so, download the Chapter 4 folder at www.peachpit.com/prodesignCS3.

1. Choose File > Place, and navigate to the file named 100_**Nameplate.psd**. Resize and scale to fit as needed. The nameplate will overlap the gutter rules that were placed on the verso master.
2. Shift+Command-click (Mac OS) or Shift+Ctrl-click (Windows) the left gutter rule to release it from the master. Delete the gutter rule.
3. To flow in your text, choose File > Place, and navigate to the **newsletter0807.txt** file. Click Open to load the text icon with unformatted text.
4. Click and drag across the first two columns beneath the nameplate from the upper left to the lower right to create one wide column of text. The text in this column will be specially formatted to create an opening for the newsletter.
5. With the two-column frame in place, use the Selection tool to click on the red plus sign (overset text icon) found in the lower right of the column. This will reload the text icon with the rest of the story.
6. With the loaded text icon at the top of the third column, press and hold down the Shift key, and then click to have InDesign automatically flow the text (Figure 4.13). Depending on your default settings, autoflowing the text should generate at least three pages automatically.

With the bulk of your text now in the newsletter, it's time to begin formatting the copy with style sheets.

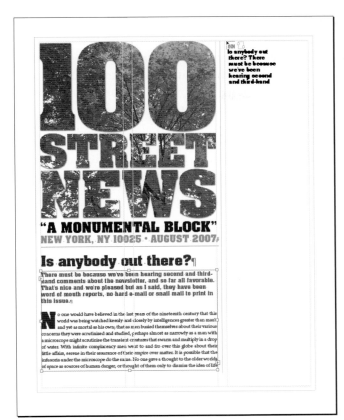

Figure 4.13 InDesign will automatically flow the text when you press Shift and click.

Work Smart with Styles

Even if you don't know how to create or use styles, chances are you've heard people talk about styles or style sheets. The concept is simple. Creating documents involves lots of formatting, most of it repetitive. By creating styles, designers save formatting attributes such as what fonts are used, how paragraphs are aligned, and how a drop cap should appear. The next time around, the designer needs to select only the word, the paragraph, or the drop cap and click the saved style name to apply its attributes. To make matters even easier, keyboard shortcuts can be saved with styles so that designers never need remove their hands from the keyboard to apply a style. And for those who want to go even further into simple automation, InDesign provides advanced methods to apply multiple styles with just one keystroke or mouse click.

That sounds pretty attractive, doesn't it? After all, isn't this why you use a computer for design? It's so you can save time with repetitive drudgery in order to concentrate on the fun part, the design.

Yet odd as it may seem, many designers either avoid using styles or use them incorrectly. Most of these people will tell you they can do the job just as fast, if not faster, by not using styles. This may be true, because for these people creating styles takes too much time. And it's time they'd rather use designing. Yet once you know and understand styles and recognize how easy they are to create and apply, you'll probably never want to work without them.

Understanding Paragraph and Character Styles

Part of the problem with using styles stems from the confusion about paragraph and character styles. So before you create styles, it's important to understand how each behaves.

Very simply, paragraph styles apply to *every* letter, number, symbol, space, or even graphic in a paragraph. Conversely, character styles apply *only* to those letters, numbers, symbols, spaces, or graphics that are selected (highlighted) in the paragraph. This concept is pretty easy to follow, no? Now with this concept comes another concept: hierarchy. Hierarchy is the importance between paragraph and character styles, with character styles taking precedence over paragraph styles.

For example, the paragraph you're now reading has a paragraph style specifying the font as Garamond Premier Pro, Regular, 11 pt on 13.2 pts of leading. There's also a character style called Italic, which is defined as Garamond Premier Pro, Italic, 11/13.2 (shorthand for 11-pt type on 13.2 pts of leading). Now selecting the words *For example* and clicking the Italic character style changes those words to italic (wow!), even though the paragraph style calls for Regular. This is because the Italic character style has precedence over the Regular paragraph style. This is also referred to as an *override*, as in the character style overrides the paragraph style.

NOTE: If you're wondering what the number sign is at the bottom of the text, that's the end-of-story symbol. A story, according to InDesign, is anything that falls between the beginning of a text thread and the end-of-story character. This means a story can be one character or one million characters. Stories can also occupy one text frame or multiple linked text frames.

Although this sounds simple, the confusion starts with designers not knowing what's a paragraph and what's not. You see, a paragraph can be three words, three letters, or even three spaces. In other words, a paragraph is anything that sits between the end of the last paragraph and the beginning of the next. An easier way to see for yourself what constitutes a paragraph is to always work with hidden characters turned on (in InDesign or Illustrator, choose Type > Show Hidden Characters). With hidden characters turned on, it's easy to spot the end of paragraph mark, which is called a *pilcrow* (¶). In Figure 4.14, if you count four separate paragraphs, then you get the picture.

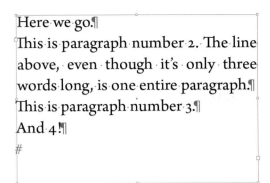

Figure 4.14 Each pilcrow marks the end of a paragraph.

A logical question might be, if character styles override paragraph styles, why not just format all text with character styles (which I've seen designers do) and eliminate paragraph styles? The answer is that to apply paragraph styles, all you need to do is click and put your insertion point in the paragraph and then click to apply the style. Nothing needs to be selected or highlighted. In fact, you can even apply paragraph styles by clicking with the Selection tool on the text frame alone if the frame is not part of a series of threaded frames. So, you can see that this is much faster than highlighting every little thing and then applying character styles.

Creating Paragraph Styles

Now that you know something about what a style is and how to use it, it's time to learn how to create styles. InDesign provides three ways to add styles: style your text on the page and make a new style based on it, open a blank style and define the style, or import styles from an existing document.

With just two fonts (Aachen Std and Arno Pro), keeping the number of styles down is not hard. Even so, you might be surprised to learn that 16 paragraph styles and 3 character styles are employed in this newsletter. In addition, you'll find 1 table style and 5 cell styles, for a total of 25 styles. But once you see how easy it is to create most styles, you'll never live without them. You'll start by creating the opening H1 headline style followed by the Body Lead-in:

1. Choose Type > Show Hidden Characters.
2. Go to page 1. Triple-click with the Selection tool to select the entire first line and end-of-paragraph mark in the double-column opening frame.
3. With the line *Is anybody out there?* highlighted, format the text using Aachen Std Bold, 25/30 pts.

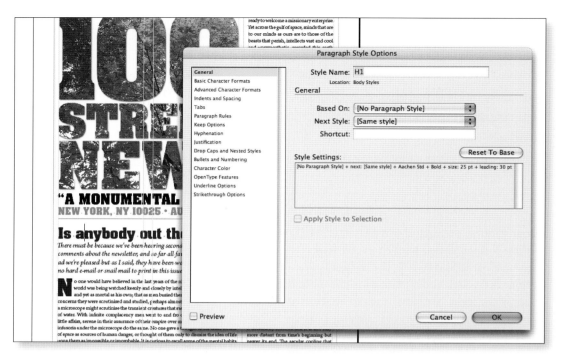

Figure 4.15 Create the opening H1 headline style from the text in the project.

4. In the Paragraph Styles panel, choose New Paragraph Style from the panel menu.

5. Name the style H1, base the style on No Paragraph Style, and select Apply Style To Selection. Click OK to close the dialog (Figure 4.15).

Great. You've just created a paragraph style based on text you formatted locally. Next you'll make a style by entering paragraph attributes directly in a New Paragraph dialog.

1. Click to put the insertion point anywhere in the first paragraph.

2. In the Paragraph Styles panel, choose New Paragraph Style from the panel menu.

3. Name the style Body Lead-in.

4. Base the style on No Paragraph Style, and set the font to Arno Pro Italic, 14/16.5. Set the alignment to Left, click Apply Style To Selection, and click OK.

Notice how this time the entire paragraph took on the style you created, even though nothing was highlighted. This is because paragraph styles apply to *all* the text in the paragraph. This means that whenever you want to apply a paragraph style to a paragraph or multiple paragraphs, all you need do is click anywhere in the paragraph or paragraphs. Doing so tells InDesign to which paragraph to apply the style.

The last way you'll learn to apply styles is probably the easiest, assuming someone else did all the heavy lifting (that is, created the original styles). InDesign can append styles from other documents. Appending styles simply means that you point your document to another document whose styles you want to use. When you do, InDesign displays a clever dialog that lets you choose all (or some of) the incoming styles, and how those styles should be mapped or defined in light of already existing styles. For this project you'll now append styles that have already been created for you:

TIP: Any item listed in the Character panel or its menu is a character-level attribute. This includes font style, size, leading, kerning, tracking, underlines, and baseline shifts. Likewise, paragraph attributes are any items found in the Paragraph panel or its menu. This includes type alignment, indents, space before or after, drop cap, number of lines and characters, hyphenation, justification, align to grid, bullets and numbering, and paragraph rules. Knowing which is which will save time when applying styles.

1. In the Paragraph panel, choose Load All Text Styles from the panel menu.
2. Navigate to the Chapter 4 folder, and select the file named **newsletter_styles.indd**. This file has no content other than the styles you'll use to complete the project. Click Open.
3. In the Load Styles dialog, select all incoming styles.
4. Deselect the two incoming styles you already made, H1 and Body Lead-in, and click OK (Figure 4.16).

Now that was easy, wasn't it? Also notice how the styles are organized in folders, or what InDesign calls *style groups*, making them easier to find.

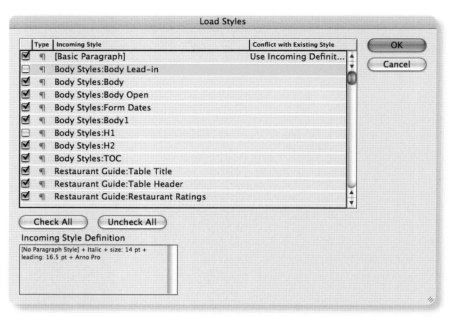

Figure 4.16 Append styles that have already been created from other documents.

Creating and Nesting Character Styles

So far you've learned about making and applying paragraph styles. Now you'll see how to create character styles and how to use character styles to create one of the most powerful formatting tools in InDesign: nested styles.

For an example of a nested style, open the PDF of the newsletter called **newsletter_done.pdf** that's in the Chapter 4 folder. Notice how each article begins with a large drop cap that's set in Aachen Std Bold. Not only does the drop cap provide a nice visual hook for the eye, showing where an article begins, but it also helps break up what might be a boring page filled mostly with text. Because the drop caps use a different font from the rest of the body text, you'll need to create a character style to tell InDesign how to treat the first letter of a new article. Once you create the drop cap style, you'll see how easy it is to embed, or *nest*, the character style in the paragraph style.

1. Choose New Character Style from the Character style panel menu.
2. Name the style Aachen DC, and base the style on No Style.
3. Follow the settings in Figure 4.17; notice how the style specified only the Aachen Std font family and its Bold font style.
4. Click OK to create the style and close the dialog.

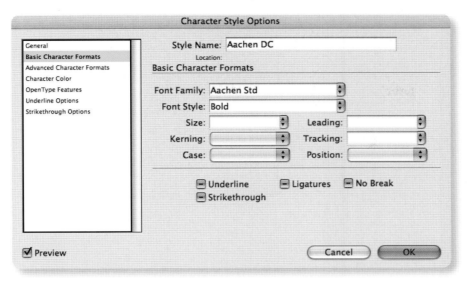

Figure 4.17 This style uses the Aachen Std font family, with a Bold font.

As you saw, the character style did not indicate font size, leading, case, kerning, tracking, or other typical attributes—although it can. How you define character styles is a matter of choice.

So, why wouldn't you want to define everything possible about a character style? Again, you could, but when you do, you limit where and how that style can be used. In other words, you narrow its use. Creating a broader, less-specific character style allows you to use the style in a greater number of formatting situations.

In this case, all you need to care about is that the drop cap uses Aachen Std Bold. That's it. The size, color, or other attributes will be determined by the paragraph in which it's used. So, now it's time to set up the nested style:

1. In the Paragraph Styles panel, double-click the Body Open style to edit it.
2. Choose the Drop Caps and Nested Styles pane in the dialog.
3. Choose 3 for the number of lines, set the Character Style to Aachen DC, and select the Align Left Edge check box (Figure 4.18). Click OK.
4. Now double-click to put your insertion point in the next unformatted paragraph and apply Body Open. Assuming all is well, your text should now begin with the Aachen drop cap and then continue using the Arno Pro Regular 10/13 definition.

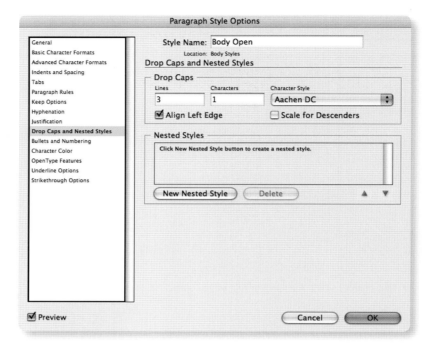

Figure 4.18 Creating nested character styles will save you hours of time with your InDesign projects.

Although simple, this is a great example of a nested style. If you like this kind of automation, you'll find many more examples of nested styles in future chapters, so hang on.

The Zen of Baseline Grids

Imagine a world where the baselines of printed text never align across multiple columns. Horrible, isn't it? Actually, this world already exists. It's called newspapers. Pick up any newspaper to see what I'm talking about. Of course, newspapers are all about having words crammed into fixed spaces as quickly as possible. Rarely do newspaper compositors enjoy the luxury of massaging text until it all looks nice and even.

But newsletters, magazines, and other kinds of publications differ. Although a few beautiful publications don't hew to this philosophy of the importance of the baseline grids, most do. And for good reason. Grids give structure and unity to text not only visually but also to the content and the ideas the content supports (Figure 4.19). Think of grids' benefit in terms of being all part of a good reading experience.

100 STREET NEWS • AUGUST, 2007

Local Restaurant Reviews

Name	Address	Cuisine	Rating	Price
107 West	2787 Broadway	Tex-Mex, Cajun	★★	$$
Alouette	2588 Broadway	French	★★★	$$$
Bistro 1018	1018 Amsterdam	American	★★	$$
Café du Soleil	2723 Broadway	French	★★★	$$$
Carne	2737 Broadway	Steaks	★★	$$$
Flor de Mayo	2651 Broadway	Peruvian/Chinese	★★	$$
Indus Valley	2636 Broadway	Indian	★★★	$$$
Le Monde	2885 Broadway	French	★★	$$
Mamá Mexico	2672 Broadway	Mexican	★★★	$$$
Métisse	235 West 105	French	★★★	$$$
Mill Korean	2895 Broadway	Korean	★★★	$$
PicNic	202 Broadway	European	★★★	$$$
Rack & Soul	2818 Broadway	Barbecue, Southern	★★	$
Regional	2607 Broadway	Italian	★★	$$
Terrace in the Sky	400 W. 119th St.	French, Mediterraean	★★★★	$$$$
Tokyo Pop	2728 Broadway	Sushi	★★	$$
Turkuaz	2637 Broadway	Turkish	★★★	$$$
V&T	1024 Amsterdam	Italian	★★	$$
Yuki	656 Amsterdam	Japanese	★★★	$$$

about either pole and periodically inundate its temperate zones. That last stage of exhaustion, which to us is still incredibly remote, has become a present-day problem for the inhabitants of Mars. The immediate pressure of nece

No one would have believed in the last years of the nineteenth century that this world was being watched keenly and closely by intelligences greater than man's and yet as mortal as his own; that as men busied themselves about their various concerns they were scrutinised and studied, perhaps almost as narrowly as a man with a microscope might scrutinise the transient creatures ■

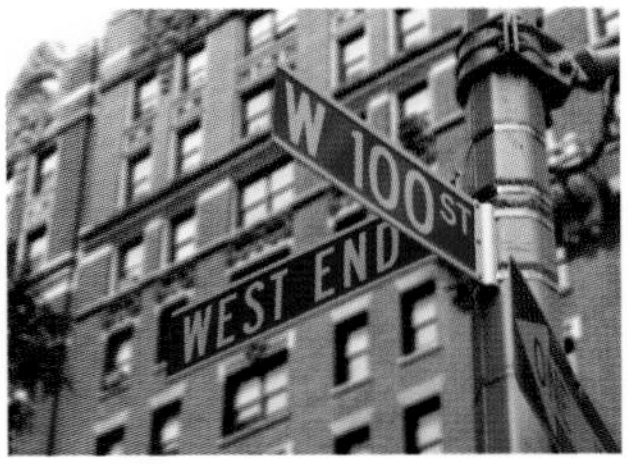
W 100 ST
WEST END

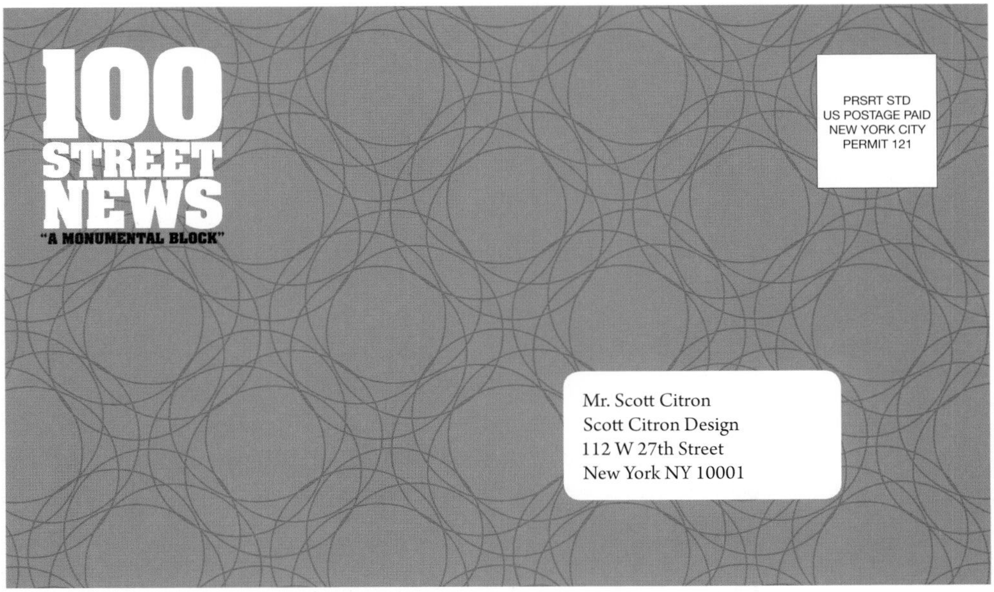
100
STREET
NEWS
"A MONUMENTAL BLOCK"
PRSRT STD
US POSTAGE PAID
NEW YORK CITY
PERMIT 121
Mr. Scott Citron
Scott Citron Design
112 W 27th Street
New York NY 10001

Figure 4.19 Grids give structure to the ideas you are presenting.

Figure 4.20 The default baseline grid for InDesign can be accessed by choosing View > Grids & Guides > Show Baseline Grid.

Every InDesign document comes preinstalled with its own default 12-pt baseline grid. To see the grid, choose View > Grids & Guides > Show Baseline Grid (Figure 4.20). If you followed these steps and you still can't see your grid, it's because either you're viewing your page in a Preview mode (instead of Normal view) or you're viewing your page at a magnification less than its View Threshold (Preferences > Guides & Grids).

But just because a baseline grid exists in every InDesign document doesn't mean your text is aligning to the grid. For that, you have to enable grid alignment by clicking into or selecting a paragraph and choosing Indents & Spacing > Align to Grid > All Lines from the paragraph's style sheet. You can also use the Align to Baseline Grid icon in the Control panel, but assuming you're using style sheets, then that's the place to enable grid alignment.

But how do you set up a baseline grid in the first place? And what value do you use for your grid? For the answer, click in your body text, and take note of your leading value. This number (by default 120 percent of your text size) goes into the Grids panel in Preferences > Grids. In the newsletter the body text is 10/13, so you need to set the increment value to 13 pts, which can be typed as p13, 0p13, 13pt, 13 pts, or 1p1 (Figure 4.21).

For now, apply as many of the paragraph and character styles as you can.

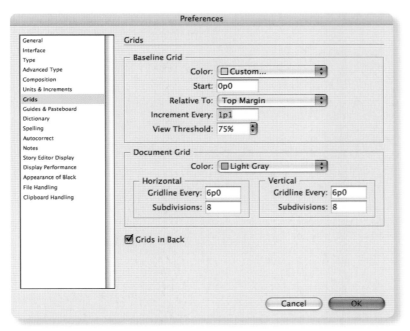

Figure 4.21 Set an increment value for your baseline grid according to the leading of your body text.

Adding Interactivity

Embedded objects such as text anchors and hyperlinks add to the newsletter's value when read as a PDF. Creating hyperlinks is easy in InDesign and makes reading a PDF online a pleasure because you're providing convenient links to people or places mentioned in the publication. Text anchors are great. The idea behind them is that when viewing a PDF document, the reader can click an anchor and be taken to a related destination in the document.

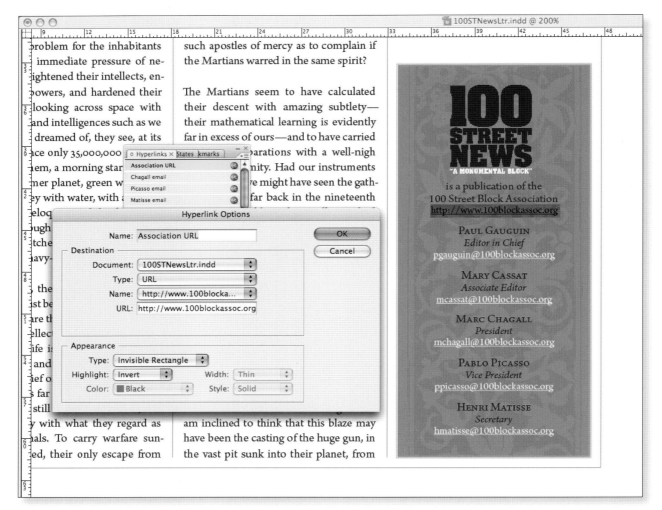

Figure 4.22 If you plan to distribute your newsletter electronically, you can add hyperlinks to your document.

Adding Hyperlinks to the Masthead

Look at the masthead, and you'll see a brief list of names of those responsible for creating the newsletter. Because the newsletter will be distributed electronically and by mail, you'll want to set up hyperlinks for the email addresses listed under the name of each participant, plus create a link to the Web site of the 100 Street Association (Figure 4.22). You'll start by setting a hyperlink for the group's Web site and then for those involved with the group and the newsletter:

1. Choose Window > Interactive > Hyperlinks to open the Hyperlinks panel.
2. Using the Type tool, highlight the group's URL in the masthead, and choose New Hyperlink From URL from the Hyperlinks panel menu.
3. Double-click to open the hyperlink, and change its name and appearance as in Figure 4.23 before closing.
4. Back in the masthead, highlight the email address of Paul Gauguin, the newsletter's editor-in-chief.
5. In the Hyperlinks panel, choose New Hyperlink from the panel menu.
6. Rename the Hyperlink to Gauguin email, and set the dialog as in Figure 4.24.
7. Continue creating hyperlinks for all the others listed in the masthead.

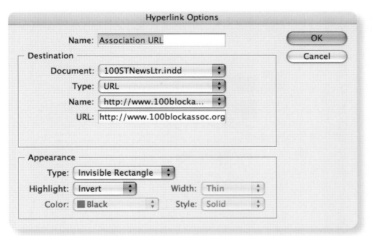

Figure 4.23 Change the name and appearance of your hyperlink.

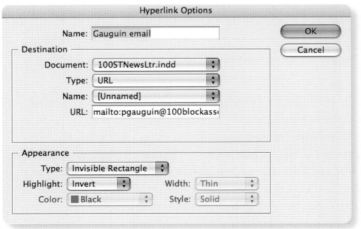

Figure 4.24 You can add as many hyperlinks as you want, adding urls or email addresses.

Adding Text Anchors to the Table of Contents

Although creating text anchors for a four-page newsletter might be considered overkill, you'll learn how easy it is to add this feature for the next time you create a long document.

Text anchors have two parts: the source and the destination. To create a text anchor, you first establish the destination and then configure its source. To practice, you'll work with the table of contents found at the bottom of the newsletter's front page.

1. On page 2, highlight the headline *Paving paths in Riverside Park?*
2. In the Hyperlinks panel, choose New Hyperlink Destination from the panel menu.
3. Configure the destination settings to match those in Figure 4.25.

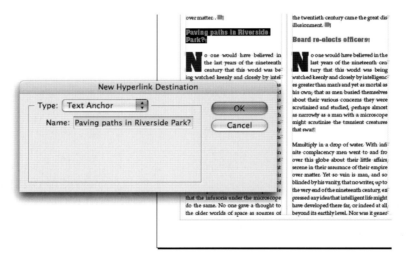

Figure 4.25 Text anchors are great for creating quick navigation inside of PDFs.

4. On the front page, highlight *Paved paths p2*, and choose New Hyperlink from the Hyperlinks panel menu.
5. Make sure your settings match those in Figure 4.26, and click OK.
6. Continue creating the three other text anchors, starting with the hyperlink destination first and then setting its source from the table of contents.

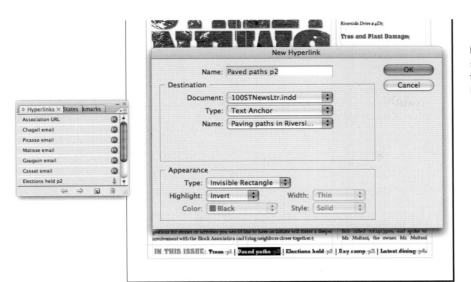

Figure 4.26 You can even set the appearance of the hyperlink in the New Hyperlink dialog.

Working with Graphics

Let's face it. A newsletter without graphics is pretty boring. Sadly, most newsletters fall short when it comes to graphic content. Either they have none, or what they use is mostly crummy clip art from some equally crummy source. But just because your newsletter is done on the cheap doesn't mean it has to look cheap. In the following sections, you'll see how to find and take advantage of interesting and affordable graphics and also how to create your own great-looking pie chart with 3D effects, built easily in Illustrator CS3 (Figure 4.27).

Adding Photos

Depending on the kind of newsletter you're producing, photography can add much to your overall content. Today, in the era of the ubiquitous digital camera, gathering photos to place in a newsletter has become a lot easier. Gone are the days of shooting film, developing photos, and scanning snapshots just to drop a few pictures of the office picnic into the monthly newsletter. In its place, the photographer now downloads the photos from her camera and emails them to you, the designer, whose job it is to place the best shots into the layout.

This section hardly replaces a more in-depth book about photography, but here are a few worthwhile fundamentals about working with images in publications. The concepts are simple. Pay attention to them, and you'll get more out of the images you use in future projects.

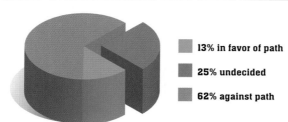

- 13% in favor of path
- 25% undecided
- 62% against path

New paths in Riverside Park?

Yet so vain is man, and so blinded by his vanity, that no writer, up to the very end of the nineteenth

century, expressed any idea that intelligent life might have developed there far, or indeed at all, beyond its earthly level. Nor was it generally understood that since Mars is older than our earth, with scarcely a quarter of the superficial area and remoter from the sun, it necessarily follows that it is not only more distant from time's beginning but nearer. ■

Board re-elects officers

No one would have believed in the last years of the nineteenth century that this world was being watched keenly and closely by intelligences greater than man's and yet as mortal as his own; that as men busied themselves about their various concerns they were

scrutinised and studied, perhaps almost as narrowly as a man with a microscope might scrutinise the transient creatures that swarm and multiply in a drop of water. With infinite complacency men went to and fro over this globe about their little affairs, serene in their assurance of their empire over matter. It is possible that the infusoria under the microscope do the same.

No one gave a thought to the older worlds of space as sources of human danger, or thought of them only to dismiss the idea of life upon them as impossible or improbable. It is curious to recall some of the mental habits of those departed days. At most terrestrial men fancied there might be other men upon Mars, perhaps inferior to themselves and ready to welcome a missionary enterprise. Yet across minds as ours are to those of the beasts that perish, intellects vast and cool and unsympathetic, regarded this earth with envious eyes, and slowly and surely drew their plans against us. And early in the twentieth century came the great disillusionment

Yet so vain is man, and so blinded by his vanity, that no writer, up to the very end of the nineteenth century, expressed any idea that intelligent life might have developed region the midday temperature barely there far, or indeed at all, beyond its earthly level. Nor was it generally understood that since Mars is older than our earth, with scarcely a quarter of the superficial area and remoter from the sun, it necessarily follows that it is not only . ■

2008 Central Park Day Camp applications now available

Even though this summer's hardly over, it's already time to start thinking about sending your kids to camp for next summer. According to the parks department, over one million New York kids attend city summer camps, and competition is fierce for those who want to attend. As a service to those who'd like to reserve a place in line for their children, we've published an application (above) that can be filled out electronically (using the free Adobe Reader) or manually and returned by fax. The immediate pressure of necessity has brightened their intellects, enlarged their powers, and hardened their hearts. And looking across space with instruments, and intelligences such as we have scarcely dreamed of, they see, at its nearest distance only 35,000,000 of miles sunward of them, a morning star of hope, our own warmer planet, green with vegetation and grey with water, with

100 STREET NEWS

"A MONUMENTAL BLOCK"

is a publication of the
100 Street Block Association
http://www.100blockassoc.org

PAUL GAUGUIN
Editor in Chief
pgauguin@100blockassoc.org

MARY CASSAT
Associate Editor
mcassat@100blockassoc.org

MARC CHAGALL
President
mchagall@100blockassoc.org

PABLO PICASSO
Vice President
ppicasso@100blockassoc.org

HENRI MATISSE
Secretary
hmatisse@100blockassoc.org

Figure 4.27 Add some life to a newsletter by combining graphics and charts.

Central Park Summer Day Camp
2008 Application

Parent First _____ Parent Last _____

Address _____ City _____ St ___ Zip _____

Home Phone _____ Work _____ Mobile _____

Child First _____ Child Last _____

Address _____ City _____ St ___ Zip _____

Home Phone _____ Work _____ Mobile _____

Date of Birth _____

Doctor's Name _____ Tel _____

Choose the session(s):

☐ June 2–6, 2008 .... $450.00

☐ June 9–13, 2008 .... $450.00

☐ June 16–20, 2008 .... $450.00

☐ Horseback riding lessons $100.00

Grand total $ _____

Choose method of payment:

☐ Visa ☐ MasterCard ☐ American Express

Card Number _____ Expiration Date _____ Code _____

Signature _____

Submit (electronic registration only) ☐

(This form can also be faxed to NY City Parks and Recreation at 212.555.1212)

and closely by intelligences greater than man's and yet as mortal as his own; that as men busied themselves about their various concerns they were scrutinised and studied, perhaps almost as narrowly as a man with a microscope might scrutinise the transient creatures that swarm and multiply in a drop of water. With infinite complacency men went to and fro over this globe abou their little affairs, serene in their assurance of their empire over matter. ▪

Spate of new restaurants open on the Upper West Side

Once considered a desert of decent dining, the last few years has seen a string of better restaurants open in our neighborhood. No one would have believed in the last years of the nineteenth century that this world was being watched keenly and closely by intelligences greater than man's and yet as mortal as his own; that as men busied themselves about their various concerns they were scrutinised and studied, perhaps almost as narrowly as a man with a microscope might scrutinise the transient creatures that swarm and multiply in a drop of water. With infinite complacency men went to and fro over this globe about their little affairs, serene in their assurance of their empire over matter. It is possible that the infusoria under the microscope do the same. No one gave a thought to

2008 Central Park Day Camp applications now available

Even though this summer's hardly over, it's already time to start thinking about sending your kids to camp for next summer. According to the parks department, over one million New York kids attend city summer camps, and competition is fierce for those who want to attend. As a service to those who'd like to reserve a place in line for their children, we've published an application (above) that can be filled out electronically (using the free Adobe Reader) or manually and returned by fax. The immediate pressure of necessity has brightened their intellects, enlarged their powers, and hardened their hearts. And looking across space with instruments, and intelligences such as we have scarcely dreamed of, they see, at its nearest distance only 35,000,000 of miles sunward of them, a morning star of hope, our own warmer planet, green with vegetation and grey with water, with a cloudy atmosphere eloquent of fertility, with glimpses through its drifting cloud wisps of No one would have believed in the last years of the nineteenth century that this world was being watched keenly

Understanding Image Size A few years ago I designed a book where the authors provided me with scans they had made of the images to be used. When I opened the scans in Photoshop, I discovered them to be huge, massive files, each weighing in at several hundred megabytes per image. When I asked about why the scans were so big, the authors told me they figured that if scanning the images at 300 pixels per inch made a good-looking image, that scanning them at 600 ppi would make a *great*-looking image! Ah, if it were only that easy.

This story represents the kind of confusion that surrounds discussions of image size and resolution. Compounding this are digital cameras that typically capture images at 72 ppi. So, without going into this subject much further (there are many good books on the subject), here are a few simple guidelines.

The amount of image resolution you need depends solely on the device to which you are printing. The accepted rule of thumb is that if you are printing to a commercial offset printer, 300 ppi is the magic number. The fact is 300 is really just an arbitrary number and, depending on other factors such as line screen and output size, may or may not be enough resolution. In fact, 300 ppi may be too much resolution, particularly for low line-screen environments such as a newspaper, because more is not better when it comes to pixels per inch and image quality as my book authors learned.

Further muddying the waters is that InDesign can be confusing for beginners trying to predict whether the photo they just placed will print well. Fortunately, InDesign provides the necessary information about images, assuming you know where to look.

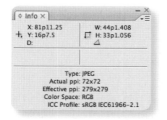

Figure 4.28 Effective ppi for this particular figure is 279, making it a good resolution for high quality printing.

Using the Effective ppi Take any image and place it on a blank InDesign page. With the image frame selected, open the Info panel. There, for all the world to see, under Actual ppi, are the words *Effective ppi* (Figure 4.28). This is the image resolution as a result of scaling the picture larger or smaller and is the only number you need concern yourself with. Actual ppi (72 in this case) is of little importance. For fear of generalizing after just stating that there's no magic number for correct image resolution, allow me to venture that for most devices where you might output a typical newsletter (ink-jet printer, laser printer, or commercial press), images need to possess an effective resolution of between 240 and 300 ppi. In practice, I've gotten away with lower and higher values, so also take that into consideration.

Once again, these values are general guidelines. But as long as you're aware of an image's effective ppi and understand that too much resolution ultimately degrades image quality, you should be in good shape.

Cropping Creatively   As any good photographer will tell you, the difference between a good shot and a great shot is the right crop. Many a ho-hum photo or graphic can be dramatically improved with proper cropping. When done well, cropping forces the viewer to see what you want to be seen. Just like the relationship between an editor and the writer, the designer must know what to use and what to lose.

Look at the photo on the left in Figure 4.29. Now look at it after it has been cropped. See how much stronger the image is? The eye focuses on only what's important, without any interference from nonessential information. The key to cropping is figuring out what's important and what's not. Once you know what's important, it's easy to know what to discard. Not every photo benefits from tight cropping. In fact, many feel constrained or constricted, even claustrophobic, when they're cropped too tightly. But when an image is properly cropped, it's like pruning a rose. By cutting off what's not needed, you ultimately make the final product stronger and more beautiful.

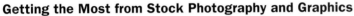

TIP: As tempting as it might be to crop images in Photoshop in an effort to save file space, resist this urge. Unless you always save multiple copies, once you've cropped an image in Photoshop, you have no way to change your mind later. Smart designers always leave the door open for change by leaving final cropping to InDesign or Illustrator.

Getting the Most from Stock Photography and Graphics

Before the digital explosion, decent stock imagery was not only expensive but also slow to acquire. Stock houses printed large, expensive books of photography and artwork they'd send by mail. Images would be ordered by phone or fax and delivered days later on CDs. Today, of course, things are different.

Photo credit: Barry Schwartz

Figure 4.29 Cropping an image draws the eye to what is important in the shot.

Thanks to high-speed Internet connections, designers are able to search through millions of images anytime, anywhere, all instantly downloadable with the swipe of a credit card. As a result, the Web is a dense forest of stock sites, each brimming with every kind of content imaginable. And as any student of Economics 101 knows, as supply goes up, prices go down.

One of the best examples of how the sale of digital imagery has changed over recent years is iStockphoto.com. In case you're unaware, iStockphoto (www.istockphoto.com) was one of the first Web sites to pioneer the idea that anyone with a digital camera could upload and offer images for sale on their site. For years customers could buy images for between $1 and $3 each. As the popularity of this model grew, so did iStockphoto and the number of its imitators. Recently iStockphoto was bought by Getty, the stock image behemoth. Prices for individual images may have risen, but so too have the quality, depth, and variety of these Web site assets. Video and Flash content has been added for download, too, along with photos and other graphic formats.

This leads back to the issue of making great-looking newsletters. With all the available resources of wonderful (and often inexpensive) images, there's no longer any excuse for even a neighborhood newsletter to look like it came off the Mimeograph machine. If you examine the finished 100 Street News newsletter, you'll see several examples of stock photography and artwork. In fact, the only original photos are the two I took with my digital camera: the shot of the trees that are used to fill the nameplate and the street sign found on the back. The rest I bought for very little.

There Is Such a Thing as Good Clip Art

Clip art is another one of those phrases that gets a bad rap among designers. Years ago the rap was justified; just like most stock photography was boring and predictable, most clip art shouted "amateur," "low-budget," or "church bazaar" when used. Today there's still plenty of dross to wade through, but fortunately there's lot of good stuff, too.

For years one of the better suppliers of inexpensive clips have been the folks at Dover Publications. This Mineola, New York-based company has carved itself a comfortable niche by reprinting royalty-free artwork into neat books such as *Old-Fashioned Floral Designs*, to which I turned for two of the illustrations used in the 100 Street News newsletter. To make its offerings even more irresistible, many Dover titles such as the one I just mentioned include CDs that contain all the artwork shown in the book, most of it in multiple file formats. At about $13 per book, these gems are hard to pass up, and I have many. And if you're working

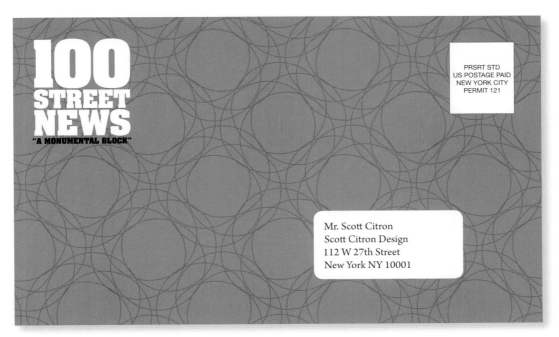

Figure 4.30 This pattern was a perfect backdrop for the look I wanted to achieve for the mailer panel on the newsletter.

late at night and just can't get to the bookstore, you can find the Dover collection online at Clipart.com, a subscription-based, all-you-can-eat Web site that offers millions of images for very little.

For the two Dover images I used in the newsletter (the front-page flowers and the masthead background) I placed single-bit TIFF files and then applied a splash of color to these wonderful etchings. Instead of using clip art for the circular pattern of the self-mailer panel, I decided to create my own artwork in Adobe Illustrator. To create this effect I used the Wallpaper tool, one of the many powerful components that are part of the Xtreme Path plug-in from CValley, Inc. (Figure 4.30).

Charts, Forms, and Tables

If doing newsletters is considered by some to be the torture rack of the design business, creating charts, forms, and tables for newsletters must be its thumb-screws. I'm always amused by the look on student's faces when I ask them how they feel about doing this kind of work. Yet it's no wonder why designers disappear to make very important phone calls when art directors poll the office for someone to do the latest table or form. Before InDesign came along, designers created tables and charts by assembling small boxes of text or graphics like pages of Legos.

Fortunately, those days are over. Today, Adobe Creative Suite 3 has made creating tables, charts, or forms (shall I dare say?) fun. In the next sections, you'll learn how to love what used to be one of graphic design's nastiest jobs.

Pie Charts à la Mode

Let's start by taking a look at the pie chart on the second page of the newsletter. The purpose of the chart is to visually show how the local 100 Street community is divided over an issue of asphalt-paved paths in nearby Riverside Park. Although the same information could be presented any number of other ways (including simply with text), the pie chart adds an appealing visual element to the page. For the next series of steps, you'll begin working in Illustrator and then switch over to InDesign. Follow these steps to create your own version of the pie chart:

1. From the Illustrator Welcome Screen (Help > Welcome Screen), press and hold Option (Mac OS) or Alt (Windows), and choose Create New > Print Document to skip the subsequent dialog.
2. Select the Pie Graph tool hidden under the Column Graph tool, and click once in the middle of your page.
3. Set both the width and height to 300 pts, and click OK.
4. In the table data form that appears (Figure 4.31), type **62**, **25**, and **13** (or any combination of numbers that adds up to 100) in the top three fields.

Figure 4.31 Enter the tabular data in the appropriate fields.

5. Click the Accept button (the check mark in the upper-right corner) to place the data into the chart.
6. Replace the black stroke that's automatically added to the chart with None.

The next step from here would be to recolor the pie segments to something a little snappier than their grayscale defaults. You can do this either manually or by using the Illustrator Live Color feature (see the "Recoloring Your Pattern with Live Color" section in Chapter 2, "Creating Effective Typography"). Whatever you choose, note that the segments are grouped; you'll need to use the Direct Selection tool to select individual pieces. You may also want to separate the segments to emphasize one or two pieces. Again, use the Direct Selection tool for this task to maintain the grouping relationship. Now you should be ready to add the 3D effect. Beware that physically changing the chart at this stage means you can no longer edit the data it represents and expect the chart to update.

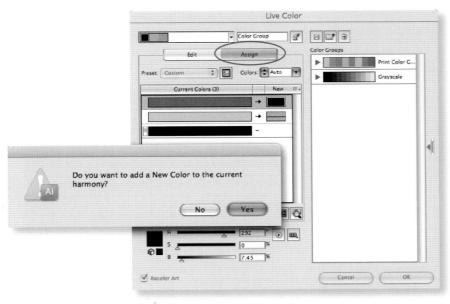

 NOTE: By default Live Color protects the color black. This means if you use Live Color to select a new color scheme for your pie graph, black will stay black. To edit black, select the Assign tab, and click again in the blank column space to the right of the black swatch. A dialog appears asking whether you'd like to add a new color to the harmony (Figure 4.32). Click Yes, and you'll see that black now becomes an editable color.

Figure 4.32 Create an editable color by making this change in the Assign tab.

1. In Illustrator, with the entire pie graph selected, choose Effect > 3D > Extrude & Bevel.
2. Follow the settings in Figure 4.33, or experiment with your own.
3. Click OK to apply the settings.
4. If you're satisfied with your pie graph, save the file, and return to the InDesign document.
5. In InDesign, place the pie graph (File > Place) as shown in the finished file, and apply a text wrap to the bottom of the graphic (Window > Text Wrap).

 TIP: Holding down the Shift key while setting lights in the Extrude & Bevel dialog lets you see the effect update dynamically.

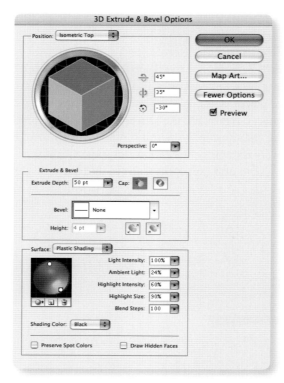

Figure 4.33 Try these settings to create the pie graph in the project newsletter.

The last step is to add the legend for each color in InDesign. You can easily do this by creating three swatches from the graph:

1. With the Eyedropper tool, click the unshaded portion of the largest segment.
2. In the Swatches panel, click the New Swatch button at the bottom of the panel to add the color.
3. For the remaining segments, Option-click (Mac OS) or Alt-click (Windows) an unshaded segment to select the color, and then click the New Swatch button in the Swatches panel to add the color. Option-clicking (Mac OS) or Alt-clicking (Windows) with the Eyedropper tool clears the previous color.
4. Draw a small square, and fill it with the first color from the graph you picked up.
5. Choose Edit > Cut to cut the colored square to the clipboard.
6. Draw a text frame, and choose Edit > Paste to paste the square into the text frame.
7. Choose Type > Insert White Space > En Space, and then type the proper percentage the segment represents, including a short description (Figure 4.34).

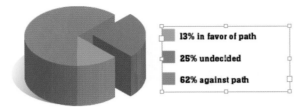

Figure 4.34 Enter the percentage for the various segments of data.

8. Repeat steps 4 through 7 for the other segments. If your text is missing, choose Object > Text Frame Options > Ignore Text Wrap to disable the text wrap that was applied to the pie graphic.

Summer Camp Registration Form

The next step will be to create the Summer Camp form on page 3 (Figure 4.35). The text for the form is available in the Links folder of the Chapter 4 folder and is named **summer_camp_form.txt**.

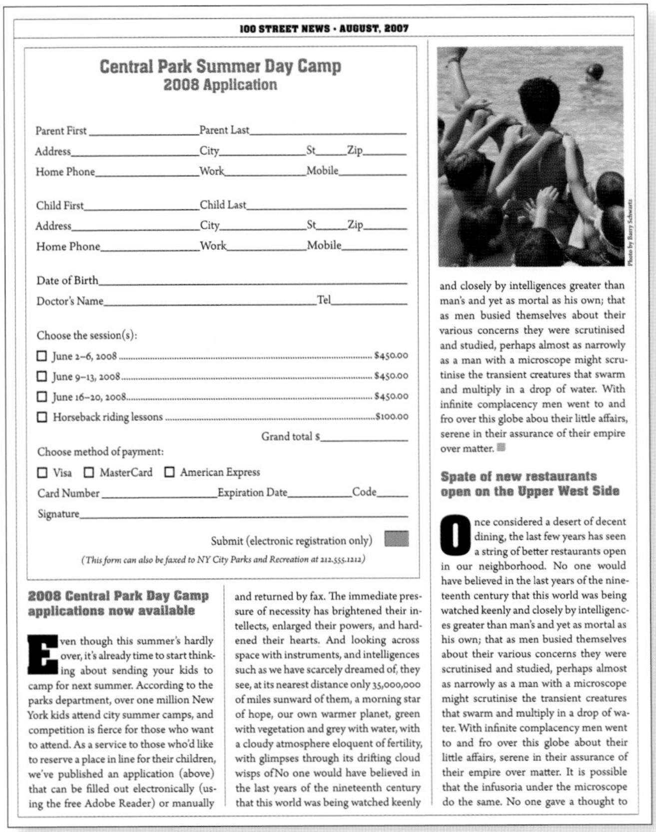

Figure 4.35 Next we'll create a simple and elegant form for the newsletter.

You'll start by placing the text and insetting it:

1. Choose File > Place, and navigate to the form text file. Place the text in a frame that's two columns wide.
2. Choose Object > Text Frame Options, and add a 1p inset on all four sides of the text frame.

The next process involves setting tab stops to create the lines of the form:

1. Select all the text from Parent First through Submit (electronic registration only). Apply Arno Pro Regular 11/18, and set the Figure Style to Proportional Oldstyle from the OpenType submenu found in the Control panel menu.
2. Just as you did for pie graph legend, create a small square with the 0.25 stroke weight, and cut (Edit > Cut) and paste it (Edit > Paste) into the text to create check boxes for the four camp sessions and the three credit card choices.
3. Insert an en space between each box (Type > Insert White Space > En Space) and the text it precedes. Use Baseline Shift to adjust the vertical position of the boxes if necessary.
4. Continue setting tab stops as needed to complete the form layout.

NOTE: It might seem easier to just use a font that contains a small box such as Zapf Dingbats. However, the autoform field recognition function of Acrobat Professional consistently fails to see the box glyph as something it should convert into a digital field. Pasting in your own box, for some reason, solves this problem.

Creating a Dot Leader

Tab leaders are objects that lead your eye from tab to tab. The "Choose the session(s):" part of the form uses dots as the leader to separate the three camp sessions and the horseback riding lessons choice from their prices. To create the dot leader, click to select the tab stop, and type a period in the Leader field in the Tabs panel for each line (Figure 4.36).

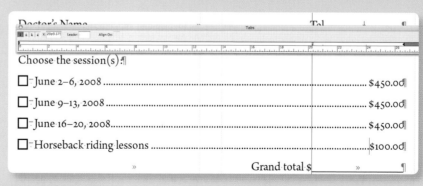

Figure 4.36 Dot leaders can help keep items on a form organized.

100 STREET NEWS · AUGUST, 2007

Local Restaurant Reviews

Name	Address	Cuisine	Rating	Price
107 West	2787 Broadway	Tex-Mex, Cajun	★ ★	$$
Alouette	2588 Broadway	French	★ ★ ★	$$$
Bistro 1018	1018 Amsterdam	American	★ ★	$$
Café du Soleil	2723 Broadway	French	★ ★ ★	$$$
Carne	2737 Broadway	Steaks	★ ★	$$$
Flor de Mayo	2651 Broadway	Peruvian/Chinese	★ ★	$$
Indus Valley	2636 Broadway	Indian	★ ★ ★	$$$
Le Monde	2885 Broadway	French	★ ★	$$
Mamá Mexico	2672 Broadway	Mexican	★ ★ ★	$$$
Métisse	235 West 105	French	★ ★ ★	$$$
Mill Korean	2895 Broadway	Korean	★ ★ ★	$$
PicNic	202 Broadway	European	★ ★ ★	$$$
Rack & Soul	2818 Broadway	Barbecue, Southern	★ ★	$
Regional	2607 Broadway	Italian	★ ★	$$
Terrace in the Sky	400 W. 119th St.	French, Mediterraean	★ ★ ★ ★	$$$$
Tokyo Pop	2728 Broadway	Sushi	★ ★	$$
Turkuaz	2637 Broadway	Turkish	★ ★ ★	$$$
V&T	1024 Amsterdam	Italian	★ ★	$$
Yuki	656 Amsterdam	Japanese	★ ★ ★	$$$

the older worlds of space as sources of human danger, or thought of them only to dismiss the idea of life upon them as impossible or improbable. It is curious to recall some of the mental habits of those departed days. At most terrestrial men fancied there might be other men upon Mars, perhaps inferior to themselves and ready to welcome a missionary enterprise. Yet across the gulf of space, minds that are to our minds as ours are to those of the beasts that perish, intellects vast and cool and unsympathetic, regarded this earth with envious eyes, and slowly and surely drew their plans against us. And early in the twentieth century came the great disillusionment. ■

Figure 4.37 Use prebuilt styles when designing a table.

The Local Restaurants List

The final major component in the newsletter is the table of local restaurants on the back page (Figure 4.37). This element begins life as a Microsoft Excel document that's placed into InDesign and formatted for looks and readability. To create the table, you'll begin by placing the Excel document and then apply prebuilt styles:

1. Choose File > Place, and navigate to the file named **RestaurantList.xls** in the Chapter 4 folder. Click Open to place the file on your page.
2. Select all the text, and choose Table > Convert Text To Table.
3. Place the Type tool in the upper-left corner of the table, and click when you see a diagonal-facing arrow.
4. With the whole table selected, go to the Table Styles panel, and click to apply the Restaurant Table style.
5. Place the Type tool just to the left of top row, and click when you see a small black arrow facing right.
6. With the row selected, choose Table > Merge Cells, or click the Merge Cells button in the Control panel (Figure 4.38).
7. With the top row still selected, apply the Table Title paragraph style.
8. Select the entire second row, and apply the Table Header cell style, which formats the type and applies a black fill to the row.
9. Drag with the Type tool to highlight all the cells beneath the Ratings header cell, and click to apply the Restaurant Ratings cell style.

Figure 4.38 Click the Merge Cells button.

Once you're happy with your newsletter, you're ready to export the file to PDF for others to proofread and review:

1. Choose File > Export.
2. In the Export PDF dialog, select the Smallest Size preset, and choose General > Include > Hyperlinks (Figure 4.39). Select the View PDF After Exporting check box. Notice that Bookmarks (provided you created some) and Page Thumbnails can also be enabled if you'd like.
3. Click the Export button to export the file to a PDF.

From the PDF you can convert the camp registration form into a digital form that can be filled out by anyone using the free Adobe Reader. Form data can then be extracted from the PDF and returned by email, as you'll see in the next section.

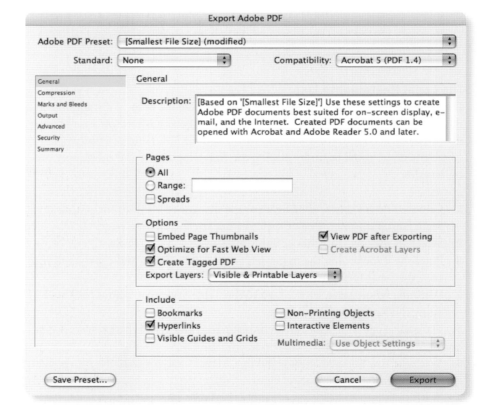

Figure 4.39 Finally, export your file as a PDF.

The Acrobat 8 Professional Component

Acrobat 8 Professional wins hands-down as the jack-of-all-trades component in Creative Suite 3. Nimble, flexible, and athletic, it's no wonder the program was named Acrobat years ago. Today Acrobat continues to do a little bit of everything and wins my vote for least understood and appreciated CS3 component.

With Acrobat 8 Professional, Adobe has added two landmark features: auto-form field recognition and the ability to create PDF forms that can read and be returned from Adobe Reader 7.0 and later. Without this last addition to the free Adobe Reader, creating PDFs with on-screen editable form fields would be of limited use. Thankfully, Adobe finally recognized this limitation and changed Adobe Reader accordingly.

Sending the Newsletter for Review and Comment

Prior to turning your summer camp registration form into an electronic document, you'll want to pass it around first to friends and colleagues for quick review (Figure 4.40). Traditionally, this process was done on paper and required someone to cull and collate reviewers' comments and manually type them into the original document.

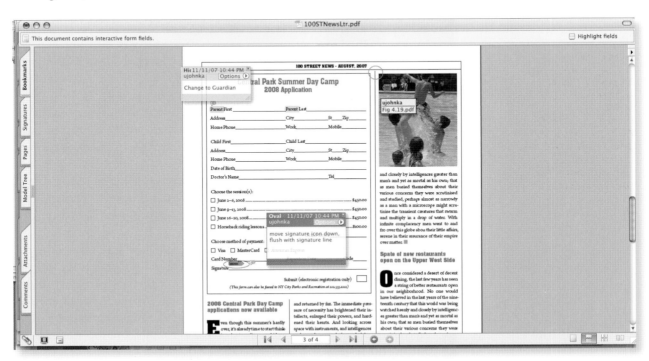

Figure 4.40 Sending your newsletter out for review is a simple task in Adobe Acrobat 8 Professional.

In the next section, you'll see how easy it is to send your newsletter or other document for electronic, on-screen review and how returned comments can be simply reconstituted into your original.

Types of Reviews   Acrobat 8 Professional has four flavors of review types, so before enabling your document for review, you'll want to review the reviews:

- *Shared reviews* are the most feature-rich and are designed for reviewers working behind firewalls who have access to a remote file server. Reviewers outside the firewall can review documents using their email and return comments to those within the firewall, who then publish the comments to the shared PDF. Shared reviews also have a notification feature, letting reviewers know when new comments are available regardless of whether Acrobat is open. Acrobat 8 or Adobe Reader 8 is required to view other reviewers' comments in a shared review.
- *Email-based reviews* are for those who don't have access to a remote server and who don't require real-time review collaboration. In this situation, a member of the group initiates the review by sending the PDF as a file attachment. Reviewers are invited to participate in the review and add comments and markup to the document. Those comments are then returned to the initiator with the PDF. Reviewers using Acrobat Professional also have the option to export only their comments and return them using the Form Data Format (FDF). Once the initiator receives the comments, the comments can be merged back into the master document. To participate in an email-based review, Acrobat 6.0 or newer and Adobe Reader 7.0 or newer is required in addition to a WebDAV-enabled server to host the review.
- *Browser-based reviews* are similar to shared reviews in that participants have access to a shared server. The PDF document is uploaded to the server, and reviewers are invited to participate via email. When the invitation is clicked, a setup file that's included in the email opens the PDF in the reviewer's browser. Comments are then sent back via the browser and stored on the shared file server. The disadvantages of browser-based reviews are that they have no mechanism for tracking changes and users of Adobe Reader can't participate.
- *Acrobat Connect meetings* are another way to conduct an interactive review using any Web browser. The initiator needs an Acrobat Connect account and then invites reviewers by email and an enclosed link to participate in a virtual meeting. Acrobat Connect meetings allow different levels of reviewer involvement, including two-way audio and video communication, and they even allow reviewers to control the screen and computer of the person conducting the review.

Initiating an Email-Based Review Of the four kinds of reviews listed earlier, an email-based review makes the most sense for your newsletter. This type of review will let you track the status of the review and merge comments into the PDF. During the process of initiating an email review, you'll want to enable commenting in Adobe Reader 7.0 or newer. When commenting is enabled in Reader, the document adds a message bar, instructions on how to add comments, and various commenting tools that otherwise don't exist.

1. From the Acrobat 8 task bar, click the Review And Comment button and select Attach For Email Review, or choose the same command from the Comments menu.
2. Fill out the Identity Setup dialog, and click Complete when done (Figure 4.41).
3. Follow the on-screen instructions, being sure to click the Customize Review Options button in the Review Options dialog to allow Reader 7.0 users to comment (Figure 4.42).

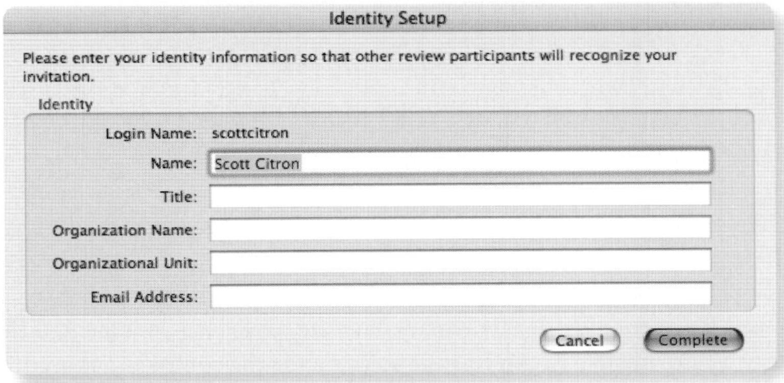

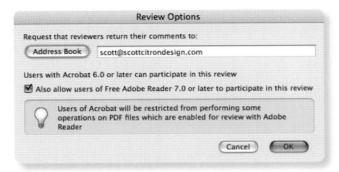

Figure 4.41 Determine how you want your identity to appear.

Figure 4.42 Make sure to allow those with only the Reader version of Acrobat to comment.

Figure 4.43 In Step 3, you're ready to send your invitation to review the PDF.

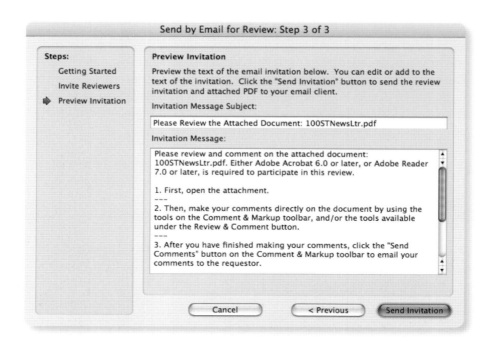

4. Preview the invitation in the Step 3 Of 3 dialog, and when finished, click the Send Invitation button (Figure 4.43).

Viewing and Merging Comments   Adobe has done a thorough job of closing the review circle when it comes to receiving notes and comments in an email-based review. To view the comments, the recipient opens the email attachment in Acrobat and is presented with this statement at the top of the document: "This is a copy of a PDF file in a managed review. To merge the comments from this copy into your tracked master copy, click Merge Comments." Or you can choose to Merge Comments Later (Figure 4.44).

Also at the top of the document is a button clearly marked Merge Comments, which merges comments from all marked-up PDFs into the original master document (Figure 4.45).

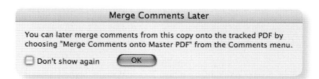

Figure 4.44 Merging the comments makes it much easier to review them all.

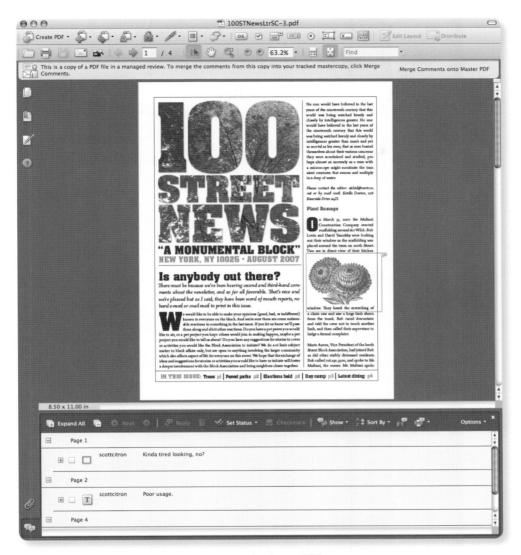

Figure 4.45 You can view all the comments together in one PDF.

Creating Electronic Forms

Once final design and copyediting changes to the newsletter have been made and accepted, the last mile of this project involves enabling the summer camp registration form for on-screen completion. Filling out forms by hand and then mailing or faxing them can really be annoying. By creating forms in Acrobat, readers of your newsletter are spared this tedious process. Not only does this make readers happier, but it tends to increase the amount of responses returned since doing so is painless.

Prior to Acrobat 8 Professional, designers could create electronic forms in Acrobat, but the process of creating and formatting form fields was done manually. With the release of version 8, most of the work is now handled through the Form Field Recognition feature:

1. From InDesign, export a final, corrected version of your newsletter to a PDF file.
2. In Acrobat 8 Professional, open the exported file.
3. Navigate to page 3, and choose Forms > Run Form Field Recognition.
4. For help with problems or questions, check the Recognition Report that's automatically generated by Acrobat.

Chances are all the fields were turned into forms except the Submit button at the lower right. One of the keys to successful form field recognition is using clearly legible type for form labels followed by a line to indicate fields. Without lines, Acrobat doesn't understand where to place form recognition fields.

No Lines Required

Just because Acrobat needs lines to know where to create form fields doesn't mean your form has to have lines when it's distributed. To create form fields without lines, place your lines on a separate layer in InDesign. Export the PDF as an Acrobat 6 or newer file, and select the Enable Acrobat Layers option. In Acrobat, run Form Field Recognition as usual. When you've finished, click the Layers button in the left navigation panel, and hide the visibility of the layer with your lines. As a last step, choose Flatten Layers from the Layers Options menu. Save your new file, which has electronic form fields minus form field lines!

Without a Submit button, your form is going nowhere. The last step in this project is to enable the Submit button to automatically return the form data to its home. Follow the next series of steps to accomplish this:

1. Click the Button tool in the Forms toolbar (View > Toolbars > Forms), and draw a button to match the size of the rectangle you created in InDesign (Figure 4.46).
2. In the General panel of the Button Properties dialog, complete the form as in Figure 4.47.
3. Choose a color for the button in the Appearance panel as in Figure 4.48.
4. Set your button options as in Figure 4.49.

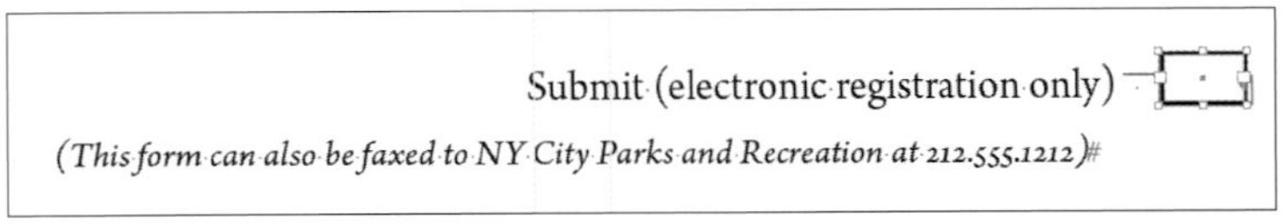

Submit (electronic registration only)

(This form can also be faxed to NY City Parks and Recreation at 212.555.1212)

Figure 4.46 Draw the button first.

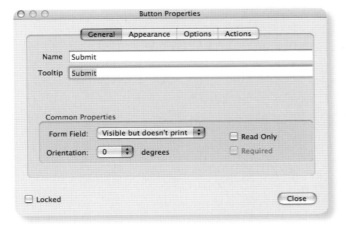

Figure 4.47 Assign the button properties.

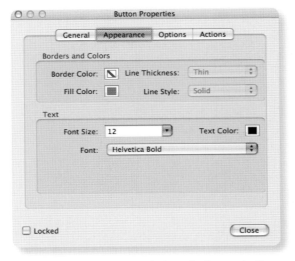

Figure 4.48 You can even select a color for your button.

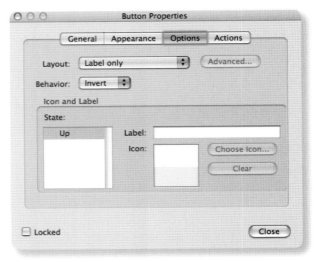

Figure 4.49 Set the options.

5. In the Actions panel, set the action to submit a form on mouse up (Figure 4.50).
6. Click the Add button, and type a URL or mailto: address for the Submit action (Figure 4.51). Be sure to select the FDF and All Fields radio buttons. Then click OK.
7. Return to the Actions panel, and click Close to complete the Submit action.

Figure 4.50 Add an action.

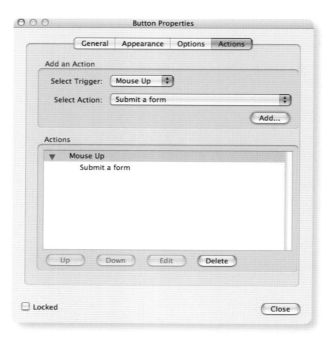

Figure 4.51 Set the return address last.

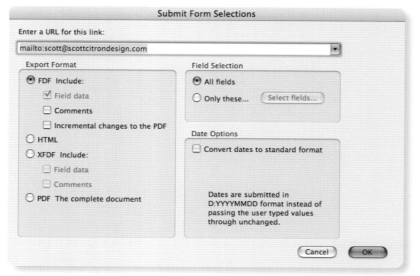

As you can see, you can choose numerous options when creating a Submit button, including the highlight style, tool tip display, button label options, and so on. For now you should have a simple green button that displays *Submit* in a tool tip when your mouse hovers over it. This green button appears only when the PDF is viewed on-screen and won't appear in the printed version of your newsletter.

Project Wrap-Up

After working through this project, you can appreciate that a lot goes into making a great newsletter. Fortunately for you, the hard work is now over. Subsequent issues of the newsletter will be easier once you've established a look and feel for your publication. By using style sheets, master pages, tables, and forms, designers free themselves from the drudgery of producing a monthly document, and they reap the rewards of more time to play with the creative side of design.

Chapter 5 | Designing Magazines and Newspapers

"EVERY PUBLICATION NEEDS *FIZZ*: AN ELEMENT OF SURPRISE THAT SEPARATES IT FROM THE REST.... IT IS A SPECIAL TOUCH THAT CAN LIFT A HEADLINE, A STORY, A PAGE DESIGN, HOW A PHOTO LOOKS ON THE PAGE. IT HAS LITTLE TO DO WITH WHAT ONE HEARD IN THE FOCUS GROUP AND ALL TO DO WITH THE EMOTION OF THE MOMENT." — Dr. Mario R. Garcia

Perhaps the most surefire way to gauge the health of the magazine business is to talk to advertisers. According to *Advertising Age*, "The top 100 U.S. advertisers last year (2006) increased ad spending by a modest 3.1% to a record $104.8 billion. But most of that growth came from 'unmeasured' disciplines. In a troubling sign for traditional media, the marketing leaders increased measured media spending by just 0.6%, the smallest gain since the 2001 recession."

The news for newspapers isn't much better. If you've opened the *New York Times* lately, you've probably noticed it has gone on a diet. The *Times*' management recently trimmed 1½ inches off the paper's width to save money on paper and printing costs. It was the same thing at the *Wall Street Journal*, which was recently swallowed by Rupert Murdoch's mammoth News Corporation.

So, does this bleak forecast portend the end of magazines and newspapers? Admittedly the future looks dim, but don't rush to eulogize such long-standing forms of communication quite yet. Instead, this trend more than anything underscores that good magazine and newspaper design is now more critical than ever. As publishers move toward digital delivery via the Internet, only the strong will survive on paper. This chapter shows how to create great-looking magazines and newspapers. You'll learn what makes these kinds of publications stand out and how you can build your own magazine or newspaper using the wealth of tools in Adobe Creative Suite 3.

What Makes Great Magazines and Newspapers?

Much as I'd like to credit the power of great design as the cornerstone of success when it comes to magazines and newspapers, the fact is that even the most handsome publication will fail if the stories stink. In other words, content is still king. If readers have nothing worth reading, then even the most captivating publication won't last. Unfortunately, graphic designers generally have no control over the quality of the writing in their magazines or newspapers. So in this regard, they're stuck with what they're given. But, assuming the writing is good (or good enough), then designers have a chance. And in the end, it's the editorial content that the design must serve. Often young designers get this relationship between words and pictures backward. They are so intent in making their voices heard that they drown out that of the writer. Yet when the design works in concert with the words, when both voices sing together harmoniously, publications soar.

Stacey King, in her inspiring book *Magazine Design That Works: Secrets for Successful Magazine Design* (Rockport Publishers, 2001), distills the principles of magazine design into what she calls the Four Fs: format, formula, frame, and function. For examples of excellence in magazine design, look no further than last year's award winners chosen by the Society of Publication Designers (www.spd.org). Among those consistently cited by the organization for their outstanding design are *GQ* (www.gq.com), *Martha Stewart Living* (www.marthastewart.com), *Details* (http://men.style.com/gq), and *Real Simple* (www.realsimple.com).

Designing for Magazines and Newspapers

Good design is good design, but when it comes to designing for magazines and newspapers, it helps to understand how they differ. And the way in which they differ has more to do with shelf life than any other factor. Think of the newspaper as a frail flower; here today, gone tomorrow. In its short life span, the daily newspaper must grab the attention of readers quickly, deliver cogent content, and then fold up at night. Since they're around only for 24 hours, newspapers behave similarly to a short story. They start fast, hook their reader, tell their tale, and then abruptly end. Magazines, conversely, are more like a novel. They open slowly, introduce their characters (sections), build toward a meaty center, reach their height, and then trail off quietly. Magazines are something you pick up, read, put down, pick up later, read some more, put down, pick up once more, and so on. Now of course there are exceptions to this portrayal, but most newspapers and magazines follow this basic pattern. Whereas magazines can go for pages without ads sharing space with editorial content, newspapers rarely do. Newspapers also tend toward fewer graphic elements in favor of column after relentless column of copy. Only special newspaper sections like a Sunday magazine or a weekly book review are afforded space to do much of anything graphically. An interesting trend to follow these days is how, because of the convergence of print and digital, many newspapers are supplementing written stories with audio, video, and even interactive pieces on the Web. The once very conservative and staunchly traditional *New York Times* is one such example. Today many stories in the daily *Times* are fleshed out in greater detail at www. nytimes.com.

Typography for Magazines and Newspapers

So, how do these factors affect the way each is designed? Renowned publication designer and consultant Dr. Mario Garcia concludes his excellent book *Pure Design* (Miller Media, 2002) with his top 10 myths of magazine and newspaper design. Of the 10, several of these myths revolve around type. For example, Dr. Garcia contends that, based on his research and experience, the notion that justified type is more readable than ragged right is pure myth. And he states that the tightly held beliefs that italics are hard to read and that readers don't like reversed-out type are also unsubstantiated. Yet despite Dr. Garcia's lofty credentials as an award-winning publication doctor, just see how far you get with your executive editor the next time you try to flout one of these conventions. Although attitudes are changing, most newspaper and magazine decision makers keep designers on a very short leash when it comes to breaking the so-called rules of type. Magazines, on the other hand, generally offer more room to experiment with less conventional solutions. For examples of creative uses of type in the magazine world, look again at some of the award-winning titles mentioned at the beginning of this chapter.

Parts of a Magazine

Before you design a magazine, it helps to familiarize yourself with the vocabulary of magazines and the magazine business. The first third of a magazine is referred to as the *front of the book* (FOB), the last third is called the *back of the book* (BOB), and the middle or meat of the magazine is called the *well*. Typically the well is free of advertising. Pages that contain both editorial content and advertising are called *fractional pages* or simply *fractionals*. See Figure 5.1 for more of a breakdown of the magazine's parts.

Figure 5.1 Here are some terms used to describe various parts of a magazine, or what's called in the business "*the book.*"

A Headline (or Hed)
B Deck (or Dek)
C Byline
D Caption
E Body Text
F Subhead
G Folio
H Footer
I Sidebar
J Pull Quote or Call Out
K Gutter

Let's Design a Magazine

The project for this chapter is an article called "Tutte Le Strade Portano a Roma (All Roads Lead to Rome)" for a fictitious magazine named *Food + Travel*. Not unlike other great magazines such as *Food & Wine*, *Travel + Leisure*, or *Condé Nast Traveler*, *Food + Travel* celebrates great places and great cuisines around the globe. For a taste of *Food + Travel*, visit the book's companion Web site at www.peachpit.com/prodesignCS3, and open the file named **Food_Travel.pdf** in the Chapter 05 folder (Figure 5.2). In terms of design mechanics, this project is simple and uncomplicated. You'll start by setting up master pages, folios, and footers. Then you'll move on to developing a grid, creating a color system, importing text, and exploring the advantages of OpenType fonts. So if you're ready, let's get started.

Figure 5.2 Download the files from www.peachpit.com/prodesignCS3 if you'd like to follow along with the project for this chapter.

Setting Up the Document

Before you begin, it's important to load the fonts for this project. You'll find the fonts in the Chapter 5 folder. Use your font manager of choice to load and activate these fonts before continuing.

In InDesign, choose File > New Document, and use the settings as shown in Figure 5.3. Click the Save Preset button, and name the document preset *Food+Travel*. Click OK to exit the dialog.

Note that this layout uses six columns, instead of the usual two, three, or four. The reason you want to work this way is to add flexibility to your page layout.

TIP: No font manager? No problem. Adobe InDesign has its own Fonts folder inside the InDesign CS3 application folder. Any fonts placed in this folder (or any alias or shortcut to an outside fonts folder) will become instantly available to InDesign once they're placed in this folder. In fact, if you'd like your fonts available to any Adobe application, place them in the Application Support/Adobe/Fonts folder.

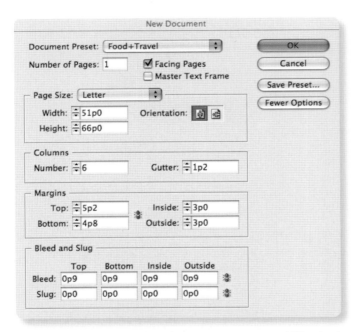

Figure 5.3 Choose a six-column layout so you can use additional columns when you need them.

You'll see this if you study Figure 5.4 for a moment. As you can see, some pages employ two columns of text, with each column spanning three page columns. Other pages use three columns of text, with each column spanning two page columns. Another page uses two text columns, with each column spanning only two columns each. This particular setup leaves two extra columns that can be used for captions, sidebars, or photos or can be left empty as a visual breather. This multiple-column approach lets you use the same master page for a wide variety of design scenarios, depending on what best works for the layout.

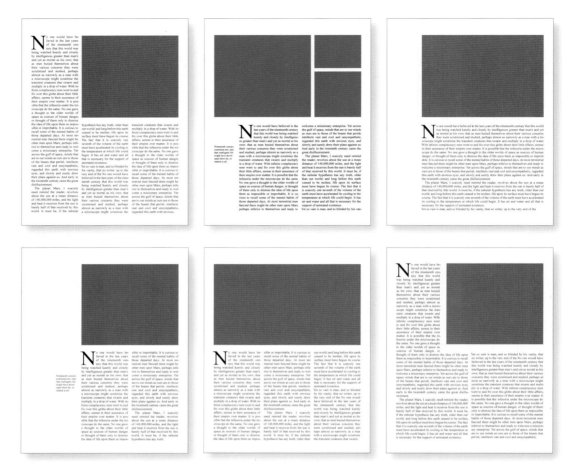

Figure 5.4 Here are several examples of how a multi-column page can add design flexibility to your layout.

Fractional Pages

In my job as a trainer and consultant I often run across magazines with 10 to 20 master pages. While it's important to have enough masters, don't feel obligated to have a master for every conceivable design possibility. Instead, design a small handful of flexible masters that can be easily repurposed to handle a reasonable variety of tasks. In our *Food + Travel* layout, I've created one A-Master (what I'll call the *Master Master*) and two more that are based on the A-Master. Both B and C masters are designed for ads that typically don't interrupt a feature story but are more commonly found in other parts of the magazine. Ad pages like these are known as *fractional pages* or simply *fractionals*.

Adding Footers

It's critical that magazines include page numbers (known as *folios*) so that readers know what page they're on. The folio is then part of the overall footer, which usually includes the name of the publication and its issue date. The folio is important for keeping the reader oriented. Because photos in magazines often bleed off the page bottom, you'll want to place your footers on a higher layer level so they won't be covered by images or conflicting graphics. Doing so is easy when using the InDesign Layers panel.

1. From the Layers panel menu, choose New Layer. Name the layer Footers.
2. With the Footers layer targeted, click and drag a text frame with the Type tool.
3. With your text cursor blinking in the text frame, click to select the Type menu and choose Insert Special Characters > Markers > Current Page Number. This will insert the letter A into the frame as a placeholder for the folio, which will appear on the document pages.
4. Add the name of the publication and the issue date to the footers.
5. In the Layers panel, create a New Layer and double-click to rename it text.

Choosing a Color Palette

Did you ever notice that spring and summer editions of magazines tend to use lots of pastel yellows, greens, and blues? And that fall and winter editions are filled with rich oranges, reds, and browns? Was that the communal sound of all readers thumping their foreheads in unison and saying "Duh"?

As obvious as this may sound, the point remains that colors trigger innate, deeply ingrained responses in people. White signals purity, black connotes stealth, blue equals serenity, pink evokes softness, yellow means warmth, and so on. So without knowing anything about color, you probably know more than you think. Perhaps this is oversimplifying. Have you ever left your house wondering whether your shirt matched your pants? At one point I considered wearing only white shirts just to avoid this kind of daily color-matching uncertainty. What about choosing paint chips at a hardware store? It's a nightmare, right? So in reality, sometimes mixing color *is* hard. But working with color doesn't have to be hard. Today a number of sophisticated solutions make the job easier. In addition, by following a few simple rules when working with color, the job of what to wear with a blue suit need not be so traumatic.

NOTE: After following these steps, you should have three layers: Layer 1, Footers, and text. All graphics should be assigned to Layer 1, your folios and the magazine name and issue information should be on the Footer layer, and all other text should be placed on the text layer (Figure 5.5).

Figure 5.5 There are three layers at this stage in the project.

Keeping Cool with kuler

One of the best things to come along for the color-challenged is the new Adobe Web site kuler (lowercase *k* intentional). This Flash-based interactive color picker is one of my favorite places to play online. Aside from the pure fun of using kuler, it is just plain useful when it comes to choosing compatible colors. Here's how to use kuler for this magazine spread. Start first by opening http://kuler.adobe.com in your browser. Look around or jump to the tutorials at kuler.adobe.com/tutorials. As you'll see, kuler is more than just an online color-harmony finder/creator; it's a community of color aficionados. The idea is simple. Choose a base color, and then select any color harmony type based on the base color. Does that sound a little like the Live Color feature in Illustrator CS3?

Here's how to choose a base color from which kuler will generate the rest of a palette:

NOTE: Once swatches are saved to your kuler collection, click the middle button shown here to download the swatches as an Adobe Swatch Exchange file (.ase).

1. In Adobe Photoshop CS3, open the file in the Chapter 05 folder named **TiberView.psd**. This image will occupy most of the opening spread.
2. Choose Filter > Blur > Average. Select the Eyedropper tool in the Toolbox, and click anywhere in the image. Write down the CMYK formula for the image. Click to close the image without saving the changes.
3. By running the Average filter, you now have a set of numbers to plug into kuler to use as the base color. After registering and logging in to kuler (it's free), click the Create link on the left side of the page.
4. Click the far-left swatch to establish it as the base color (Figure 5.6). Set the color rule to Triad. Click to activate the CMYK sliders. Drag the CMYK sliders, or type the corresponding values you wrote down in Photoshop. Name your colors, and save them to your mykuler space. Click to download your saved colors in Adobe's .ase file format (Adobe Swatch Exchange).
5. Now return to InDesign, and import your kuler swatches before you begin. Choose Load Swatches from the Swatches panel menu, and navigate to your .ase file. Click OK to add your kuler swatches to the InDesign Swatches panel. As you'll see as you get further into designing the article, these swatches will be very useful for small touches of accent color.

Beginning the Layout

Now you're ready to start the layout. Your next step is to change the first page of the layout from a right page to a left page. The easiest way to do this is by resetting the document's page section options, as follows:

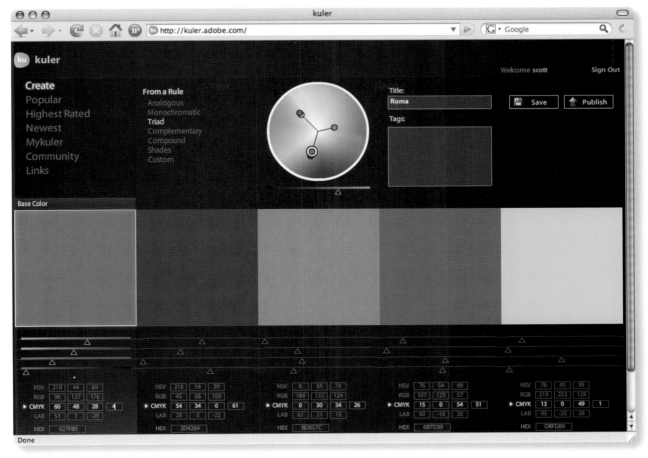

Figure 5.6 Light blue is selected here as the base color.

1. In InDesign, click the icon at the upper left of the Pages panel to open the Pages panel menu.
2. Choose Numbering & Section Options.
3. Click the button next to Start Page Numbering At, and type any even number. For now, type **24**. Click OK to apply the new section number.

When you return to the Pages panel, you'll see that the first page is now a left page, with the *24* beneath it. Now add another page by clicking the Create New Page button at the bottom of the Pages panel (Figure 5.7).

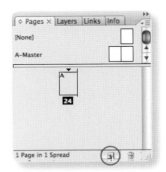

Figure 5.7 Create another page by clicking here.

Figure 5.8 There is some distortion in the photograph that should be fixed.

Correcting Distortion in the Opening Image

With your blank spread in view, begin the layout by placing the **TiberUncorrected.jpg** image across two-thirds of the spread (File > Place). You might notice that the photo is badly distorted because of the nature of the small point-and-shoot camera used to take the shot. See how the bridge railing and the statue curve upward at the right side of the photo (Figure 5.8)? Before continuing, you'll correct the distortion using the Lens Correction filter in Photoshop:

1. In InDesign, click to select the image, and then double-click it while holding Option (Mac OS) or Alt (Windows). This keyboard shortcut opens any image or graphic in its original parent application.
2. In Photoshop, select the Background layer and choose Filter > Convert for Smart Filters. Converting the layer to a Smart Layer gives you the freedom to change filter settings anytime, even after the file has been saved.
3. Choose Filter > Distort > Lens Correction. The Lens Correction dialog opens.
4. Click the image to turn on the grid. This will give you something to check your horizontal and vertical elements against (Figure 5.9) Start by setting Remove Distortion to 4.00. This will correct what's known as *barrel distortion* introduced by the lens.
5. In the Transform area, set the angle to -1.90. The bridge railing should not appear parallel with the horizontal lines of your grid. To compensate for the distortion introduced when shooting upward toward the statue, set Vertical Perspective to -14. Check the vertical of the statue base to ensure that it's now parallel with the grid verticals.

Figure 5.9 Correct distortion by making some minor tweaks in the Lens Correction dialog.

6. Before exiting the dialog, drag the Scale slider to about 111% so the corrected image fills the view. Check once more to make sure horizontals and verticals line up as much as possible. Turn the Preview on and off. You should see a big difference from where the image began.

7. Return the Scale slider to 100%, and click OK to commit the changes.

Adding Some Drama

The next step is to make the image a bit more dramatic since it is the opening image for the story. You'll do this by adding two adjustment layers and then finish by sharpening the photo using a technique you may have tried already:

1. At the bottom of the Layers palette, click the New Adjustment Layers button, and then choose Levels to add a new Levels adjustment layer.

2. In the Levels dialog, drag the black input slider slightly to the right to increase the contrast (Figure 5.10). Click OK to close the dialog.

   Next you'll warm up the image and give it more of an afternoon glow by adding a Photo Filter adjustment layer.

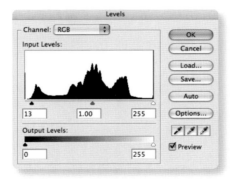

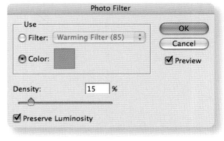

Figure 5.11 Warm up your image by choosing Warming Filter (85).

Figure 5.10 Increase the contrast by dragging the black input slider to the right.

3. At the bottom of the Layers palette, click the New Adjustment Layer button, and choose Photo Filter.

4. In the Photo Filter dialog, choose Warming Filter (85), and set Density to 15% (Figure 5.11). This setting simulates a #85 filter used with traditional film cameras to add a slight yellow-orange tint to images.

5. Select the Preserve Luminosity option. This setting ensures that the brightness of the image (or luminosity) is maintained despite the filter.

6. Click OK. Save the file as a native Photoshop file, and name it **TiberView.psd**.

Adding the two Levels adjustment layers not only improves the overall look of the image but does it nondestructively and without making the file larger, because adjustment layers don't increase file size. Next you'll sharpen the image slightly, which will also help make it pop off the page.

Sharpening the Image

It's safe to say that all digital images can benefit from some degree of sharpening. Although sharpening can occur in the camera when the image is processed, most professionals leave this important step to Photoshop to maintain maximum control. The problem with most sharpening routines is that they don't discriminate between what they sharpen. The Unsharp Mask filter in Photoshop works well but sharpens noise along with everything else in the image. The Smart Sharpen filter is an improvement over unsharp masking and is duly named because it can sharpen shadows and highlights separately. The following method uses the best of both worlds and allows a great degree of adjustment for just the right amount of sharpening:

1. Presa and hold the Shift key, and click to select all three layers of your **TiberView.psd** image in the Layers palette.

2. Merge all three layers, and place the new merged layer at the top of the Layers palette by pressing Shift+Option+Command+E (Mac OS) or Shift+Alt+Ctrl+E (Windows).
3. Change the blend mode of the new layer to Overlay.
4. Choose Filters > Other > High Pass.
5. With the Preview check box selected, drag the filter slider to a radius of about 2.0 pixels. Click OK to close the dialog.

What's great about this technique is that you can control the amount of sharpening by adjusting the layer's opacity. Also, areas where you want no sharpening to occur (such as with the sky, for example) can be held back by adding a layer mask. Try using the Magic Wand tool to select all but the foreground (hold down Shift and click with the Magic Wand until the entire sky is selected). When you've made your selection, add a Layer Mask by holding Option (Mac OS) or Alt (Windows) and clicking on the Add Vector Mask button at the bottom of the Layers palette. This will fill the selection of the layer mask with black, thereby preventing the sharpening from being applied to the sky. Resave the file. You'll return to InDesign to continue working on the opening spread.

What Makes a Good Opening?

Just like the old saying that you can't tell a book by its cover, you can't tell an article by its opening page or spread. Although this axiom may be true, chances are your readers won't even read your article if the opening lacks punch. Even if readers do read on, a lifeless or boring opening subconsciously suggests to them that a lifeless or boring article is about to follow. So, what then makes readers want to turn the page? Bright colors? Large headlines? Dull colors? Tiny headlines? Although there's no recipe for success when it comes to openings, the secret is to engage the reader in some way.

Think of the opening as a pair of closed velvet curtains at the theater. You have no idea what's behind the curtains, but the music coming from the orchestra pit sets a tone of intrigue or expectation that is meant to increase feelings of excitement and anticipation. In the same way, the opening page or pages of a magazine article must also build excitement and anticipation and make the reader pause instead of flipping past the article. For graphic designers, the article opening is often the most fun to design. And, as would be expected, magazine editors typically spend hours laboring over multiple openings in search of the one that sets just the right tone. A common exercise in design schools is to create multiple openings using the same elements in each, as I've done in Figure 5.12. Would you have chosen the same opener? If not, why, and how might it be better?

Figure 5.12 You may want to experiment with a variety of styles until you hit the right tone.

TUTTE LE STRADE PORTANO A **ROMA**

There's a reason they say all roads lead to Rome. In this exclusive for Food+Travel we walk the streets to bring you the best of the Eternal City.
Text and photographs by Scott Citron

TUTTE LE STRADE PORTANO A

ROMA

There's a reason they say all roads lead to Rome. vvIn this exclusive for Food+Travel we walk the streets to bring you the best of the Eternal City.
Text and photographs by Scott Citron

The Devil Is In the Details

Some small details deserve mention. Otherwise unnoticed by the casual viewer or student, these details collectively make the difference between good design and great design:

The pizza O on the opening page of the project bothered me for days until I realized that it was too red. Desaturating the image in Photoshop using a Hue and Saturation adjustment layer toned down its color and made it blend more harmoniously with the other elements on the page. Removing a slice from the pie in Photoshop also gave the photo more character.

In the FOOD + TRAVEL footer, the plus sign (+) is 7 pts, while the rest of the text is 8.5 pts. The plus is also shifted 1 pt up from the baseline to make it center vertically between the words *FOOD* and *TRAVEL*.

The photo on the left in page 26 of the project and the large photo on page 27 started out distorted but were fixed with the Lens Correction filter in Photoshop.

In addition, the sky of the photo on page 27 was enhanced with a Multiply mode applied to a blank Levels adjustment layer. A layer mask was used to confine the adjustment to the sky only. To see how this image was transformed, open the file in Photoshop, hold down Option (Mac OS) or Alt (Windows), and click the Background layer visibility icon (the eye) to hide or show all layers except the Background layer.

In the Ingredients part of the pasta recipe, the amount of each ingredient is 1 pt smaller than the ingredient itself. This was done for the sake of visual balance. Try increasing the ingredient amount size by 1 pt to see whether you agree.

The rainfall graph on page 29 was created in Illustrator using the Bar Graph tool. Colors were added to the graph from a group of harmonious swatches generated in kuler.

The two black-and-white images on pages 30 and 31 were converted from color using the new Black & White feature in Photoshop CS3, applied as a nondestructive adjustment layer.

Optical Margin Alignment was applied throughout the article. As a result, the justified body text maintains clean and crisp edges uninterrupted by punctuation as normally occurs without this feature.

Pouring Copy

At this point, you should be ready to bring in your text file and place it on the first few pages. This process, known as *pouring text* or *pouring copy*, generally occurs before photos and graphics are placed. Don't worry too much about where the copy falls; the important thing is to just get it somewhere on the page. Once it's all there, then you can begin formatting the copy and moving it as needed.

Getting Your Team on Board

One of the most vexing problems for print and publication designers is placing text files into a layout. Ideally, text comes in preformatted with all the proper styles so the designer can spend more time designing and less time formatting. Sadly, this is rarely the case. Instead, a more typical scenario is that some text comes in correctly, but most doesn't. Even worse, text that has been formatted by the writer to indicate bold or italics ends up losing its attributes. As a result, designers waste more time trying to replace the lost formatting. If this problem sounds familiar, there is hope. But also know that the fix requires some effort and a bit of diligence on the part of writers and editors to make it work. Provided everyone on your magazine staff is willing to follow the rules, the process of pouring text can still require some post-pour formatting.

Learning to Love Character Styles

The key to all this formatting business is based on understanding and using character styles. Character styles, to refresh your memory, are styles that are specific to characters only. Unlike paragraph styles, which apply to *all* characters in a paragraph, character styles apply only to selected (or highlighted) characters. For example, the word *all* has been formatted with a character style called Italic. Couldn't you just click the little slanted *I* button in Microsoft Word to do the same thing? Well, yes and no. Yes, in that clicking the little slanted *I* button in Word would make the word look italic. No, because creating italics that way (described as *local formatting*) may come at a price. The price is that if, after pouring your Word document into InDesign, you then apply a paragraph style and use the Option (Mac OS) or Alt (Windows) key to override any other unexpected styling, you'll wind up wiping out your beloved italics. But, if you use a character style to italicize or bold words you want to emphasize, applying a paragraph style to your text in InDesign won't eliminate your styling. Why not? Well, in the hierarchy of style sheets, character styles trump paragraph styles. So, what's the big deal? Why does it sound so hard? The fact is, it's not! What's hard is getting people to change how they format text and remembering to use character styles.

More About Microsoft Word Documents

For years I tried to exert my will over Word to force it to behave, to outthink it into submission, but in my dotage I've given up the fight. Despite my best intentions and those of the mighty InDesign engineering team, trying to import Word documents perfectly into InDesign remains a hit-or-miss proposition. Fortunately for all of us, I've learned of a better, less-hair-pulling solution. It goes something like this:

1. Create a blank page of any size in InDesign.
2. Choose File > Place, and navigate to your Word .doc file. Click OK to place the file on your page.
3. Click to insert your text cursor in the document.
4. Choose File > Export > Rich Text Format.
5. Close the blank page file, which is no longer needed. Choose File > Place, and now place the exported RTF document.

What's cool about this technique is that the RTF file supports all the intentional formatting done in the Word file (the stuff you want) while eliminating the underlying and annoying styles Word tends to bring along for the ride. If something still goes wrong when you place your text, make sure your Character style is set to None. If not, the selected style will apply itself automatically and override your intended style when text is placed.

Just one final note: saving a Word .doc file as an .rtf file does *not* get you the same result, so don't bother. Often you'll find it more convenient to simply copy and paste text from Word into InDesign. This approach makes sense when text is broken up into lots of chunks, where flowing large quantities of text won't work. If you decide to use this technique, be aware that InDesign brings along Word styles only if you deselect the default preference that controls this function (Preferences > Clipboard Handling > When Pasting Text and Tables from Other Applications). Again, this means that if the document's creator used local formatting to indicate bold and italics, those attributes will be lost when the text is pasted into InDesign.

Type and Tone

Imagine, if you will, that when you wake up tomorrow you learn that the *New York Times* has changed its body font from Cheltenham to Comic Sans. And that the *Wall Street Journal* now uses Marker Felt for all its headlines. Over at the *New Yorker*, Sabon is out and Hobo is in. Scary, huh? Fortunately, the chances of this happening are slim to none, but never say never. The point of this painful exercise is to make you aware of how type sets a mood or a tone for a publication and how the wrong font can upset an otherwise harmonious balance of words and pictures. Just as color has personality, type has its own personality, too. Generally designers understand this fact, but sometimes the obvious bears repeating. In other words, choose your fonts carefully, and make sure the personality of your type matches the personality of the page. Occasionally this maxim can be turned on its head to great effect, and like all rules, this one can be broken when appropriate. Pay close attention to the tone of the piece—let it guide your choice of type. In this project I've chosen all OpenType fonts: Arno Pro for the body text, Memphis LT Std for the headlines and other display needs such as the deck and the quote from Emperor Augustus (Figure 5.13), and Myriad Pro for the photo captions and the pasta recipe (Figure 5.14). With its support for true fractions, Myriad Pro lends itself well to designing a clean, clear page that's easy to follow.

Figure 5.13 Memphis LT Std gives this quote a classic, elegant look when placed with the photographs surrounding it.

Bucatini all' Amatriciana

Named for the town of Amatrice outside of Rome, this rich dish is quick to prepare and uses common ingredients. The addition of balsamic vinegar gives it a wonderful depth that compliments the taste of the onions and pancetta. Makes 4–6 servings.

Ingredients

3	tablespoons extra virgin olive oil
4	ounces pancetta sliced into 1 x ⅛ inch strips
1	medium onion, chopped
½	tablespoon balsamic vinegar
5	large tomatoes, peeled, cored, and chopped
2	tablespoons tomato paste

¾	cup freshly grated Parmesano Reggiano
⅔	teaspoon dried red pepper flakes
1	pound bucatini or linguini
	Italian parsley, chopped (optional)
	salt and pepper to taste

Core tomatoes and score the bottom with an X. Place into boiling water for one minute and then remove. Run under cold water until cool. Peel tomatoes, cut in half and remove seeds with your fingers. Using your hands, crush well and place in a bowl to rest.

Heat enough oil to cover the bottom of the pan. Add onions and pancetta and cook until nicely browned. Add dried pepper flakes and cook for one minute. Clear an area at the bottom of the pan and add tomato paste. Cook to carmelize the paste for one minute. Add vinegar, mix with other ingredients and cook one minute. Add crushed tomatoes and simmer for 6–8 minutes.

Boil pasta until very al dente. Reserving one cup of water, drain pasta and toss into sauce. Continue cooking in the sauce until the pasta is done, adding additional water if needed. Ladle into bowls and freshen with a quick drizzle of olive oil. Sprinkle with grated cheese and parsley and serve.

Figure 5.14 Myriad Pro is a good choice for its readability and clean look.

A lifetime ago when I was studying to be a film director, a wise acting coach once told me, "You can't muscle comedy." By that she meant that forcing something to be funny only ends up being forced. And forced ain't funny. Over the years as I drifted away from showbiz and toward the design biz, her sage words about comedy still resonate whenever I'm stuck wondering what to do with a pile of words and images. For me the answer always lies in simplicity. When a design is not working, it's usually because I'm trying too hard to force a structure onto it; I'm trying to muscle the page into submission. Be aware of falling into the same trap. When you catch yourself forcing your design, try taking a deep breath to relax. Sometimes removing everything from the page helps, too. Staring at the blank page tends to calm me down and allows me to begin slowly reapplying elements one by one until a new balance emerges.

Project Wrap-Up

The strength of the *Food + Travel* layout is an elegance that's anchored by a simple grid. Helping to accentuate the grid is lots of whitespace and mostly single-column text frames. As an experiment, try moving the text frames elsewhere on the grid. You'll find that depending on where the text is placed, some configurations create tension while others don't. Whereas tension in life is usually a bad thing, tension in design can often be just the opposite.

On page 29 of the article, however, notice that the text and rainfall graph violate the grid out of necessity (Figure 5.15). Sometimes breaking the grid is as important as following it.

Also pay attention to the sequencing and pacing of the pages and spreads, as described in Chapter 1, "Getting Started." The layout is a great example of this concept when designing multipage publications. Look at Figure 5.16 to see a linear progression of thumbnails that reinforces this point.

Figure 5.15 The grid is an excellent guide but you should feel free to break out of it if needed.

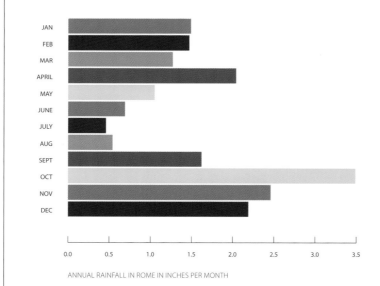

LEFT: What more can you say about the interior of the dome at San Giovanni in Laterano?

OPPOSITE: Piazza del Popolo acts like a hub for the three main streets that feed into it: Via di Ripetta, Via del Corso, and Via del Babuino.

Rome's Rain

Although Rome enjoys a typically southern climate, it does get its fair share of rain. In the graph below note how the rainy season begins in October but tapers off by March, despite a brief spike in April. All amounts in inches.

JAN
FEB
MAR
APRIL
MAY
JUNE
JULY
AUG
SEPT
OCT
NOV
DEC

0.0   0.5   1.0   1.5   2.0   2.5   3.0   3.5

ANNUAL RAINFALL IN ROME IN INCHES PER MONTH

Figure 5.16 Sequence and pacing is achieved in this series of spreads from the project.

Chapter 6 | Books and Longer Documents

"THE WORLD IS COMPLEX, DYNAMIC, MULTIDIMENSIONAL;
THE PAPER IS STATIC, FLAT. HOW ARE WE TO REPRESENT THE
RICH VISUAL WORLD OF EXPERIENCE AND MEASUREMENT ON
MERE FLATLAND?" — Edward R. Tufte

Unlike many design projects whose brief life can be compared to that of a beautiful butterfly, what makes longer documents such as books fun to create is their permanent nature. You can knock yourself out designing the greatest invitation, newsletter, or magazine spread, but before long it's bound for the trash. Books, on the other hand, are often revered, collected, deified, and displayed for years or lifetimes on one's shelf like a literary trophy. It's no wonder the buying and selling of antiquarian books is a healthy profession for many. Whereas the book you design today might fetch thousands of dollars years later, it's doubtful anyone will give a hoot about the cool flyer you did for the church bazaar.

What Makes a Good Book?

When pondering what makes a good book, keep in mind that I'm not talking about snappy dialogue or happy endings. Yes, yes, I know, ask any writer or fledgling writer, and they'll tell you that what makes a book good are the words,

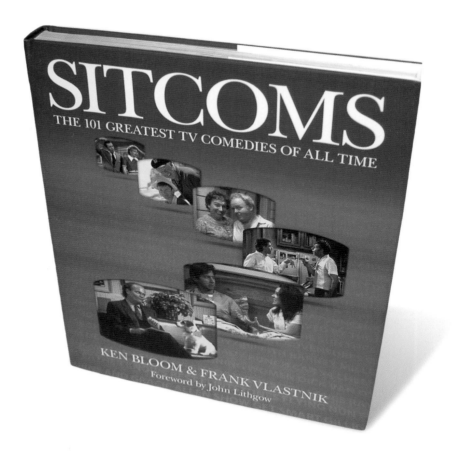

Figure 6.1 The project for this chapter is based on real pages from *Sitcoms: The 101 Greatest TV Comedies of All Time* (Black Dog & Leventhal Publishers, 2007). On the facing page are several iterations of the cover as it was being designed.

not the pictures. In the case of a novel or piece of nonfiction, such an analysis is largely true. Nobody ever read *The Brothers Karamazov* for the breathtaking photos. But then not all books are about the words. Some, like the *Sitcoms* book around which this chapter's project is based, relies heavily on a visual hierarchy of photos and graphics to communicate the subject of television comedies (Figure 6.1). Books like this, known as *illustrated books* in the publishing business, offer designers page upon page of opportunity to ply their wares. Unfortunately, it's exactly this reliance on graphic freshness that makes designing illustrated books so challenging. Not only must each page look somewhat unique, but unlike novels where designers can pour in 300-plus pages of one-column continuous text, illustrated books are built from scraps, snippets, and bits of text.

How to Begin Designing a Book

As a book designer, I'm often asked whether I read the book before I design it, which always gives me a little chuckle. The fact is that most books I design aren't even written when I begin. Typically I'll start with only a chapter or two and work almost in parallel with the author or authors. As new chapters are written and sent to the editor, to the copyeditor, and back to the writers and editor for a final pass, I keep plugging away on whatever finished text I have at the time. Yet to understand how books are designed, it's helpful to understand how they're sold.

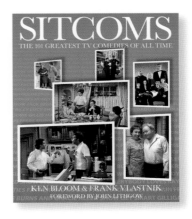

Books, much like movies, are presold before they're sold. This means a publisher peddles the idea of the book to resellers and distributors long before committing an army of writers, editors, and designers to the project. By preselling a book, the publisher knows going in whether there will be any interest in the publication when the finished books come off the trucks. If there is early interest, resellers and distributors often commit to buying x amount of final copies, which naturally affects which books get made and which don't.

As part of preselling a book, it's common for me to design not only a sample cover or two of the book but to also put together a few interior spreads. With color ink-jet or laser prints in hand, the publisher can then venture forth into the urban jungle in the hope of drumming up presales for the book. For special projects, publishers will even commercially print and bind a smattering of pages from the proposed book with its cover into a slick presentation piece called a *blad*. The better the blad, the bigger the sale, so much care is taken early on to craft a compelling presentation.

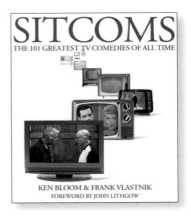

Blad or no blad, it's often early in a book's genesis that a designer becomes involved. This period is often the most fun because it's at this stage that creative playtime is encouraged. This is the time where different layout approaches, fonts, and graphic styles are tried on in an effort to see which best fits the book. Of course, having some photos or real text always helps but can't be expected.

If given the choice, I always like to start by designing the jacket or cover first (Figure 6.2). Since the cover is what the reader sees first, establishing the graphic style of the cover, a controllable one page, goes a long way to help establish the style of what will follow. This is not to say that the interior must mimic the cover in color, font, or graphic approach, yet the cover's ability to set the stage for what's inside can't be overlooked. Worth noting is that in larger publishing houses the jobs of cover design and interior design are strictly divided. Rarely does the cover designer also design the interior pages, except in the area of children's books, which operate under their own set of rules.

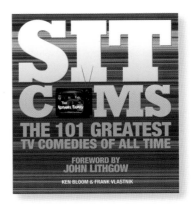

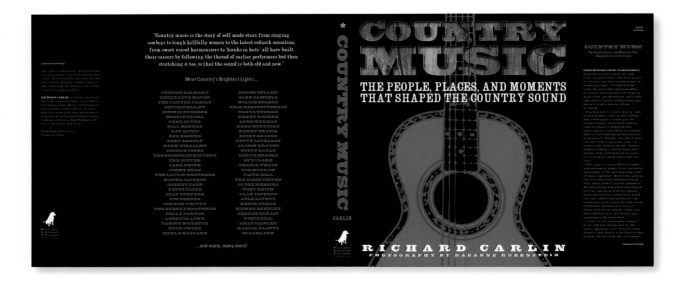

Figure 6.2 Here are two examples of covers that I designed. Notice the design is followed through to the book's spine, back cover, and flaps.

The Strategy of Working with Long Documents

Most designers would agree that less is more. Sometimes, however, more is all
you've got: more content and more pages. So far, we've tackled smaller projects
with few enough pages to be handled as a single file. Larger, multidocument
projects, however, are well within the scope of the Creative Suite, specifically
Adobe InDesign CS3.

For many large-scale projects, a good approach is to break down the job into
smaller, manageable chunks. A logical approach, for example, would be to separate each chapter or section into its own file. Doing so on a book project makes
sense for several reasons. First, there's the danger of keeping all of your eggs in
one basket, so to speak. Bad things sometimes happen to good files. They can
become damaged, corrupted, accidentally deleted, or otherwise lost. When that
file is a 400-page book that's 95 percent ready to go to the printer, think about
what redoing that work will cost you in time, money, and your relationship with
your client.

Another argument for breaking up a large book project into multiple files is
that several people can work on the project simultaneously. At any given time,
new text can be flowed into one chapter and formatted while another is with a
production artist adding photos and captions. Concurrently, a finished chapter
can be out to the editor for proofing and revisions. Everyone is simultaneously
working on a part instead of waiting for the whole.

For a large project, many InDesign features can help organize, synchronize, accelerate, and automate much of the production process. When used together, these features actually build upon one another, increasing their usefulness.

Despite my love of order, I don't employ checklists or style sheets when designing books. All of the information on particular styles, fonts, transparency, image resolution and sizes, page sizes, and so forth, resides in the file. There's no reason to make extra work for yourself. For most of my projects, I'm handing off press-ready PDFs, so everything is self-contained—and available if the recipient has questions about the project. See the section "Mass Production: Preflighting, Packaging, and Exporting a Book" at the end of the chapter for more on press-ready PDFs.

To see how a book's components interrelate, let's take a look under the hood.

Structure and Navigation: Master Pages

As a car is built on a frame, a well-designed book is built on a grid, margins, and columns. All of the design concepts discussed in earlier chapters—balance, whitespace, and so on—are factors in deciding the structure for your book pages. When it's time to build your book documents, you'll want those margins, columns, guides, and any repeating elements set up on well-built master pages. Even for the smallest projects, master pages are a good idea, but for a book, they're absolutely essential.

Master pages can be as rigid or as flexible as you need them to be. You can have many, many master pages that account for every possible difference in your page layouts, or you can have just a few that are built to allow for variations in the basic structure. My preference is for the latter. Limiting the amount of master pages means fewer master pages to manage. The *Sitcoms* book project for this chapter (which can be downloaded at www.peachpit.com/prodesignCS3) is already 336 pages with more than 100 chapters, so the simpler its components, the better. To that end, the book uses only two master pages: a 2-column master that handles most of the standard layouts (Figure 6.3) and a 12-column version that honors the 2-column format with each of the 2 columns subdivided into 6 narrow columns. This 12-column layout allows the page to be arranged asymmetrically (ideal for sidebars and photo placement) while maintaining equal spacing between columns and other objects on the page (Figure 6.4).

Figure 6.3 A two-column master page is used throughout the *Sitcoms* project.

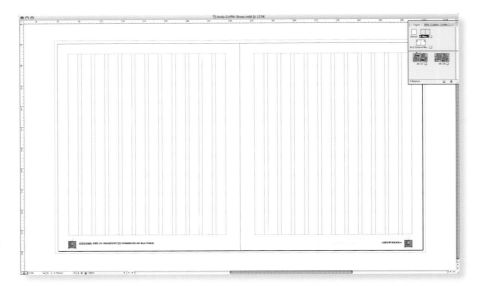

Figure 6.4 The columns are divided further to create a 12-column version, which is useful for arranging additional elements on the page (below).

Staying Inside the Lines: Margins and Columns

Your page size sets the limits of your printable area, but within that physical constraint are other, self-imposed limits—margins and columns, which act simultaneously as boundaries, buffer zones, and alignment aids for all elements on the page, especially text. If you look at the individual chapter files for the *Sitcoms* book, you can see that some chapters have pages with two equal columns of body text, and some have pages with three (Figure 6.5). Some sidebars span two columns, and some span only one. Photos are even less consistent—spanning one to three columns, small sidebar insets, and many sizes in between. Some photos stay within the margins, and others bleed off the page (Figure 6.6).

Yet, for all the variation on the individual pages and spreads, the page margins and column widths exert invisible influence over the structure of each and every page. Viewed in Normal screen mode (View > Screen Mode > Normal) with guides showing (View > Grids & Guides > Show Guides), that structure is obvious. Whether 2- or 3-columns wide, all of the body-copy text frames align left and right within one of the guidelines in the 12-column format.

Figure 6.5 Some spreads in the *Sitcoms* project have three columns.

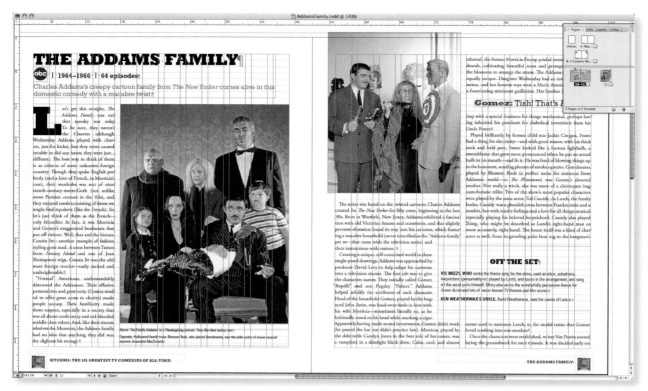

Figure 6.6 You can create a lot of variety while maintaining consistent page margins and column widths.

Similarly, the 1-pica spacing between each column is adhered to throughout, creating easy pathways for the eye that divide content into distinct regions.

For example, all photos have a 1-pica text wrap (Window > Text Wrap) so that text is pushed away exactly far enough to create a gutter consistent with all other spacing on the page (Figure 6.7).

All sidebars have a 1-pica text inset (Object > Text Frame Options) that keeps the text away from the stroke on the frame (Figure 6.8).

Photos that "break" a sidebar edge and page margin (like the black-and-white photo on page 27 of the project) typically do so by only 1 pica.

Figure 6.7 1-pica text wraps allow for a consistent look.

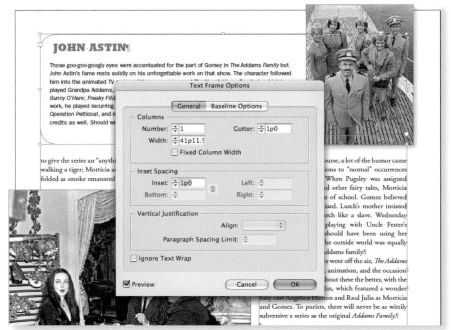

Figure 6.8 The 1-pica text inset allows enough space between the sidebar frame and text.

You Are Here: Page Folios

All that structure helps guide the eye through each spread, but it takes a level of navigational guidance to help move the reader through the whole book. These days, navigation typically means a web strategy rather than a strategy for print work, but the bigger something is, the more people need to know how to get through it and where they are at any given time. Think of a shopping mall. Without a directory to show where you are and an indication of where else you can go, it's going to take you much longer than necessary to find the Orange Julius. Typically, your map for a book is its table of contents, but guideposts also should appear throughout, such as folios with chapter names and graphic elements that identify sections (Figure 6.9). The ideal location for these repeating elements is, yet again, on a master page.

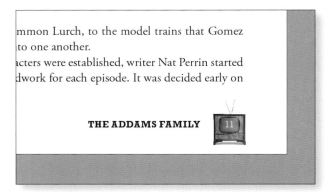

Figure 6.9 A reader can identify what chapter he is in by consulting the folio.

Folios on master pages benefit designers in several ways. First, you have to position and format them only once to get them to appear consistently on all pages to which the master as been applied. Second, using automatic page numbering for individual chapter files adds a level of automation that will pay off significantly later. Finally, information in the folio that changes based on page content (the show name in this example) can be set up on the master to update dynamically using text variables, a powerful new feature of InDesign CS3.

Setting Standards with Text and Object Styles

If you're designing a book, odds are you're dealing with a lot of text. For text formatting, styles are an absolute must. Consistent typographic settings for body copy, subheads, captions, sidebars, chapter titles, and folios are the lifeline upon which readers depend to understand the hierarchy of information in front of them. Within a few pages, stylistic conventions should be familiar to the audience, whether they realize they've picked up on them or not. The best way to manage that text is a strategic and consistent use of InDesign paragraph and character styles. (See "Work Smart with Styles" in Chapter 4, "Creating Newsletters and Forms.") As you continue formatting this project, styles will become increasingly important, allowing you to automate other tasks such as running footers and tables of contents.

In the same vein, you can tag graphic frames with object styles to control their fill, stroke, text wrap, transparency, and other attributes including how images fit and are positioned within those frames. Object styles for text frames can include attributes that specify text inset, paragraph styles, custom baseline grids, vertical justification, and optical margin alignment (Figure 6.10). So, it's no surprise that assigning all of these options to an object style dramatically speeds up long-document formatting.

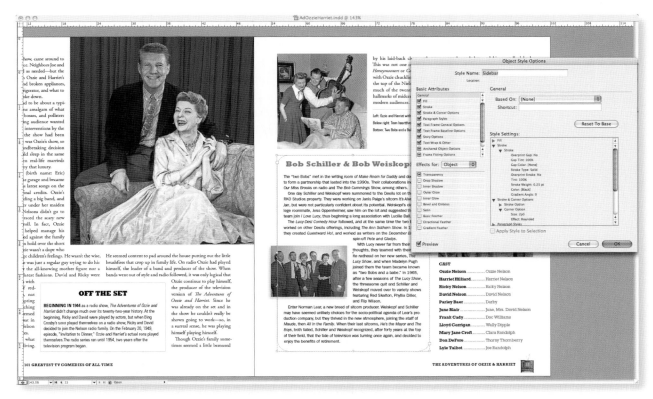

Figure 6.10 Use object styles for all the components of your book.

Using the Book Panel

Managing all of these parts and extending automation options over multiple documents is the key to working with books in a consistent and efficient way. When working in InDesign CS3, the nexus of long-document production is the Book panel (Figure 6.11). For long documents, it is the hub for your project and will keep you organized.

But first, let's clear up a misnomer. Although it's called the Book panel and the word *book* appears frequently in this chapter, your project does not need to be a novel, textbook, catalog, or traditional book to take advantage of the Book panel. Any document that can be split into multiple files and that could benefit from the consistent application of master pages, swatches, styles, and consecutive page numbering from document to document is a likely candidate for the Book panel.

In truth, the Book panel is a file manager with a specific set of features. It classifies and organizes a particular group of InDesign files as part of a single project, keeping the files separate but establishing order and consistency on all of them and then gathering them together as needed to print, package for output, or export to PDF. Icons in the panel indicate the status of documents along the way. For example, if more than one designer or editor is working on the book project, an "in use" icon appears next to the name of any file that's open by someone other than you. The panel also displays missing, open, or modified icons for any document in the book.

Creating a new book is simple:

1. Choose File > New > Book.
2. Name the book in the dialog, choose a location for it on your computer, and click Save.

The file you saved uses an .indb extension, and a new panel opens with the book filename shown in the tab. To work with an example of an existing book, open the file **Sitcoms Book Final.indb** in the Chapter 6 folder at www.peachpit.com/prodesignCS3, or follow along using files of your own.

You add documents to your book by simply dragging them into the Book panel from any Finder (Mac OS) or Explorer (Windows) window. You can also click the Add Documents button at the bottom of the panel (Figure 6.12) or choose Add Documents from the Book panel menu. As you add documents, their page ranges appear to the right of the filename. If your master pages are set up with automatic page numbering, the Book panel automatically renumbers the pages

Figure 6.11 The Book panel displays the various files in your project, with page ranges included for easy reference.

Figure 6.12 One way to add documents to your book is to click the Add Documents button.

in each document you add to keep them sequential. You can change the order of documents in the panel at any time by simply dragging a document name above or below any other listed document. Page numbering adjusts accordingly, based on settings in the Book Page Numbering Options panel menu (Figure 6.13).

Some books have specific conventions for how and where chapters start. A requirement for your book project may be that all chapters begin on a right-hand page or as a spread. By default, pages simply continue from the previous document, but you can choose to continue them on the next odd (right-hand) page or even (left-hand) page in the Book Page Number Options menu. With either of those options chosen, you can select the Insert Blank Page option to have InDesign add pages wherever they're needed at the end of the preceding document in the book. As content continues to change during the editing and design process, InDesign will continue to add or delete pages to maintain your settings.

 TIP: Once you've added your documents, remember to always open them in the Book panel by double-clicking their name. If you open files that are part of the book from the Finder (Mac OS) or Windows Explorer (Windows) and then save them, a modified icon will appear next to that document's name in the Book panel indicating that the document has been modified "outside" the book. You can clear the icon only by reopening the file in the Book panel and resaving it.

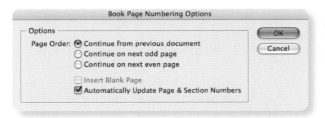

Figure 6.13 If you prefer to change your page order from the default setting, you have a few options available in Book Page Numbering Options menu.

Synchronizing Styles

Page numbering and document organization are just two of the big payoffs for your up-front work establishing efficient master pages and well-organized styles. Even better, you can synchronize those masters and styles across all documents. In any InDesign book, one document acts as the style source. By default, it's the first document added to the panel, but you can change that at any time by simply clicking the box to the left of the filename. A small icon appears in that box next to whichever document is the style source for the book.

Synchronizing styles to a single document means that any changes made to the character, paragraph, cell, table, and object styles in that document will update the corresponding styles in all other documents in the book the next time you choose Synchronize from the Book panel menu. In addition to styles and master pages, you can synchronize swatches, numbered lists, text variables, and trap presets (Figure 6.14). To exclude any of these from synchronization, choose Synchronization Options from the Book panel menu, and deselect the appropriate choice for your needs. I prefer consistency throughout, so I tend to keep all options selected. You can also synchronize only selected documents in the book. To do so, highlight only those documents you want to synchronize. To synchronize all documents in the book, either highlight all the documents in the book or select none at all. Both methods will synchronize all your Book documents to the selected style source.

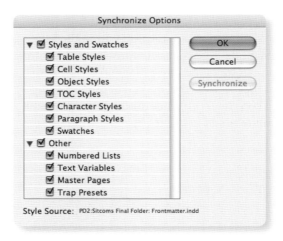

Figure 6.14 There are many options available for synchronizing, such as paragraph styles and numbered lists.

Adding Object Styles

Object styles take the fundamental idea behind paragraph and character styles—a set of attributes that can be saved for later reapplication—and extend it to frames, shapes, and strokes. Virtually any attribute you can think of can be part of an object style, including paragraph styles. The sidebars in the *Sitcoms* book project are a good example of object style formatting. If you haven't done so already, download the Chapter 6 folder at www.peachpit.com/prodesignCS3. Then follow these steps:

1. Open the file **Sitcoms Book Final.indb**.
2. In the Book panel, double-click the Andy Griffith Show chapter name to open the file **Andy Griffith Show.indd**.
3. Open the file and navigate to page 27, which is the second page in the document, and use the Selection tool to select the sidebar in the upper right.
4. Open the Object Styles panel (Window > Object Styles), in which you'll see the style named Sidebar highlighted in blue.
5. In the Object Styles panel, Control-click (Mac OS) or right-click (Windows) the Sidebar style name, and choose Edit Sidebar from the panel menu to open the Object Style Options dialog (Figure 6.15).

This sidebar has several attributes assigned to it. Specifically, it has a 1-pica text inset, a 0.25-pt black stroke, rounded corners, and a 1-pica text wrap. It also has a headline that uses a particular paragraph style, followed by a sidebar body copy style that differs in font, size, and leading from the overall text of the book. All of these attributes are part of the Sidebar object style, are editable in this dialog, and can be applied in a single click.

In a way, an object style is like Wal-Mart for attributes. It has everything you'll find in individual panels gathered together in one place for your convenience and savings (time savings, that is). In this one dialog you'll find all of the options available in the Transparency, Stroke, Text Wrap, and Story panels. The Text Frame Options, Anchored Object Options, and Frame Fitting Options are reproduced here in their entirety (Figure 6.15). You'll also find options for applying paragraph styles and swatches but won't be able to modify or create styles or swatches.

TIP: Attributes can be specifically ignored as part of an object style by unchecking the settings group in the Basic Attributes section on the left. For instance, if you use an object style on four text frames that are formatted identically in every way except their fill color, you can uncheck Fill and apply the object style to all four frames while retaining their respective fill colors. This is not considered a local override since Fill is not a predefined part of the style.

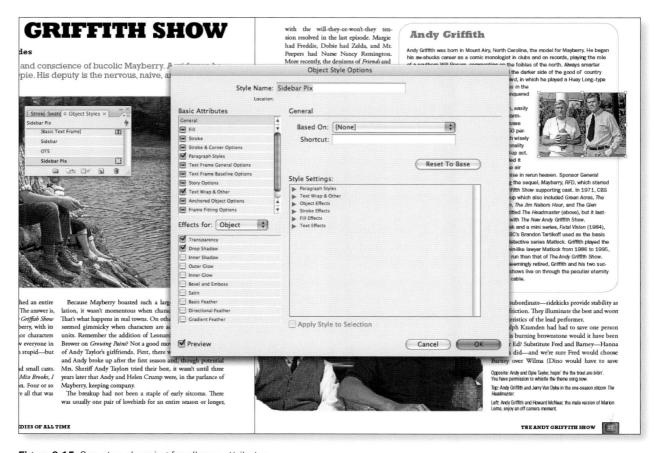

Figure 6.15 One-stop shopping for all your attributes.

TIP: Changing a style using the dialog is one thing, but it's not the most intuitive or creative working method. I prefer to work more naturally on the page, making decisions and adjustments a little bit at a time until everything looks right and then locking in that formatting as a style. Fortunately, object styles don't force me to change how I work. Just like paragraph styles, which pick up formatting from the current pointer location or selected text, object styles pick up the formatting of whatever is selected with the Selection tool and automatically build all of its attributes into a new style when you choose New Object Style from the Object Styles panel menu. All of the on-the-fly, intuitive work I've done is recognized and included, ready to be applied to many other objects in my project.

TIP: To synchronize all documents, either all documents in the panel must be selected or no documents must be selected. Expanding the panel to show all the documents in the book or scrolling down to the bottom of the panel reveals a small blank area. Click in that area to deselect everything; then choose Synchronize Book.

Using this example, I'll demonstrate how quickly style changes can be made first document-wide and then throughout the entire book:

1. With the sidebar on page 27 still selected and the Object Style Options dialog still open, click Fill in the Basic Attributes pane of the dialog.
2. Select any swatch other than Paper or None, and then select the Preview check box in the lower left to view your changes to the style on the page behind the dialog. If necessary, change the Tint percentage to keep the text legible against the new Fill color.
3. Click Stroke in the Basic Attributes pane of the dialog. Then select any swatch other than Black, None, or Paper, and change Weight to 1 pt from 0.25 pt. If necessary, select the Preview check box again to see your changes on the page.
4. In the Effects For Object pane, click Drop Shadow to automatically apply the default drop shadow settings.
5. Click OK to exit the dialog and save these changes to the Sidebar style.
6. In the Pages panel, double-click the page numbers 28–29 below the page thumbnails to display that spread. Notice that the Ron Howard and Sheldon Leonard sidebars also reflect your fill, stroke, and drop shadow changes.

So, one chapter in the book has a new sidebar look that needs to be applied to all of the other chapters. Using the Book panel, applying this style change to more than 100 documents can be accomplished in a few simple steps:

1. Save and close **Andy Griffith Show.indd**.
2. In the Book panel, click the empty box next to the name Andy Griffith Show to make that document the new style source for all other documents in the book.
3. Click the name Addams Family near the top of the panel. Then Shift-click the name Andy Griffith Show to select both documents and all documents in between.
4. Choose Synchronize Selected Documents from the Book panel menu. If alert dialogs appear regarding overset text, dismiss them by clicking OK (Figure 6.16).
5. Click OK when the final synchronization alert appears.
6. In the Book panel, double-click the name Alice. Notice that the Linda Lavin sidebar on page 17 also reflects the changes made to the Sidebar object style that were made in the Andy Griffith chapter.

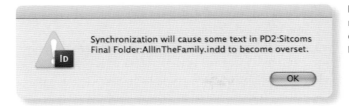

Figure 6.16 You may receive warnings about overset text, which can be ignored.

Styles in Sequence

To boost efficiency even more, a paragraph style setting within an object style can include its Next Style functionality. Next Style settings are part of a paragraph style. In the General area of the Paragraph Style Options dialog, you can select any existing paragraph style from the Next Style menu, allowing you to select and format multiple paragraphs with different styles in one step.

The Paragraph Style area of the Object Style Options dialog has an Apply Next Style check box. With this option active, the object style applies the first paragraph style (chosen from the pop-up menu just above that check box) and then the style indicated by its Next Style setting. That second style could have a Next Style setting of its own, and so on, and so on, for subsequent styles. If there's an order to your styles, it can be built right into them. In this case, the Sidebar object style uses a specific paragraph style, Sidebar Heads, which includes a Next Style setting of Sidebar, to format the body copy that follows it.

Letting Styles Do the Driving

Beyond their text- and object-formatting power, styles can be put to use several other ways in a book to automate certain tasks. This saves you repetitive work and ensures consistency by taking human error out of the process. You can search for text formatted with a specific style in your project and then that text can be "found" by InDesign and reused in other places using other styles.

In the *Sitcoms* book, the left-hand page folio reiterates the name of the book and remains unchanged throughout. On the right-hand page, however, the folio contains the chapter name, which is typically the name of the show. Changing this in every chapter by modifying it on the master page isn't that difficult, but it's an additional step that runs the risk of introducing a typo and requires you to remember to update the folio if, at any point in the process, there's a change in the show name.

To take advantage of this functionality outside an object style, follow these steps:

1. Select the range of paragraphs in the document to which you want to apply styles in succession.
2. Open the Paragraph Styles panel (Window > Type & Tables > Paragraph Styles).
3. In the Paragraph Styles panel, Control-click (Mac OS) or right-click (Windows) the name of the first style in the sequence.
4. Choose Apply [your style name], and then choose Next Style from the context menu (Figure 6.17).

Figure 6.17 Use the Next Style function in InDesign to boost your productivity.

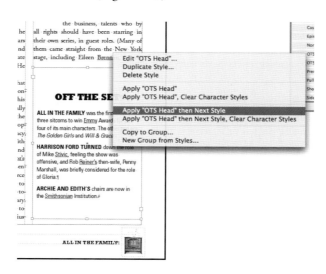

 TIP: If a set of paragraph styles repeats, set the Next Style option of the last style in the sequence to be the first style. The styles will be applied in a loop because the first style starts the sequence all over again. InDesign will keep going until it runs out of paragraphs to style. Be aware that Next Style is not smart enough to recognize more than one paragraph at a time. In other words, if you have two successive paragraphs with a Body Text style applied, InDesign will apply the Body Text next style to the second paragraph.

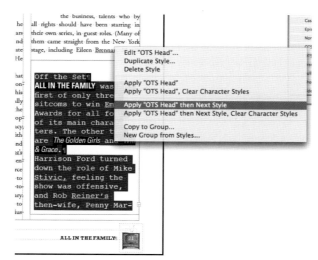

Automating Folios and Headers
with Text Variables

Each chapter starts with the show name, which uses the ShowName paragraph style. This is the only text in the project that uses this style. That's an important distinction, as you'll see. Using the InDesign CS3 Text Variables feature, any text with this style applied to it can appear elsewhere in the document automatically. If the text changes at any point, so does the variable.

Look at the right-hand page folio on the master page of any chapter in the *Sitcoms* book, and you'll notice that, rather than the name of the show, the text frame for the folio contains only a <SHOWNAME> placeholder. On the document pages, however, that frame contains the show name itself. All documents in the book share the same master pages, and this same <SHOW NAME> variable is automatically populated with the appropriate text from each chapter.

To create a text variable, follow these steps:

1. Choose Type > Text Variables > Define.
2. In the Text Variables dialog, click New.
3. In the New Text Variable dialog, name the variable **Show Name** (Figure 6.18).

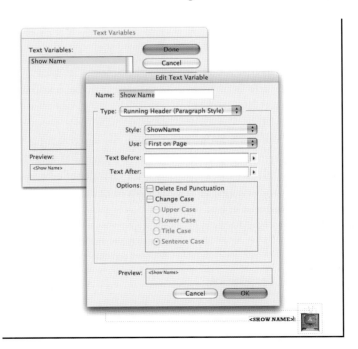

Figure 6.18 Use Text Variables for simple automation in your headers.

NOTE: Running headers can also be generated from character styles, if appropriate. In that case, you would choose Running Header (Character Style) in step 4, and the menu choices in step 5 would change to a list of character styles already in your document.

4. Choose Running Header (Paragraph Style) from the Type menu.
5. Choose the paragraph style used in the document that you want as the source of the variable.
6. Choose First On Page from the Use menu to select the first instance of text on the page where the variable is inserted that uses the paragraph style chosen in step 4. If no text on that page uses the paragraph style, the variable feature searches backward from that point to the first instance it finds. In the *Sitcom* book, the ShowName style is used only on the first page of the chapter. As a result, the variable uses the show name consistently throughout the document.
7. As an option, enter any text that your variable requires before or after it—for instance, a bullet character—in the Text Before or Text After field.
8. Leave the other options unselected unless they apply to your needs, and click OK.
9. Click Done.

Now that you have a variable defined, you need to establish where the text it represents will appear on the page by inserting the placeholder for the variable. If you're using the variable for a folio or header, the most likely location for inserting it is somewhere on your master pages.

Insert a text variable by following these steps:

NOTE: Variable place-holders are a single unit, not editable text. The variable name and the angle brackets around it can be selected only as a whole. If you need to rename your variable, you must do so in the Text Variables dialog by selecting the variable in the list and clicking the Edit button.

1. Create a text frame on the appropriate page where you want the variable text to appear.
2. With your insertion point in that frame, choose Type > Text Variables > Insert > Show Name. The Show Name variable will appear in the text frame surrounded by angle brackets (Figure 6.19).

Now take your variable for a test drive. Either in your own file or the sample files (at www.peachpit.com/prodesignCS3), change the text on a page that uses the style selected to trigger your variable. To be able to see the change reflected in the variable, you need to refresh the page, such as by switching between Preview and Normal mode or by zooming in or out.

Figure 6.19 The variable for the *Sitcom*s project.

Cruise Control:
Automated Tables of Contents

Another task that InDesign can take off your hands—and that works on the same principle as the running header text variables described previously—is the creation of a table of contents (TOC) for your book.

An InDesign TOC is driven entirely by paragraph styles. The TOC feature locates specific paragraph styles used in your documents, remembers the page number where that style appears, and collects the text (up to 256 characters) to which the style is applied. Without paragraph styles, you simply cannot generate an automated TOC.

InDesign TOCs enable you to designate several styles across all of your book documents from which to gather text, and it provides options for arranging that text in a specific order, including or excluding page numbers, and applying entirely different paragraph and character styles to the collected text that are appropriate for your TOC layout.

The *Sitcoms* book has an automatically generated table of contents in the Frontmatter.indd document (Figure 6.20). A look at how that TOC is set up will go a long way toward understanding how this feature works:

1. In the Book panel, double-click the name Frontmatter to open the Front-matter.indd file.
2. Show the Pages panel, and double-click the numbers 6–7 beneath the page thumbnails in the panel to view the Contents spread.
3. Using the Text tool, click in either of the two frames containing the show names and page numbers.
4. Choose Layout > Table of Contents to open the Table of Contents dialog.
5. Click the More Options button to reveal all the available options (Figure 6.21).

In this book, the TOC is fairly simple. With 100 TV shows to list and only two pages for the TOC, this was a practical decision. Only one paragraph style—ShowName—appears in the Include Paragraph Styles area. The list on the right contains all the paragraph styles in the book, from which you add or remove styles for use in the table of contents. Given more room, the Premise style (used for the brief summary of each show that follows the show name in each chapter) could have been included here by selecting it from the Other Styles list and clicking the Add button.

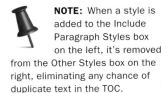

NOTE: When a style is added to the Include Paragraph Styles box on the left, it's removed from the Other Styles box on the right, eliminating any chance of duplicate text in the TOC.

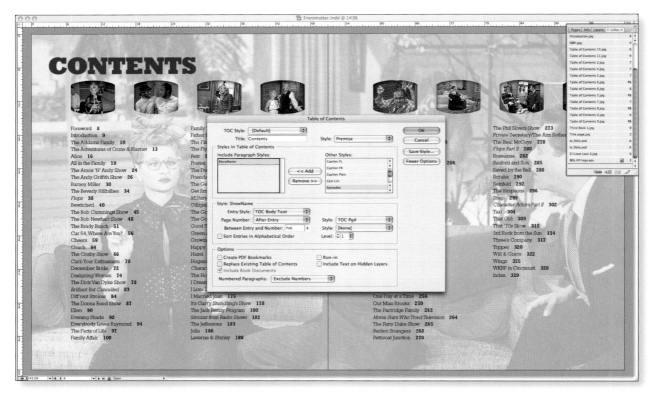

Figure 6.20 The table of contents can be generated automatically, saving you important time for designing its elements.

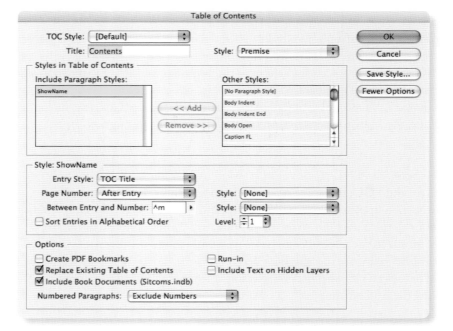

Figure 6.21 There are many options available to suit your table of contents needs.

Each style added to the TOC is called an *entry*. When a style is selected in the Include Paragraph Styles box, you can assign altogether different styles to the entry in the Style area below it in the dialog. The Entry Style menu associates any paragraph style you select to the incoming TOC text.

The Page Number menu includes options to insert the page number before or after the text of the entry or to not include a page number at all. The page number can have a character style applied to it from the adjacent Style menu, and any number of special characters (em spaces, right indent tabs, soft returns, and so on) can be inserted between the text of the entry and the page number in the Between Entry And Number field. A character style can be applied to that as well.

The bottom of the dialog reveals the Options section only after you click the More Options button, some of which are essential to a book-based TOC. The most important option is Include Book Documents. When the document that will contain your TOC is opened in the Book panel, the name of the book appears in parentheses here. This option extends the scope of the TOC to all documents in the book, not just the current document. If your book is being distributed as a PDF, check Create PDF Bookmarks to have each TOC entry translated into a PDF bookmark when you export the book.

Once you've set up a table of contents for your book, you can automatically update the TOC for changes made to the text in the book itself, changes made to the reordering of documents in the Book file, and changes made to page numbers. Simply put your insertion pointer in the text frame containing the TOC, and choose Layout > Update Table of Contents.

NOTE: You can create a completely different kind of style —the TOC style—in the Table of Contents dialog by clicking the Save Style button. A TOC style is similar to an object style or paragraph style in that it records many settings in one place. TOC styles let you try variations on the content and formatting of a TOC without having to rearrange the text manually.

TIP: Automated TOCs are not limited to projects using the Book panel. Any single document can include an InDesign-generated table of contents. In both instances, all features work the same.

Mass Production:
Preflight, Packaging, and Exporting a Book

The benefits of managing your project with the Book panel continue through to the end of the process when it's time to prepare your book for print or PDF. Rather than preflighting, packaging, printing, or exporting each document individually, you can perform those processes on all documents at once using options in the Book panel menu (Figure 6.22). InDesign handles the task of going through each file for you.

Figure 6.22 Select your options for preflighting, packaging, or exporting directly from the Book panel menu.

InDesign's Preflight feature checks files for missing images and fonts to identify any potential problems prior to printing or exporting a document and summarizes its findings in the Preflight dialog (Figure 6.23). Preflighting identifies images with RGB color and pages where transparency is used in the document. Using the Preflight dialog you can relink any missing images and generate a report on the document, its links, and its fonts details as a text file for your output service or print provider.

If you are providing your print provider with native InDesign files for print, use the Package Book option to collect all the InDesign documents in your book, along with their linked files and fonts, and copy them to single folder.

TIP: As with synchronization, performing batch actions like these on an entire book requires that either all documents or no documents be selected in the Book panel. To preflight, package, or export only some of your book files, select just the desired files in the panel, and choose the appropriate option from the Book panel menu.

You can export the entire book from the Book panel into a single PDF file with the Export Book To PDF option. Similarly, you can print all files in the book from the Book panel with the same settings without having to open each file. Of course, preflighting, packaging, and exporting are not limited to the Book panel. These features are available for any single InDesign document in the File menu.

Books are big projects, and they require a big-picture approach from the beginning to ensure that, at the end, you've accomplished what you set out to do. Up-front preparation and planning are the keys to an organized process.

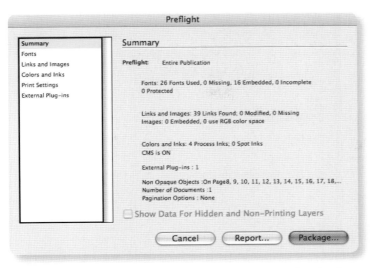

Figure 6.23 Although basic in nature, the InDesign Preflight function flags essential problems like missing links, fonts, and non-CMYK images.

Automation-friendly features such as master pages, styles, text variables, tables of contents, and the file-management capabilities of the Book panel keep the execution phase efficient and flexible, allowing you to easily accommodate changes and achieve a result in which quality is not compromised by deadlines or the scope of the job.

Keep It Organized and Back It Up

You can never be too organized when working on projects like this, particularly books with a hundred or so chapters. Be vigilant about using Save As each time another iteration is developed. By adding "v1, v2, v3..." to each version, it's easy to keep track of the design's progression.

Maintaining a strict folder structure is essential to knowing what's where (Figure 6.24). Too many designers litter their desktops with files like leaves scattered by the wind. When it's time to find something, it's no surprise they wind up in a tizzy. My mode of work is to create one project folder ("Sitcoms," for example). Inside of Sitcoms I create a folder named "Layout" which holds only my InDesign documents. I create another folder in the main folder called "Links." The Links folder is sometimes divided into subfolders ("Logos," "Stock Photos," and so on). I also create another top-level folder called "PDF" for all the PDF files.

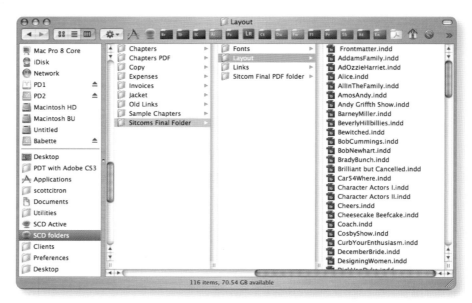

TIP: For more information about backing up, an excellent and inexpensive resource is the eBook, Take Control of Mac OS X Backups by Joe Kissel (www.peachpit.com/store/product.aspx?isbn=0975950304). If you don't back up, this may be the best $10 you ever spend. As the saying goes, it's not a question of if your hard drive will fail, but when.

Figure 6.24 Sticking to an organized folder structure will save you time and anxiety when searching for files, regardless of the document length.

Another folder is labeled "Copy." Inside of the Copy folder is often another folder or two to separate initial copy from final copyedited copy. If I'm designing the cover or jacket I also make a separate folder for that, inside of which are folders named Layout, PDF, Links, and Copy. This way when you need something there's never any doubt about where it is, or if it's the latest version.

Also, you must follow the most important and most overlooked rule: back up your files. If there's a file you can't afford to lose, you must back it up. For years I've employed a couple of different backup systems and have never regretted the effort that went into creating this layer of protection.

An effective backup system excludes human intervention. Too many times I've heard users say "Oh, I forgot to back up." If your backup system requires you to remember to use it, you're in trouble. For the last few years I've been using SuperDuper on the Mac, inexpensive shareware that runs a script each evening and backs up everything on my computer to an external hard drive. As an added layer of protection I use a remote backup system called Mozy, which also backs up key folders to a remote server. This way if both my computer and external back up drive fail or are wiped out in a fire, I still have all my files on Mozy.

Project Wrap-Up

Although most books literally tell a story, the process of designing a good book must also tell a story. Thinking of a book like a stage play or a movie helps enormously in setting up a dynamic rhythm and flow. The job of the cover is to intrigue potential readers to buy the book and then open it. The job of the title page is to begin setting a tone for what's to come. It's the same for the table of contents. More than a simple list of a book's contents, the TOC should also make readers want to flip to the next pages. Chapter openers are also important, and here again the designer has the chance to play God by manipulating the reader visually and emotionally by setting a tone for what's on the other side of the page wall. If you remember these principles, what Malcom Greer calls *sequencing* and *pacing*, you'll understand and appreciate the power of designing books and other long documents.

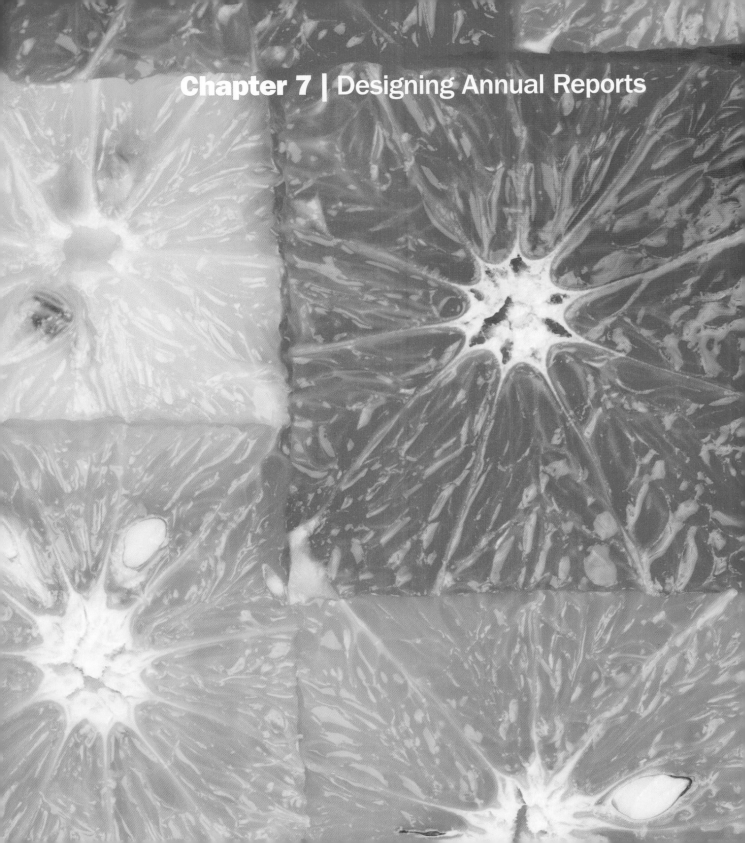

Chapter 7 | Designing Annual Reports

"BEAUTY OF STYLE AND HARMONY AND GRACE AND GOOD RHYTHM DEPEND ON SIMPLICITY." — Plato

mong the handful of jewels in the crowns of graphic designers is the annual report. Partly this is because so much attention is paid to annual reports. There, encapsulated in a sleek and slender booklet, is the distillation of an entire company for all the world to see. Of course, at the heart of it, the annual report is really just a thinly veiled, multipage advertisement whose job it is to paint a pretty picture of the company it represents, with the hope of enticing monetary participation from potential investors.

With big bucks riding on the success of each year's annual report, it's not uncommon for companies to lavish large budgets on the creation of the report. Likewise, on the creative side, landing an award from one of the many prestigious annual report competitions held worldwide results in one more coveted feather in a designer's creative cap.

When tackling the creation of an annual report, designers have the opportunity to stretch their creative wings with the layout and design of the introductory and editorial matter. Yet at the same time, they're faced with the certainty that eventually they'll have to deal with page upon page of dry (excuse me: deeply fascinating) financial data.

So, therein lies the challenge. How do you put a positive spin on the yearly progress of a business or corporation without running afoul of the Securities and Exchange Commission (SEC), all the while couching it all in an attractive and compelling package? A tall order, you say? Exactly.

In this chapter, I've chosen to create a fantasy annual report for my own company, Scott Citron Design (Figure 7.1). As you work through the project, you'll be exposed to a number of new tools and techniques that will help further broaden your repertoire of essentials skills when working with Adobe Creative Suite 3. Among the concepts will be that of using workspaces and numbering documents and sections in Adobe InDesign, using Live Paint in Adobe Illustrator, using Smart Objects and Smart Filters in Adobe Photoshop, and designing complex and compelling tables with OpenType in InDesign.

Figure 7.1 The opening pages from the Scott Citron Design annual report.

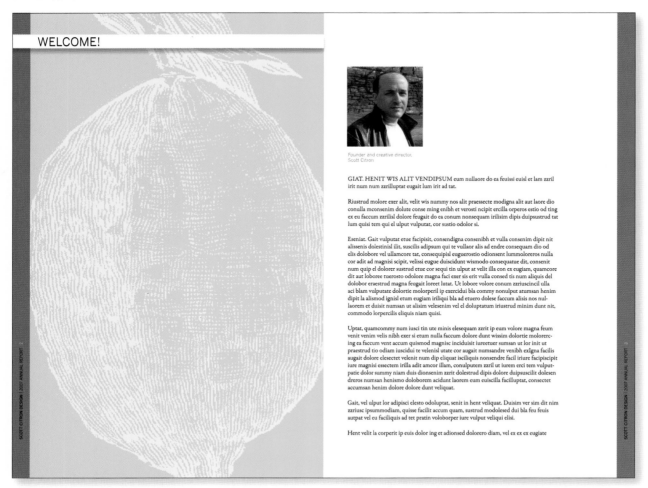

Creating a Custom Workspace

Although the Creative Suite 3 components strive to conserve screen real estate, sometimes the components are a bit *too* efficient in hiding panels—slamming them shut when you switch to another panel. Often, you don't need all the available panels visible (especially because there are more than 40 of them). And you may need to consult a couple of panels repeatedly, so you'd like to keep them open instead of having to manually open them every time. For example, in a long InDesign document, it can be handy to have the Pages panel open all the time for quick navigation while leaving other panels in icon mode (Figure 7.2). Make InDesign work the way you want by customizing your environment. Here's how:

1. In InDesign, collapse the docked panels by clicking the small ribbed control at the upper-left corner of the dock area and then dragging to the right until only the panel icons are visible.
2. Open the Pages panel by clicking its icon (Figure 7.3).
3. Detach the Pages panel from its group by dragging it by its name tab and releasing the mouse button once you're clear of the docked panels. Then collapse the remaining open panel.
4. Drag the Pages panel to the right until a bright blue vertical bar appears to the left of the row of panel icons, and release the mouse button.
5. Reduce the width of the Pages panel by dragging on the ribbed control at the top, and set the height by moving the bottom edge of the panel.
6. Although your panels will remain in this configuration between work sessions, it's a good idea to save panel positions in a custom workspace so you can always return to your favorite arrangement.
7. Choose Window > Workspace > Save Workspace, and name your new workspace.

Figure 7.2 Less-frequently used panels are in icon mode, while the Pages panel (which is in constant use in a long document) is permanently expanded. Like it? Save it as a custom workspace.

Figure 7.3 Click the icon shown here to open the Pages panel.

Numbering and Section Starts

In a long document, it's helpful to divide the content into sections, determined by topic or purpose, in order to aid readability and navigation. For example, introductory information is often set off from the "heart" of the document by differences in formatting and page numbering. Pull several books from your shelf, and note that many of them assign lowercase Roman numerals (i, ii, iii, iv...) to the front matter. There's no need to place such content into a separate document; you can use *sections* in InDesign to control numbering styles within a single document.

TIP: Illustrator and Photoshop also allow you to create and save workspaces. Workspaces for all three applications are stored separately from other application preferences, so they aren't lost if you reset your preferences. That way, if your friends envy your elegant workspace, you can share it.

A little word of advice: when working with sections, always start at the first physical page of the document and work your way through it. Don't create a second "page 1" in the document, or InDesign will give you a (justifiably) snippy alert to warn you that this is, essentially, irrational. If you persist, you'll deeply confuse InDesign when you ask it to print page 1. You can imagine the internal dialog: "*Which* page 1?"

Before you begin, download the Chapter 07 folder from the book's companion Web site at www.peachpit.com/prodesignCS3.

1. Open the first annual report file, **scd_annual report_start.indd**, and then double-click page 1 in the Pages panel. (A single click isn't sufficient; a double-click tells InDesign, "Hey! I'm talking to page 1!")
2. Choose Numbering & Section Options from the Pages panel menu. Choose i, ii, iii, iv from the Style pop-up menu in the Page Numbering section. For now, your entire document is numbered with lowercase Roman numerals. You'll rectify that in the next step. The first "real" page of the annual report is the third page of the file, currently numbered iii.
3. Double-click page iii to target that page. Again, choose Numbering And Section Options from the Pages panel menu.
4. Click the Start Page Numbering At radio button, and make sure the adjacent field is set to 1.
5. Set the style to 1, 2, 3, 4.
6. Delete any text in the Section Prefix field. Although this is a nice gesture by InDesign to identify sections, it gets in the way when you print the document. If you left the default of Sec 1: in the Section Prefix field, you'd have to request Sec 1: 1 if you wanted to print page 1 of the file, which would be very annoying! Clean out the field, and life will be easier. Note the small triangle over page i and page 1; these are visual indicators of section starts (Figure 7.4).
7. Double-click one of the triangles to reopen the Numbering & Section dialog box. This dialog box also offers options for assigning chapter numbers. When you knit multiple documents together in a book file, this allows InDesign to synchronize chapter numbers.

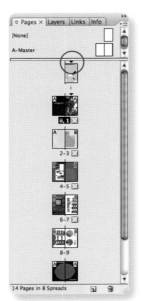

Figure 7.4 A small triangle over specific pages indicates the beginning of a section.

A Tasty Cover: Using Live Paint

Although blending modes in Illustrator and InDesign are quick ways to add visual interest, they have some limitations. Specifically, they may display incorrectly (see the sidebar "Misleading Display of Blending Modes"), and you have no control over the specific color that appears in the overlap area of shapes being blended.

For both these reasons, you may find that the Live Paint feature in Illustrator is a great solution. It's easy to use and quite flexible, so you'll use it to create the cover art for the annual report:

1. In Illustrator, open the file **cover_lemons_start** in the Links folder for Chapter 7. Initially, the lemons are just simple shapes with a fill of None and a black stroke.
2. Select all the lemon shapes, and then choose the Live Paint Bucket in the Tools panel. Then, select Citron Yellow in the Swatches panel and click inside one of the lemons, and the selected shapes immediately become a Live Paint group. Click to paint the other lemon shapes, and notice that the overlapping areas aren't painted (Figure 7.5).
3. Choose another swatch (I used Dark Yellow), and use the Live Paint bucket to fill the overlapping areas.

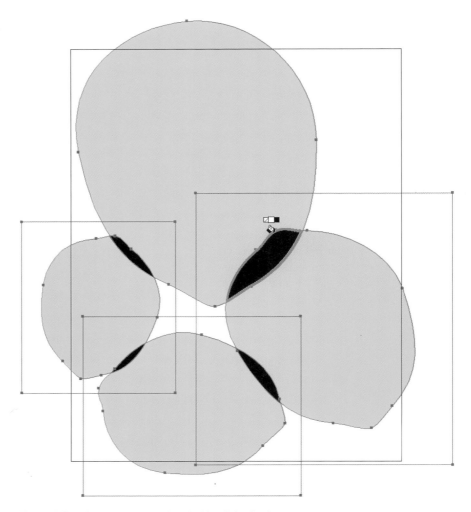

Figure 7.5 Paint the lemons using the Live Paint Bucket.

4. Using the Group Select tool (hidden under the Direct Selection tool), select one of the lemons, and reposition it. The overlap area keeps its color because it's part of a Live Paint group. Modify one of the lemon shapes with the Direct Selection tool or the Pen tool, and you'll see that the color boundaries are live, as if the paint were fluid. That's why it's called Live Paint!

5. Save the file as cover_lemons_final in the Links folder. Open the **scd_annual report_start.indd** file in InDesign, and place the lemon artwork in the existing frame on page i.

Focus on What's Important in Images

Sometimes you want to call attention to a particular component in an image. Whether it's one person in a group shot or a single building in a street scene, you often have the twin goals of accentuating a single subject while still showing its context. Silhouetting the subject removes its environment, and a big red arrow is out of the question.

But there are effective, subtler methods for calling attention to a subject within an image. You can desaturate the background and slightly increase the saturation of the subject. You can blur the background and slightly sharpen the subject. Or you can combine these methods to lure the viewer to concentrate on one element in an image, without being obvious.

You'll try some subtle methods in the image on page 1 of the annual report. Although the two lemons are clearly the focal point of the image, the background is busy, and the bright sky competes with the lemons for the viewer's attention. Let's fix that:

1. In Photoshop, open the file **LemonTreeStart.psd** in the Links folder.
   To force the background to recede, you'll use two nondestructive methods to blur and desaturate the image. Once again, working nondestructively is always preferable because it allows the greatest degree of creative freedom for designers.
2. Select the background layer, and choose Filter > Convert for Smart Filters. In response, Photoshop stores the original, untouched image information for future use. Click OK to dismiss the alert that follows. Photoshop renames the layer to Layer 0 (Figure 7.6).

Figure 7.6 Work smart by using the Smart Filters option in Photoshop.

3. To sharpen the photo, choose Filter > Sharpen > Unsharp Mask. Set the filter to about 100 pixels, with a radius of 2.6 pixels. Click OK to apply the Unsharp mask filter.

4. Now that you've sharpened the photo, you'll add a blur. Choose Filter > Blur > Box Blur. Set the blur to about 30, and click OK to apply the blur.

5. Click to target the layer mask, and paint with black over the lemons with a large, soft brush set to 50 percent opacity. As you paint on the layer mask, the sharpness of the lemons will reemerge.

6. Add a Hue/Saturation adjustment layer by clicking the Add Adjustment Layer button at the bottom of the Layers palette and choosing Hue/Saturation from the pop-up menu.

7. Drag the Saturation slider to the left to about -50 to desaturate the image. Click OK to apply the adjustment layer.

    The photo now looks a little dingy. The last touch is to add a bit of zing to the contrast.

8. With Layer 0 still targeted, click at the bottom of the Layers palette to add a Levels adjustment layer. Click and drag the white highlight slider just a bit to the left to brighten the photo. Click OK when you're done to apply the Levels adjustment (Figure 7.7).

You've been working on this image so long, it may be difficult to remember how it looked originally. In the History panel, click the initial state, and then click the name of the last state to do a quick "before" and "after" comparison. Save the finished lemons image as **LemonTreeDone.psd**, and place the image on page 1 of the annual report.

Documents as Artwork

When you want to place thumbnail-like illustrations of another document (for example, showing a magazine cover on its own table of contents), the most flexible file formats are PDF and native InDesign. In the past, we used EPSs or screen shots, but these modern files are much cooler. Both formats can be placed and scaled in the same way as can PSDs or TIFFs.

- PDF files are self-contained; there's no need to gather fonts and support art.
- PDFs are compact, often taking up significantly less disk space than the original files.
- PDFs are faithful versions of the original—as opposed to a screen shot, which would convert all text and vector content to pixels.
- Individual pages (or a range of pages) of a PDF can be placed.
- InDesign files can be placed page by page like PDFs, but they offer the additional advantage of being editable.

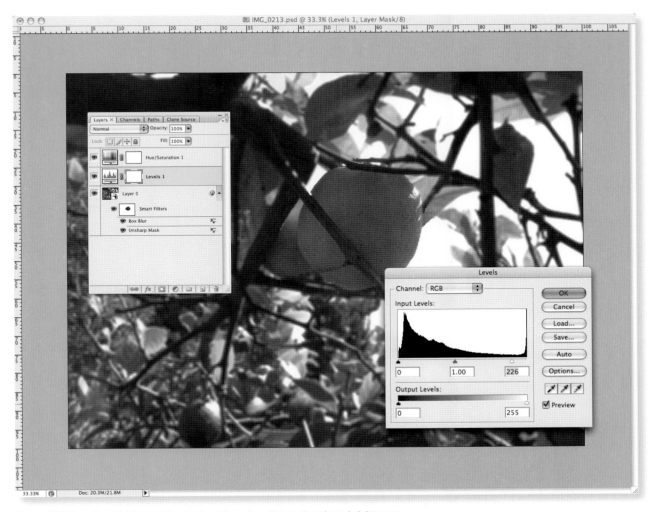

Figure 7.7 Drag the highlight slider to the left and you'll see the photo brighten up.

In the annual report, you'll place six pages of a PDF to show examples of book pages in a published project. To make this even easier, you'll use the InDesign fitting options to automatically scale the placed graphics:

1. In InDesign, navigate to page 4 of the annual report.
2. In the Layers panel, Option-click (Mac OS) or Alt-click (Windows) the lock icon for the Graphics layer. This locks all but the Graphics layer.
3. Create a graphic frame 1.7" wide by 2" tall (or 10p2.4 by 12p0), and keep it selected. Choose Object > Fitting > Frame Fitting Options. Enter the values shown in Figure 7.8.

Figure 7.8 Setting the options in the Frame Fitting Options dialog box can speed up graphic placement. These settings will center an incoming graphic and fill the frame proportionally. You might consider saving this as an object style.

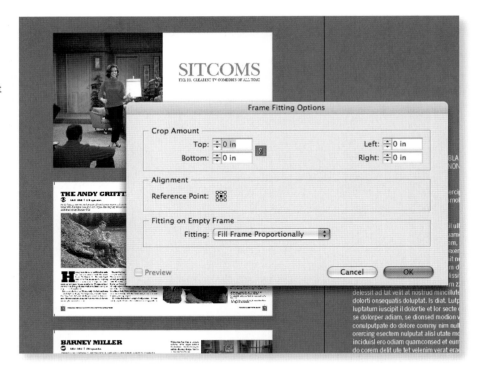

4. Option-drag (Mac OS) or Alt-drag (Windows) to duplicate the frame. Shift-click to select both frames, and open the Align panel (Window > Object and Layout > Align). Make sure Align To Selection is selected, and align the top edges of the frames. Select the Use Spacing option, enter a value of 0, and then click the Distribute Horizontal Space button. The frames should butt against each other. Group the two frames, and move them so that their top edge falls about 15p0 (2.5") from the top of the page.

   Now you'll copy the frames in pairs to align and distribute them.

5. Press Option (Mac OS) or Alt (Windows), and Shift-drag the pair of frames to create another set below; repeat this process so you have a total of six frames. Select all three groups of frames, enter **1p8** for the Use Spacing value in the Align panel, and click the Distribute Vertical Space button. Your pairs of frames should now be aligned and evenly distributed.

6. Deselect all frames. Now you'll place the PDF thumbnails.

7. Choose File > Place, being sure to select the Show Import Options option in the dialog, and select the **SitcomExcerpts.pdf** file in the Links folder. Choose All Pages, Crop To Trim, and deselect the Transparent Background option so that the pages will have an opaque white background. Click each frame in turn until you've placed all six pages.

Figure 7.9 The drop shadow gives some depth to pages.

8. Select all three groups, and add a 20 percent black drop shadow (Figure 7.9).
9. Unlock all layers by holding down Option (Mac OS) or Alt (Windows) and clicking the lock icon next to the Graphics layer.

Maximum Flexibility: Smart Objects and Smart Filters

One of the beauties of native file formats is the ability to work nondestructively: don't kill a pixel if you don't have to, don't flatten layered files—you get the idea. Give yourself a safety net whenever possible so you can exercise the luxury of changing your mind. Repeatedly.

The illustration on page 6 of the annual report (Figure 7.10) will be created out of several simple building blocks. Ultimately, it will be a painting of a lemon, hanging on a wall covered with elaborate wallpaper. But the wallpaper doesn't exist yet—it will be created out of a combination of Illustrator and Photoshop techniques.

Figure 7.10 You'll create this wallpaper using techniques in both Illustrator and Photoshop.

1. In Illustrator, open **DecorativePatternStart.ai**. Choose Select All, and then choose Edit > Define Pattern. Name the new pattern Decorative Tiles, and note that the new pattern is added to the Swatches panel. Delete the original artwork—you don't need it now. Create a rectangle that fills the artboard, and select the Decorative Tiles swatch to fill the rectangle. Save the file as **DecorativePatternDone.ai** in the Links folder.

2. In Photoshop, create a new RGB document with the following attributes: 6.75" by 10.5", 300ppi, RGB color, and a white background. Choose File > Place, and select the **DecorativePatternDone.ai** file. Choose Crop To Bounding box, and click OK. Press Return (Mac OS) or Enter (Windows) to create a new layer named DecorativePatternDone.

3. In Photoshop, double-click the DecorativePatternDone layer to edit it in Illustrator. Select the pattern-filled rectangle, and choose Edit > Edit Colors > Recolor Artwork. Click the Edit button at the top, and choose the Compound 1 set from the pop-up menu at the top. Try the settings shown in Figure 7.11, or experiment on your own. When you're satisfied, save the file, and it will be updated in the Photoshop file.

Now that you have basic wallpaper, it's time to hang the picture.

TIP: Need to scale a pattern? Double-click the Scale tool to show its options, deselect Objects, and select the Patterns option.

NOTE: Photoshop automatically converts the art to a Smart Object. In essence, a copy of the Illustrator file is now stored in the Photoshop file. There's no link to the original Illustrator file, however; any changes to it will not be reflected in the Photoshop file.

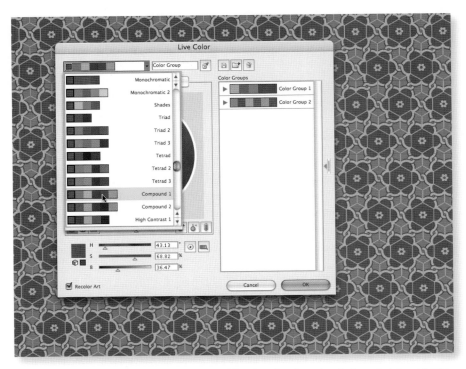

Figure 7.11 Using Live Color to experiment with colors is a freewheeling way to interactively color artwork. If you like the happy accident, save it as a color group.

TIP: If you had converted the lemon painting to a Smart Object, you would have been unable to perform the perspective correction—that's one of the limitations.

4. Open the file **LemonPaintingStart.psd**, and use the Move tool to drag the painting onto the wallpaper image. Obviously, you'll have to fix the perspective of the painting. It's helpful to place guides at the edges of the painting, then use Edit > Transform > Perspective to correct the shape, and finally scale up the painting horizontally to compensate for that distortion.

5. To make the painting look even more painterly, convert the lemon painting layer for Smart Filters, and use the Watercolor filter (Figure 7.12). Add a drop shadow to give the painting some dimensionality. If you had added the shadow before converting the painting layer for Smart Filters, the shadow would not be editable later, which is another little pitfall.

Before

After

Figure 7.12 Apply the Watercolor filter for a richer, more painterly look.

The wallpaper looks flat and fake. You'll make it look more realistic and create the illusion of depth by adding some lighting effects. In keeping with the goal of working nondestructively, you'll use a technique that allows you to add lighting effects without permanently changing the pixels of the underlying image (Figure 7.13). You'll also be able to modify the lighting effects at any time.

1. Create a new empty layer above the lemon painting layer, and fill it with 50 percent gray (choose Edit > Fill, and choose 50% Gray for Content). Set the blending mode to Overlay, which makes the layer transparent but still capable of displaying effects applied to it.

2. Convert the gray layer for Smart Filters, and then choose Filter > Render > Lighting Effects. Start with the default settings, but move the light source to the upper left by grabbing the edge of the oval that indicates the lighting coverage area. Feel free to experiment with the preset lighting effects such as Five Lights Down.

Figure 7.13 Create the illusion of depth to your wallpaper by adding lighting effects.

Now that you've created a convincing wallpaper effect, you're ready to attack what for some is the most disagreeable job for designers: creating tables. Of course, I rather enjoy working with tables; there's something sickly satisfying in seeing all those rows and columns of numbers line up neatly to attention. In the next section, you'll learn how to import and format data using the power of cell styles and table styles in InDesign CS3.

Importing and Formatting Spreadsheet Files

Chances are, you'll receive the financial data you need to incorporate into your annual report as a Microsoft Excel file or as tab-delimited text. Your challenge is to present this crucial information in a way that's intelligible ("What do these numbers mean?"), unambiguous ("Is that before or after investments?"), and attractive ("Let's write that check!"). The traditional tabular presentation (whether as tabbed text or in a formal table) lends itself to readability, and the table and cell styles in InDesign help you make it attractive.

By default, imported text and spreadsheet files have no connection with their original files. Most of the time this lack of connection is for the best. Pity the poor designer who places a lengthy text document and formats it painstakingly in InDesign, only to have all the formatting wiped out by updating the layout because the writer decided to change a period to a comma in the document. But given clients' tendencies to modify annual report data just about the time you get it all neatly formatted, linking to the original file might be a good idea, just for ease of reimport. It does save you the nuisance of completely starting over, but note that any formatting will be lost when you update text or spreadsheet files. Reread that last sentence: it means that if you reimport or update table data (such as that from an Excel file), you will need to reformat the content. But don't despair: table and cell styles can greatly speed up the application (and reapplication) of table formatting.

To establish a link with incoming text or spreadsheet files, choose InDesign > Preferences > Type (Mac OS) or Edit > Preferences > Type (Windows), and select the option called Create Links When Placing Text And Spreadsheet Files (Figure 7.14).

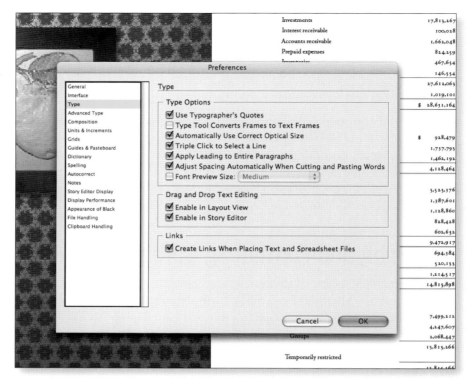

Figure 7.14 If you anticipate corrections for placed Excel files, turn on Create Links When Placing Text And Spreadsheet Files. Although it makes updating content easier, it will not retain formatting. You will have to manually reapply any formatting you've performed in InDesign.

Formatting Tables

Although you can manually format table cells and text within them in the same way you format regular text frames, it's prudent to store formatting in table and cell styles and to conscientiously use paragraph and character styles to formalize that formatting. You'll thank yourself later when it's necessary to edit table content. As you prepare to set up styles, consider some time-tested conventions for numerical formatting: right-aligned columns of numbers are easier to read, and it's important that decimals and dollar signs line up vertically.

You can facilitate readability by using OpenType fonts that contain the Tabular Lining or Tabular OldStyle feature to create numerals that are designed to line up neatly in columns. Tabular Lining numerals occupy the same vertical space as the uppercase letters of a font, while OldStyle numerals are often more readable because of their lower height (Figure 7.15).

Using Table and Cell Styles

Table styles store only very basic attributes, such as alternating fills, vertical and horizontal strokes, and the table border. Table styles offer no control over text inset or formatting.

824,259	418,259	Tabular Lining
467,654	469,945	
146,554	393,746	
27,612,063	27,505,461	
1,019,101	806,620	
$28,631,164	$28,312,081	
824,259	418,259	Tabular OldStyle
467,654	469,945	
146,554	393,746	
27,612,063	27,505,461	
1,019,101	806,620	
$28,631,164	$28,312,081	

Figure 7.15 Tabular numerals in OpenType fonts allow columns of numbers to neatly line up. You may find that OldStyle figures are more readable, since they are more easily differentiated from surrounding text.

Cell styles, on the other hand, are the powerhouses of table formatting. They can specify paragraph styles to be used, set text inset values, perform vertical text justification, separate stroke attributes for all four sides of a cell, and more. In other words, cell styles store all the table formatting you're likely to use. Once you have created cell styles, you can invoke them within a table style, specifying their use for such components as header and footer rows.

Project Wrap-Up

In this chapter, you saw once again how important clear and simple graphic design is when it comes to conveying complex information like in an annual report. Despite the smallish size of the report, the information never feels cluttered or crammed; reading it feels leisurely and surefooted. Imagine an annual report that's disorganized, chaotic, and confusing. Would you buy a used stock from those people?

Enhancing InDesign Tables

WoodWing Software's Smart Styles CS3 plug-in for InDesign (www. woodwingusa.com) can update table content while retaining formatting and can even sort table content and perform some calculations within InDesign. Prior to the introduction of cell styles and table styles in InDesign CS3, designers had to either purchase the same stand-alone plug-ins from their original developer, Teacup Software, or turn to WoodWing's Smart Styles for help. Today, the combination of both Smart Styles and built-in InDesign table styles and cell styles offers a potent punch to simplifying complex styling problems.

LUX.
Lux'bg.
Strasbourg
Danube
Munich
AUSTRIA
SLOVENIA
Ljubljana
SWITZ.
Bern
Venice
Milan
NCE
Geneva
Mt. Blanc 15,774
Lyon
Genoa
MONACO
Florence
Nice
Marseille
Corsica
ANDORRA
Barcelona
(Sp.)
Rome

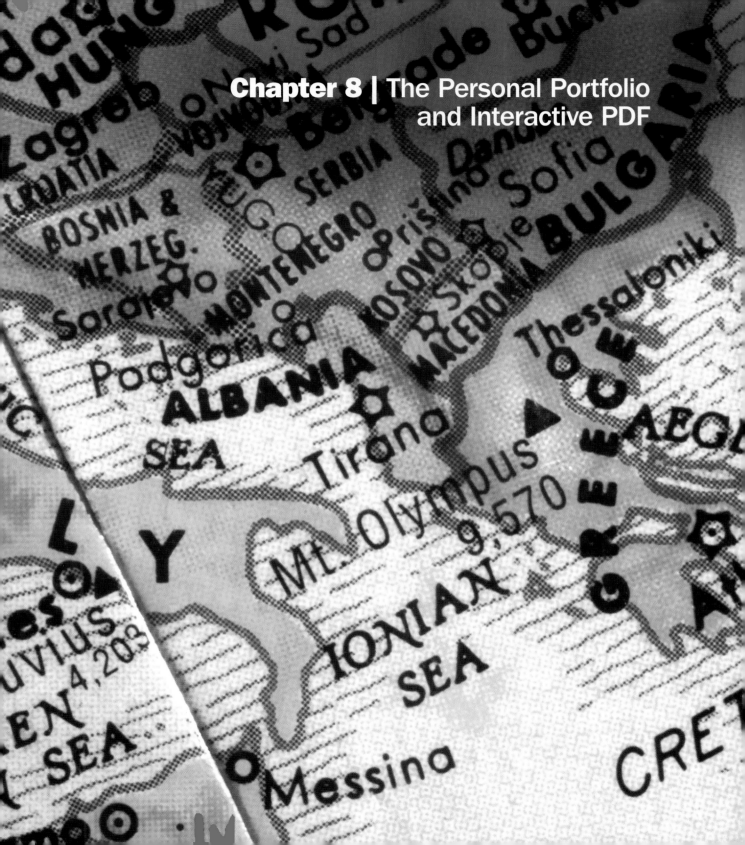

STREET SCENE

AL AT THE COLLISEUM

AT THE BORGHESE GALLERY

AL AT THE VATICAN

SPANISH STEPS

PONTE CASTEL SANT'ANGLEO

PIAZZA VENEZIA

PIAZZA DEL POPOLO

AL ALONG THE TIBER

THE FORUM (MOVIE)

VICTOR EMMANUEL
MONUMENT

"An important aspect of design is the degree to which the object involves you in its own completion." — Brian Eno

Television and the movies have long promised that by now we'd live in a world where we fly to work with jet packs, vacation on the moon, eat meals in pill form, and wax nostalgic about how our ancestors read things called *books* printed on paper. The promise of the "paperless" world seemed to be nearing fulfillment with the dawn of the Internet, but a decade into the information age, print has not met the fate so many expected, and the Web continues to evolve beyond the desktop computer to smart phones and other mobile devices. Somewhere between old and new media, there remains a middle ground. It's a place where the traditions of print (page size, layout, and typography) and the benefits of the Internet (visual feedback, hyperlinks, audio, and video) coexist. This bridge between the past and the future is a technology invented at the height of print's maturity, just prior to the online revolution, called the Portable Document Format, more commonly known as PDF.

A major complaint of print designers transitioning to the Web has been the loss of control over typography and page presentation. Web page visitors have a level of influence over what they see that never existed in print, where the format and appearance of the final piece was etched in stone, according to the decisions and preferences of the designers (and, of course, their clients). Yet, for all the convenience of the Web—nonlinear progression through information, side-by-side presentation of text, images, audio, and video—there's a limitation: portability.

When PDF was introduced, Adobe's goal for it was relatively simple: a way to reliably view, print, and share documents, independent of the user's computer platform or the software used to create the original document. With each new version of the PDF standard, however, came more features. By the mid-90s, the ability to link to external files and embed multimedia content became part of the format, and the door to interactive documents was opened.

The interactive PDF is a best-of-both-worlds solution. The tradition of the printed page is honored, but many of its limits are overcome. Text in the document can link to other relevant information in the document, in another file, or anywhere on the Web. Visual content extends beyond still images to video and animation. PDF allows easy distribution of a "package" of content—text, images, audio, video, and hyperlinks—freed from the expense of print and the connectivity requirements of the Web.

In seeking a way to capture the essence of a trip I took to Europe in 2003 with my dad, I found the interactive PDF to be the perfect solution. Since I'm primarily a print designer, I could design the interactive PDF like a book or a magazine using familiar tools and principles in Adobe InDesign CS3. But whereas books and magazines are limited to what can be printed, the PDF could easily be enhanced with short video or audio clips from our trip. When I began, little did I know how fun this project would be to create or how enthusiastically it would ultimately be received by those who saw it. For a look at the finished project, visit the companion Web site at www.peachpit.com/prodesignCS3, download the Chapter 8 folder, and open the **Travels_with_Alvin.pdf** file (Figure 8.1).

Why PDF When We Have the Web?

In the age of YouTube, social networking sites, video blogs, and rich-media content Web sites, it's natural to wonder how the stalwart PDF fits into the mix. The Web seems to be the go-to place for a hyperlinked, interactive, media-rich presentation. Or is it? Have you ever arrived at a meeting or conference where you expected an Internet connection only to find there was none? So much for your Web-based presentation. How about pointing someone to a specific Web page only to find out that they need to reconfigure their browser's media options or install a plug-in? Relying entirely on the Web can be a bit dicey.

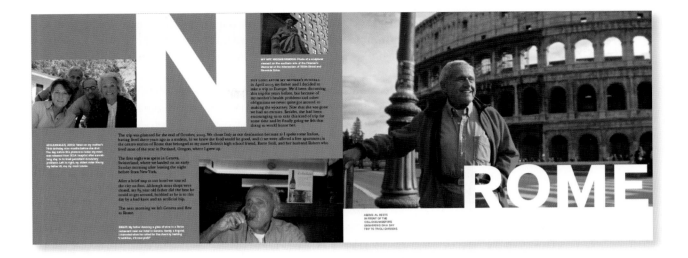

Figure 8.1 A page from Travels with Alvin, an interactive PDF embedded with video, photos, and audio.

Portability is a great advantage of PDF. As a stand-alone file, for which nearly everyone with a computer has the necessary software, a PDF can be made available for download, sent via email, or distributed on physical media such as CDs and DVDs.

For print designers, there's an irresistible incentive: your pages will look exactly like you want them to look. That, coupled with the speed and efficiency of using software with which print designers are already comfortable (InDesign), makes creating interactive PDFs an easy sell.

Imagine a product data sheet where a looping Flash animation could demonstrate the workings of a piece of industrial equipment. Or an interview where the subject's photo is also a video clip that allows his or her voice and personality to add to the context of the conversation. Or imagine a portfolio of your work that reveals your sketch concepts when the mouse moves over a photograph of a finished piece. All of these options are possible in a dynamic PDF, where enhanced Web-style content can exist in a "traditional" print layout while engaging your audience on a much deeper level.

Exploring Interactivity in PDFs

The meaning of interactivity these days is broad. A hypertext link on a Web page, an online poll that calculates results when a question is answered, and an immersive Flash-based user interface are examples of interactivity ranging from the simple to the complex.

Interactivity in a PDF is more straightforward but, in the hands of a creative designer, can produce results just as inventive as flashier and more robust tools. Together, these interactive features have the potential to transform a portfolio into a glimpse of the designer's creative process; bring an interview closer to an intimate conversation; demonstrate a process in seconds, rather than in paragraphs of detailed narrative; and connect the reader immediately to additional content.

The following sections are a rundown of the interactive options in PDF.

Hyperlinks

Figure 8.2 The lemon graphic in my signature contains a hyperlink to my email address.

Like their Web counterparts, PDF hyperlinks are navigational elements that let readers jump from one location in the document to another location, to another file, or to any online destination. Hyperlinks can be text or images (Figure 8.2). Which option to use depends on the nature of your PDF project, how the hyperlink fits in with the rest of your design, and what's appropriate for your audience.

Bookmarks

In the electronic world, bookmarks have come a long way from their cardboard-and-tassle namesake. If, unlike most people, you've bothered to actually open any of your Adobe software user guides, you've seen bookmarks—and plenty of them—put to use effectively in a PDF. Bookmarks serve two purposes. In the final PDF, they're listed in the Bookmarks panel and act as a hybrid of a menu, table of contents, and index (Figure 8.3). In InDesign, they mark parts of the document as destinations for hyperlinks and button actions.

Buttons

The name *button* is as accurate as it is misleading where InDesign is concerned. It's accurate in that a button is something you push (or, rather, *click*) to trigger an action. It's inaccurate in that it conjures up an image of the buttons we're all used to on the Web and in our software: beveled or rounded slabs with small text labels on them. In InDesign, a button can be that literal but can also be any text frame, graphic frame, shape, object, or image. Buttons can have multiple states in which their appearance changes based on user interaction. One that most of us are familiar with is the Rollover state, where a change occurs to the physical appearance of the button when the pointer passes (or rolls) over the button. States provide visual feedback for users, indicating that their interaction with the document is successful (Figure 8.4).

Figure 8.3 Bookmarks are important to add for navigation within the PDF.

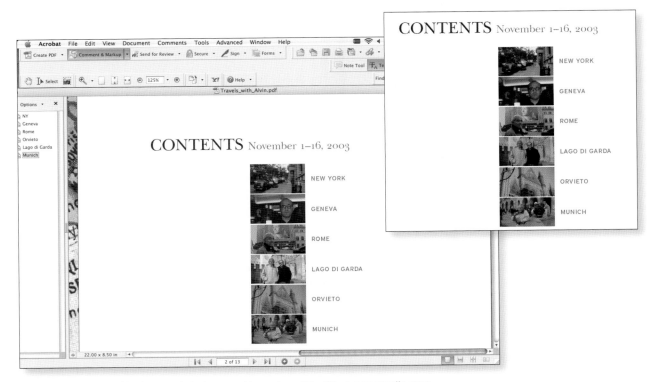

Figure 8.4 You can add a button state to a graphic such as this. When a user rolls over the image that references Lago di Garda, the tinted screen disappears from the photo.

Figure 8.5 Movies liven up a PDF page and also allow you to communicate in a different way to your reader. This cropped page from the project shows how the frame from the movie appears (upper-right).

RIGHT: Al jokes with Hans and Ernst on the ferry ride across Lake Garda. Click to play video. >

Movies

Video adds a level of immediacy, context, and interest that words and still images cannot. Effective use of video within a PDF can keep the user engaged with your project more deeply and for a longer period of time, because it requires the user to stop and watch (Figure 8.5). We are, for better or worse, a TV culture. Our eyes are immediately drawn to moving images, and their effect is hypnotic, luring us in and holding onto us whether we realize it or not. Movies can be placed (but not played) in InDesign like any other image, but that's where the similarity ends. Apple QuickTime VR, for example, is an amazing technology that lets the user see and control 360° of any scene. For more information on QuickTime VR, visit the Apple Web site at www.apple.com/quicktime/technologies/qtvr/.

NOTE: Compatible movie formats for PDFs currently are QuickTime (.mov), AVI, MPEG, or Flash (.swf) files.

Sound

Sound introduces a level of depth to an interactive PDF presentation that is entirely unique and is beyond the reach of text and images. Quotation marks around Neil Armstrong's "That's one small step for man..." moon landing statement are no substitute for hearing it spoken through the crackling microphone

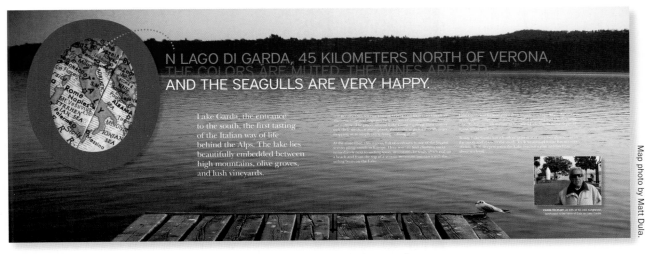

N LAGO DI GARDA, 45 KILOMETERS NORTH OF VERONA,
THE COLORS ARE MUTED, THE WINES ARE RED,
AND THE SEAGULLS ARE VERY HAPPY.

Lake Garda, the entrance
to the south, the first tasting
of the Italian way of life
behind the Alps. The lake lies
beautifully embedded between
high mountains, olive groves,
and lush vineyards.

Figure 8.6 When viewers reach this page in the interactive pdf, a gull sound greets them.

across nearly a quarter million miles. No written description of the Otis Redding classic "I've Been Loving You Too Long (To Stop Now)" can hope to capture the heartbreaking intensity heard in the song itself. Sound can be ambient, evoking a mood or an environment, or it can be fleeting, attracting attention and providing audible feedback for the user when a page turns or a button is clicked (Figure 8.6).

Together, these interactive features have the potential to transform a portfolio into a glimpse of the designer's creative process; bring an interview closer to an intimate conversation; demonstrate a process in seconds, rather than in paragraphs of detailed narrative; and connect the reader immediately to additional content.

 NOTE: Supported audio formats are WAV (8-bit or 16-bit uncompressed only), AIF, and AU sound clips.

Exploring Distribution Strategies

Some important questions to ask yourself before starting an interactive PDF project are: How will my PDF be distributed? Email? Web download? CD or DVD? Will my movies and sounds be linked files or embedded in the PDF? These are interrelated questions, and knowing how you want to distribute your final project will influence how you handle your movie files significantly.

Embedding produces a single PDF that is not dependent on any other files. This is simple and convenient, but embedding large video files will make the file size balloon up considerably, perhaps too much to send as an email attachment.

Linking to external movie files is possible in two ways: local files and Web-hosted files. If your PDF project is going out on a CD or DVD, linking to movie files in a folder on that disc is simple enough, but it will require the reader to have that disc inserted to play the movies. The second option is linking to a Web address (URL) where the movie resides. This allows the PDF itself to stay relatively small and to only go out to the Web for movies when the user chooses to view them. With short movies and a high-bandwidth connection, there should be little or no delay in the start of the movie. However, this method requires an Internet connection (to view the movies only; the PDF itself will still open, print, and so on). This takes away slightly from the stand-alone portability of PDF.

Getting Started with Interactive Options in InDesign

The one paradox when working on an interactive PDF project using InDesign is that although the tools and settings you need for an interactive document are built into it, InDesign doesn't support these features. Movies and sounds don't play in InDesign, and rollovers, buttons, and hyperlinks don't work. With the exception of bookmarks, only by exporting the InDesign file to Adobe PDF—with the appropriate interactive and multimedia options selected—and viewing it in either Adobe Acrobat Professional or Adobe Reader can any of the features be seen.

As you proceed through the project for this chapter, it's a good idea to periodically export your work-in-progress version to PDF to verify that the result of your work is what you expected. It's better—and far less frustrating—to narrow down and troubleshoot a problem with one part of a file than to spend hours adding features in InDesign that don't work as expected in the final PDF.

To start, let's pick a point of departure that's likely to be the same as what your audience will pick: the table of contents on page 3 of the project (Figure 8.7). Notice that this table of contents (TOC) does not include page numbers. Since this is an electronic document, the reader is removed from the act of flipping through the pages to find a specific page number. An interactive TOC needs to be built by converting the images on page 3 to clickable buttons that take the reader to the appropriate pages.

 If you haven't done so already, visit this book's companion Web site (www.peachpit.com/prodesignCS3) and download the Chapter 8 folder, which contains files you'll use in the step-by-step instruction below.

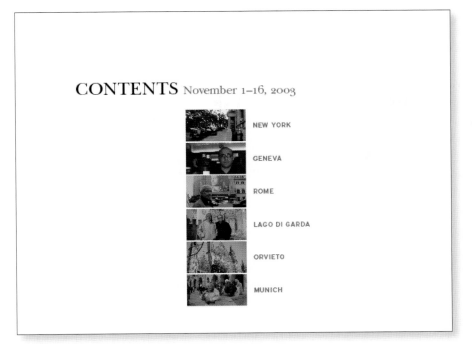

TIP: You can bypass the Pages panel by pressing Command+J (Mac OS) or Control+J (Windows) which calls up the Go to Page dialog. Type the desired page number, and then hit Return (Mac OS) or Enter (Windows). Another way to navigate through pages is from the page box at the bottom of the document window. Click the downward-facing arrow to the right of the currently displayed page number, and choose the page from the menu.

Figure 8.7 Add clickable buttons to a table of contents so users can easily navigate the PDF.

Using Bookmarks to Create Destinations

In this exercise, you'll create bookmarks that serve two purposes. First, they'll be exported when the final PDF is made, automatically populating the Bookmarks panel in Acrobat or Adobe Reader. Additionally, the bookmarks will make setting up the button options a bit more efficient and intuitive.

1. From InDesign CS3, open the Chapter 8 folder and double-click the **Travels_with_Alvin.indd** document to open it.
2. With the document open, go to the Pages panel (Window > Pages), and double-click the page thumbnail for page 4.
3. Open the Bookmarks panel (Window > Interactive > Bookmarks), and select New Bookmark from the panel menu (Figure 8.8). By default, InDesign adds a bookmark named Bookmark 1, which you can rename by choosing Rename Bookmark from the panel menu or by clicking once on the name listed in the panel itself. Name this bookmark NY (Figure 8.9).
4. Select the photo of Al at the bottom of page 4 and choose New Bookmark from the Bookmarks panel menu. Name this bookmark Geneva.

Figure 8.8 Create a new bookmark in the Bookmarks panel.

NOTE: When creating a new bookmark, be sure to first deselect previous bookmarks. Failing to do so will create a child of the selected bookmark.

Figure 8.9 The newly-created bookmark.

Figure 8.10 Test the bookmarks in the Bookmarks panel.

5. Go to page 5, and again choose New Bookmark from the Bookmarks panel menu or by clicking the button at the bottom of the panel. Rename the bookmark Rome. Repeat these steps for the spread on pages 6 and 7, page 13, the spread on pages 16 and 17, and page 21. Name the bookmarks Rome, Lago di Garda, Orvieto, and Munich, respectively.

6. Test your bookmarks by double clicking them in the Bookmarks panel to check that they take you to the proper destination in your layout (Figure 8.10).

Creating Buttons and Setting Button Options

Now that the bookmarks are in place, and the pages are marked with easily identifiable names rather than just numbers, let's put those destinations to use by turning the images in the table of contents into buttons that refer to those bookmarks.

NOTE: The Description field is optional, but any text entered here will be used as alternative text for the visually impaired and appear as a tool tip when the pointer lingers over the button in Acrobat.

1. On page 3, select the top image for New York (Figure 8.11), Control-click (Mac OS) or right-click (Windows) to access the context menu, and select Interactive > Convert to Button.

2. Double-click the image to open the Button Options dialog.

3. Under the General options, give the button a name. This can be anything, and there's no real strategy for naming buttons except that if you were writing scripts to expand the functionality of this button, or refer to it, the button name is the name to which you'd refer. In this instance, New York might be an appropriate name.

Figure 8.11 You'll add some interactivity to this image on the Table of Contents to lead viewers to that section about New York in the PDF.

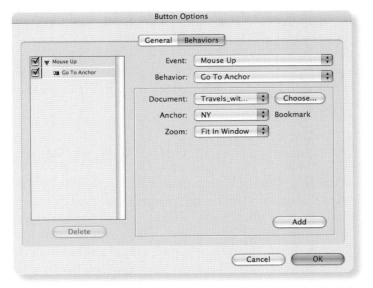

Figure 8.12 The Button Options dialog, with the Behaviors tab selected.

4. For Visibility in PDF, choose Visible. The other options—Hidden, Visible but Doesn't Print, and Hidden but Printable—are useful under different circumstances (for example, a hidden button could be placed over a country on an image of a map and trigger an action that displays a photo of that country's most recognized landmark on the opposite page), but in this instance, we want a simple button visible on the page.

5. Click the Behaviors tab at the top of the Button Options dialog (Figure 8.12). This is where you give the button one or more behaviors, or actions, to carry out when clicked. Choose Mouse Up from the Event menu. This assigns the behavior to the moment when a user releases the mouse after clicking the button.

TIP: Clicking the Choose button (next to the Document menu) allows you to select any other InDesign document as the location of the anchor. Also, anchors are not limited to bookmarks. A single word of text can be established as a text anchor within any InDesign document and set as the destination for a button. Text anchors are indicated by a small anchor icon next to the name in the Bookmarks panel.

6. Choose Go To Anchor from the Behavior menu. Once that's selected, the options below the menu change to those appropriate for your choice. In the Document menu, the current document, **Travels with Alvin.indd**, is selected by default.

7. Choose NY from the Anchor menu. Notice that the anchor type, Bookmark, appears next to your selection when you release the mouse.

8. Zoom refers to how the destination page is sized when the button brings the reader to that page. The standard PDF view options are available here for fitting the page in your window, viewing it actual size, fitting it to the width of the screen, fitting it to all be visible, or inheriting the current zoom level. In this case, choose Fit in Window so that the reader is quickly oriented when entering the new page.

9. Click Add to assign this behavior to the button, and then click OK.

10. Repeat steps 1 through 9 for the remaining images in the table of contents, assigning each its own appropriate name and anchor destination. If you want to test your work in a PDF before going any further, follow the instructions for exporting a PDF with interactive options at the end of the chapter, test your button functionality, and then return to this section to finish the steps.

Adding Visual Feedback with Button States

Now, you know and I know that the images in the table of contents are buttons, but how does the reader know? If you tested your PDF already, you may have noticed that the pointer turned to the pointer finger in Acrobat when you moved it over each image. That's a hint, but it's not the most eye-catching one, to be sure. You'll make these buttons more obvious as interactive elements by having their state (or appearance) change when the pointer moves over them.

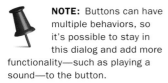

NOTE: Buttons can have multiple behaviors, so it's possible to stay in this dialog and add more functionality—such as playing a sound—to the button.

1. Choose Window > Interactive > States to open the States panel.

2. Select the first image on page 3 (New York) with the Selection tool. Notice that the States panel displays the button name you assigned in the previous section in the Name field and shows a state called Up in the list (Figure 8.13).

3. Choose New State from the panel menu. By default, a state called Rollover is added. A check mark next to the name indicates that it's now the currently displayed state. The button still looks the same on the page because this state has no content yet.

4. To add content to the state, choose Place Content into State from the panel menu, or click the Place Content Into Selected State button at the bottom of the panel.

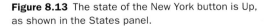

Figure 8.13 The state of the New York button is Up, as shown in the States panel.

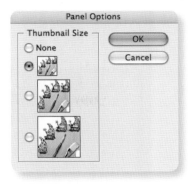

Figure 8.14 Choose view options for your thumbnails in the States panel menu.

5. In the dialog, select the file **trip001_over.jpg** found in the Links folder for this chapter, and click Open. A new, full-color image now appears as the content of the button's Rollover state to differentiate it from the tinted grayscale of the Up state. Even though this is one frame, it effectively has two images placed in it.

6. To see thumbnails of your button states, choose Panel Options from the States panel menu, and pick any of the three view options; then click OK (Figure 8.14). A small, medium, or large thumbnail of each button state (depending on your choice) will appear to the left of each state name.

7. Repeat steps 2 through 5 for the remaining images on page 3, adding the version of the file in that same folder with "_over" in the filename.

NOTE: Buttons can have a total of three states: Up, Down, and Rollover. The Down state, which we don't put to use here, changes the image's state when the user has pressed, but not released, the mouse. This third option adds another layer of visual feedback for the user, confirming that the PDF has registered the click.

An alternate way to create buttons with different states using just one file instead of two is to create Adobe Photoshop .psd files with multiple layers and blend modes to create variations of the same image (Figure 8.15). Then, use the Object Layer Options feature in InDesign CS3 to selectively turn different Photoshop layers on or off in each placed image state. Simply place the same file in each state, then Control-click (Mac OS) or right-click (Windows) the image, and finally select Object Layer Options from the context menu. Select the Preview check box to see your results in the layout as you click the visibility icons on or off for any of the Photoshop layers in the placed file (Figure 8.16). Be sure that Keep Layer Visibility Overrides is chosen from Update Link Options to maintain your selections. Repeat these steps for the content of each of your button states.

Again, feel free to export the document using the settings at the end of this chapter to test your button states before moving on to the next steps.

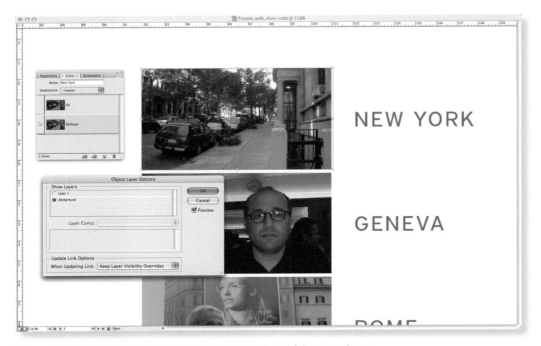

Figure 8.15 Use multiple layers when creating variations of the same image.

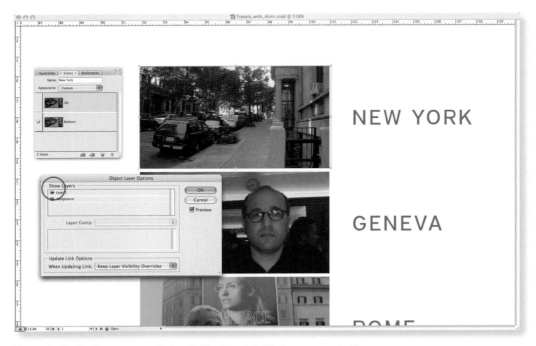

Figure 8.16 Preview your results by clicking the visibility icons on and off.

Adding Hyperlinks

Current versions of Acrobat and Adobe Reader are smart enough to automatically detect properly formatted Web site and email addresses, but any other text or images that need to act as hyperlinks must be set in the Hyperlinks panel. Much of the text in this project could conceivably link to historical or other Web-based information about the different European locations, but to keep things simple we'll manually add only one hyperlink to page 24 of this project. At the bottom of the page is my logo—a lemon—that you'll set up as a hyperlink from the interactive PDF to my Web site.

1. Open the Hyperlinks panel (Window > Interactive > Hyperlinks).
2. Choose New Hyperlink Destination from the Hyperlinks panel menu.
3. In the New Hyperlink Destination dialog, choose URL as the hyperlink type, replace the default hyperlink Name with **Scott Citron Design**, and type **www.scottcitrondesign.com** after the http:// in the URL field (Figure 8.17).
4. Click OK.
5. Using the Selection tool, select the frame containing the placed lemon logo.
6. Choose New Hyperlink from the Hyperlinks panel menu.
7. In the New Hyperlink dialog, enter **SCD Website** for the hyperlink name. By default, Travels_with_Alvin.indd should be chosen in the Document menu.
8. For Type, make sure that URL is selected.
9. Choose the Scott Citron Design hyperlink destination you just created in step 3 from the Name menu, which will populate the URL field with the full Web address (Figure 8.18).

Figure 8.17 You can add a hyperlink to make your PDFs interactive as well.

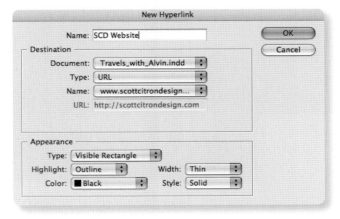

Figure 8.18 Change the New Hyperlink so it will link to a Web site.

10. In the Appearance section, set Type to Invisible Rectangle, and set Highlight to None. This will keep the lemon art looking just as it does in the InDesign layout. This link is meant to be a convenient addition to the PDF, not an overt or obvious link.

11. Click OK. The Scott Citron Design hyperlink now appears in the Hyperlinks panel, and it will be highlighted whenever this frame is selected. To enable other frames or text in the document to use this link, simply select them, and then click this hyperlink name in the panel.

To make hyperlinks more obvious to your reader, refer to the Appearance section of the New Hyperlink dialog. There you can choose among attributes to apply such as line style, weight, color, and highlight style (inset, inverse, or outline). The finished page for this project is shown in Figure 8.19.

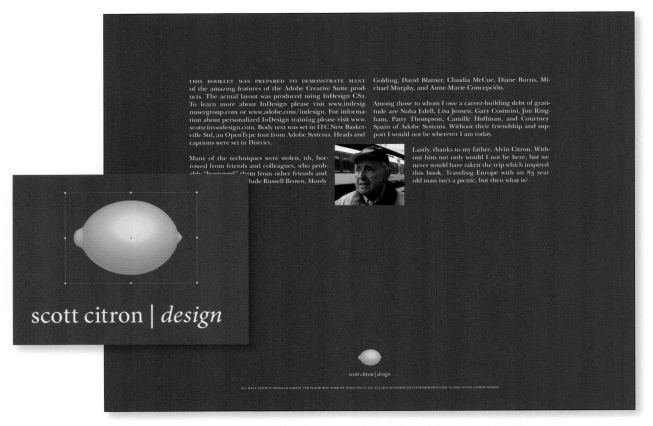

Figure 8.19 Choose from a number of attributes to make your hyperlinks more noticeable.

Adding to the Experience with Movies

Have you ever had a friend or family member force you to sit down and watch their home videos? It's painful, isn't it? One person's fond memories are another person's slow torture. The same applies with movies in an interactive PDF. Less truly is more. Keeping movies brief makes them much less taxing on the viewer's time and attention span. Short movies also mean smaller file sizes, which is an important factor to keep in mind when planning your interactive PDF project.

You can get movies into an InDesign file in several ways. Most are the same methods used to bring in any image (select File > Place, drag from the Finder or Windows Explorer, add to InDesign from Adobe Bridge, and so on), but the method described next is unique to movies and sounds.

TIP: If you want to embed the movie in the PDF, eliminating the need for external file links, select the Embed Movie in PDF check box.

NOTE: You can set your PDF to bring in a movie that's hosted on a Web server by choosing Specify a URL instead of Choose a File and then typing the full Web address of the file. After that, click Verify URL and Movie Size to have InDesign find the movie on the Web and get information about the physical dimensions of the movie. After that, all the other steps for using local or Web-based movies are the same.

1. In the **Travels_with_Alvin.indd** document, go to page 15, and then select the empty white frame in the lower-right corner of the page using the Selection tool.
2. Control-click (Mac OS) or right-click (Windows) the selected frame, and choose Interactive > Movie Options from the context menu.
3. In the Source area of the resulting dialog, Choose a File should be selected by default. Click the Choose button to the right, navigate to the Links folder in the Chapter 8 folder, select the file **Salo Sunglasses2.mov**, and then click Open (Figure 8.20).

   The Options area of the Movie Options dialog lets you establish what your movie looks like initially on the page (Poster), the method you want to use to play it (Mode), and other settings for presenting the movie once it begins playing.

Figure 8.20 Once you've selected a file to use for your movie, the details appear in the lower portion of the Movie Options dialog.

Figure 8.21 The Default Poster option ensures that the first frame of the movie appears on the PDF.

TIP: In keeping with the best-of-both-worlds benefit of PDF, a high-resolution image can be used as an image poster, allowing you to use the same InDesign file to output a press-ready PDF for print and an interactive PDF with movies. In the collage of photographs on page 12 of this project, the tinted image labeled The Forum (Movie) in the collage of images is a separate image file used as a movie poster instead of a frame from the movie file.

4. In the Poster menu, the default option is Default Poster, which is the first frame of the movie (Figure 8.21). That's good enough for this example, so stick with that. However, any frame in the movie file can be used as the poster. To pick another frame, select Choose Movie Frame as Poster from the bottom of the Poster pop-up menu, and move the playhead through the movie until you find the desired frame (Figure 8.22).

   There's also a filmstrip graphic built into InDesign that's available as the Standard Poster option. Alternatively, you can choose a completely different image file as a poster for your movie if no particular frame of the video file is appropriate within your layout.

5. Choose Play Once Then Stop, if it isn't already chosen, from the Mode menu. Other options here are Play Once Stay Open (which leaves the last frame of the movie displayed, rather than reverting to the poster frame) and Repeat Play (which plays the movie on a continuous loop that stops only when the user clicks the movie). Repeat Play is a good setting for something like a looping Flash animation (.swf file) but would be the wrong choice for a specific event or interview segment over which the user should have control. If you prefer that the movie starts playing as soon as the reader gets to the page, choose Play on Page Turn.

6. If your movie is somewhat long and you want your audience to have more control over its playback, select the Show Controller During Play check box. This will add the standard QuickTime controller below the movie once it starts playing.

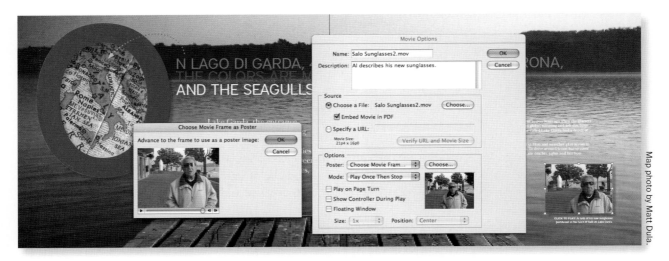

Figure 8.22 You can select another frame for the image that appears on the PDF.

7. To separate the movie playback from the page layout, choose Floating Window and then the appropriate size and position at which you want the movie to play.

   In this example, this short movie should not play automatically or have a visible movie controller, and it looks best playing in its established position, so those boxes can all remain unselected.

8. Click OK to close the Movie Options dialog.

9. Back on page 15, select the movie poster by using the Direct Selection tool, and then resize it by choosing Object > Fitting > Fill Frame Proportionally. The poster snaps to the size of the frame in which it's placed. The movie will also play at that reduced size.

   Alternately, try applying the Movie object style in the Object Styles panel. Built into the style is a 1-point white stroke, a fitting specification, and a drop shadow.

10. Go to pages 17 and 18, and repeat steps 2 through 9 for each, using the files **Chiusi.mov** and **Craftsman Alley.mov**, respectively. Feel free to experiment with some of the other poster options, playback modes, and presentation methods for these movies to see how they work.

NOTE: Optionally, you can give the movie a name in the Name field. This does not change the name of the file on disk. Primarily, this name would be used if the movie needs to be called upon by a script or referred to by a button action.

Saying It with Sound

From an implementation standpoint, sounds work almost exactly like movies. Most of their options are the same. However, sounds cannot be remote files on a Web site the way movies can, and sounds can't open in separate windows, play continuously, or display a controller when activated.

From a planning and design standpoint, there's one other significant difference. Since sounds have no visual element to them, how you present them on the page is a unique challenge. There needs to be some visual indication to the reader that audio content is available, so a text-based caption or sound icon or other indicator on the page is needed. Any image on the page can have a sound "attached" to it, so a person's photo could be clicked to start a clip of them speaking, even though it's just a still image on the page. A sound is also a more likely candidate for the Play on Page Turn option if, for example, I wanted a sound clip of water, wind, and birds to be heard when someone reaches the spread on pages 14 and 15 showing Lago di Garda (Figure 8.23).

Sounds can also be incorporated into button behaviors. The table of contents buttons, in addition to going to a specific bookmark, could play a sound when the mouse is pressed, for example, providing audio feedback to the user in addition to the visual feedback that the button states provide.

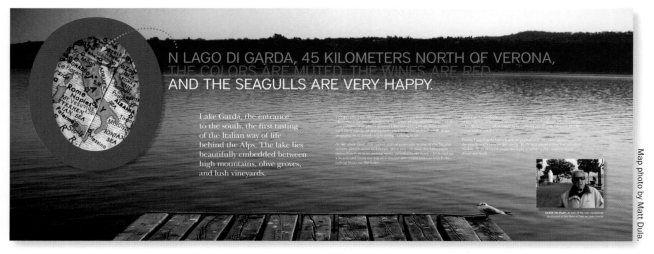

Figure 8.23 You will add the sound of gulls to this page in the project.

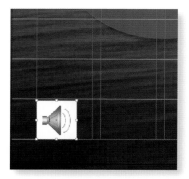

Figure 8.24 Place the AIF file and its icon will appear on the page.

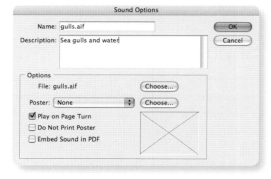

Figure 8.25 You can hide this ugly icon by changing a setting in the Sound Options dialog.

NOTE: Although Quick-Time .mov or .avi files can also be used for playing audio effects it's impossible to make them invisible. Even though their poster frames can be set to None, the file will appear as a black box in your PDF when the audio plays. For this reason, it's best to stick to dedicated audio formats like .aif, .wav, or .au.

To place an audio file on pages 14–15, follow these steps:

1. Choose File > Place and navigate to the file named **gulls.aif** in the Chapter 8 Links folder.
2. Place the file anywhere on the spread (Figure 8.24). As long as the file is placed anywhere within the live page area, its specific location is not important since you'll make the file invisible in the next step.
3. Double-click the placed file to bring up the Sound Options dialog (Figure 8.25). Set the Poster option to None to hide the physical file.
4. Select the Play on Page Turn check box to make the sound of the gulls and water play automatically when a visitor arrives at the spread.

Exporting the Finished PDF

When your PDF is fully loaded with buttons, movies, and sound, it's time to export it to a PDF in which all the settings applied in InDesign are enabled in Acrobat or Adobe Reader. When exporting (File > Export > PDF), you need to keep in mind some key settings and issues.

Compatibility

In the Export Adobe PDF dialog (Figure 8.26), the Compatibility menu has options for five PDF standards from PDF 1.3 though PDF 1.7 (Figure 8.27). If your project requires backward-compatibility to older standards (PDF 1.3 and 1.4), keep in mind that these versions have limitations that later versions do not. Movie and sound posters that are not RGB images will not be visible in the PDF. The MPEG and SWF formats are not supported, and movie files cannot be embedded. Conversely, sounds must be embedded and cannot be linked to external files.

For PDF 1.5 or newer, these limitations do not apply. However, there are some very specific behaviors and restrictions that you'll want to remember. For example, frames in which movies and sound are placed must be rectangular, with no corner options applied. Nonrectangular frames will not appear in the PDF, and neither will any masking effects applied to a movie frame. Also avoid rotating or shearing movie frames, because they will not produce predictable results.

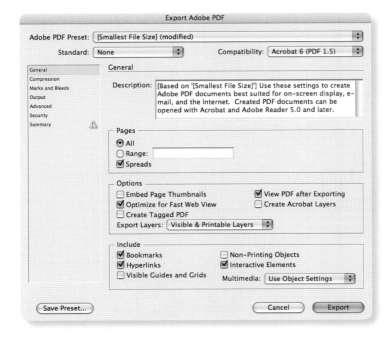

Figure 8.26 Choose your presets and compatibility in this dialog.

Acrobat 4 (PDF 1.3)
Acrobat 5 (PDF 1.4)
✓ Acrobat 6 (PDF 1.5)
Acrobat 7 (PDF 1.6)
Acrobat 8 (PDF 1.7)

Figure 8.27 Be sure the select the appropriate setting for your users.

Any objects (text, shapes, and other images) placed on top of a frame containing a movie will not be visible in the exported PDF—either they will be clipped or the movie will appear on top of them. This includes strokes that are drawn on the inside of the frame. On the other hand, drop shadows, which appear behind the frame, are perfectly fine to use with movies.

Beyond that, only a few other options in the dialog make interactive PDFs different from other PDF types. At the bottom of the General section of the Export Adobe PDF dialog, the Include area has Bookmarks, Hyperlinks, and Interactive Elements check boxes, as well as a Multimedia menu (Figure 8.28). Even though bookmarks are used in the button settings in this project, they do not need to be included upon export unless you specifically want them available as document bookmarks in the Bookmarks navigation panel of the PDF. The buttons will still function properly whether or not the Bookmarks check box is selected.

The Hyperlinks check box is necessary if any hyperlinks have been added to your PDF using the Hyperlinks panel. In this project, the hyperlinks to the InDesign User Group and Adobe Web sites on page 24, as well as the email address at the bottom of the page, will work in the PDF whether or not Hyperlinks is checked here, but the lemon logo will not. To have nonstandard hyperlinks recognized in the PDF, this box must be checked.

Interactive Elements must be checked to enable buttons, button states, and other options such as Play on Page Turn for movies. The Multimedia menu allows you either to honor all of the individual settings for embedding each of your movies

Figure 8.28 You'll find additional options for your media in the Include area of the Export Adobe PDF dialog.

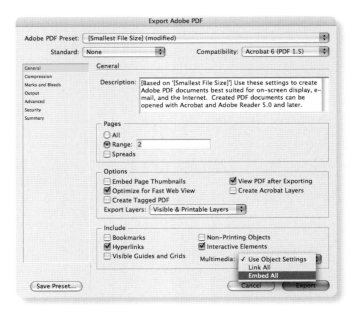

and sounds or to override those settings entirely by either linking all files or embedding all files. This can be helpful when exporting several versions of the PDF for different purposes—hosting online, bringing with you on a laptop for a face-to-face presentation, and so on.

With these options checked as needed, just click Export, and start exploring your new, interactive PDF in either Acrobat or Adobe Reader.

Project Wrap-Up

In addition to all the techniques you've learned for creating dynamic PDFs, you can explore many of the other features of the InDesign file as well. Deconstructing someone else's document is one of the best ways to learn how to create your own. In addition to the interactive elements, **Travels_with_Alvin.indd** uses the Live Trace feature from Adobe Illustrator CS3, nested paragraph styles, transparency effects, gradients and blending modes, Object Layer Options, stroke gradients, and more. Even the black-and-white background photo on page 12 has a surprise: it isn't really black and white at all (Figure 8.29). Try opening the file in Photoshop (**Italy'03_060.jpg**), and you'll see what I mean. Can you figure out how this effect was done? (Hint: it involves using blending modes in InDesign.)

Finally, if your interest in this kind of document has been piqued, visit the Web site of Bob Connolly at http://www.bcpictures.com/. Bob is one of the foremost authorities and practitioners of rich-media document creation and has written one of the few books on this topic, *Dynamic Media: Music, Video, Animation, and the Web in Adobe PDF* (Peachpit Press, 2007).

Figure 8.29 This background photograph appears black-and-white.

Chapter 9 | Making Your Workflow Work

"ALL ART IS AUTOBIOGRAPHICAL; THE PEARL IS THE OYSTER'S AUTOBIOGRAPHY." — Federico Fellini

I'm not exactly sure when the word *workflow* began replacing the word *work*, but nowadays you hear it all the time. In the same way *problematic* is now used in place of *problem*, *workflow* has tightened its grip on the English lexicon as a semi-legitimate replacement for the simpler word *work*. But although *workflow* could be accused of being a two-dollar word when a two-bit word will do, the fact is that the word *workflow* speaks more to the process of one's work than the work itself.

As the earlier chapters of this book have demonstrated, Adobe Creative Suite 3 is all about workflow. As powerful as each component in Creative Suite 3 is, it is a perfect example of how the sum of its whole is greater than its individual parts.

Take the gallery invitation project in Chapter 2, "Creating Effective Typography." Beginning in Adobe Illustrator, we created the lemon curtain pattern. From there, we brought flat art in to Adobe Photoshop, where it was transformed into a realistic undulating curtain by way of a simple displacement map. Afterward, we placed the curtain into Adobe InDesign along with a background panel sporting a realistic lighting effect that was also created in Photoshop. Once the Photoshop elements were in place, we pasted the type in and formatted it in

InDesign. To complete the project, we created a logo in Illustrator and added it to the back panel.

By leveraging what each component does best, the invitation makes a solid case for the importance of understanding workflow and its influence on one's work. No longer can man live by Photoshop alone. Or for that matter Illustrator. Or InDesign.

In this final chapter, we'll take a less local and more global look at the process of graphic design. By creating a CD package, you'll see how professional designers approach a project, analyze it, develop it, organize it, realize it, and print it. And with any luck, you'll come to understand how to make your own workflow work.

What Makes a Successful Print Project?

Although what I'm about to say flies in the face of the popular notion of creativity, failing to properly plan a print project is a recipe for failure. As obvious as this statement sounds, you'd be amazed by the number of designers who eschew early-stage planning only to regret their misstep weeks or months down the road. It's like the impetuous builder who shows up on a job with a truck loaded with 2 × 4s, plywood, concrete, bricks, and shingles but has neither permits nor blueprints. Crazy, huh? Yet many a graphic artist thinks little of launching headlong into a design project with nary a plan in mind. If this sounds like you, now is the time to break bad habits in favor of a little planning. Trust me, by investing a small amount of energy up front to properly plan your project, you'll be rewarded mightily at crunch time when your project rolls trouble-free off the press (Figure 9.1).

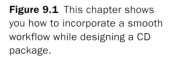

Figure 9.1 This chapter shows you how to incorporate a smooth workflow while designing a CD package.

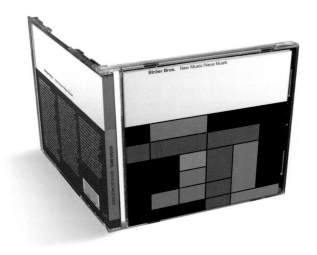

The Print Production Checklist

Few designers would argue that talking type, images, and layout is far sexier than most any discussion about inks, papers, varnishes, and folds. Yet leaving such details to the last minute is a great way to ruin an otherwise good day. So at the risk of sounding boring, pedantic, and thoroughly uncreative, I will say that planning sets you free. I'll say it again. *Planning sets you free.* By this I mean that the more you plan how your project will be printed, varnished, and folded, the more time and creative freedom you'll have to devote to the type, the images, and the layout.

For the commitment averse, planning a print project sounds like one big downer. In reality, it's not that hard. The following are among the general items worth considering:

- ☐ What's the document trim size?
- ☐ What's the document format? Portrait, landscape, or square?
- ☐ What kind of paper will be used? Coated, uncoated, vellum, or laid?
- ☐ What kinds of inks will be used? Four-color process? Pantone solids? Metallics?
- ☐ What about foils? Die cuts? Will there be embossing?
- ☐ How will the paper be finished afterward? UV coating? Varnish?
- ☐ What kind of binding, if any, will there be? Saddle stitch? Perfect bound? Smyth sewn?
- ☐ Are there special folding or perforation requirements?
- ☐ Will there be any inserts?

Of course, none of these questions can be answered without talking to the printer, which is my point. Assuming a printer has been chosen before the design begins, it is incumbent upon the designer to initiate a discussion about the project. Rarely will printers make the first move to contact you. Therefore, it is your responsibility to your client and ultimately to your reputation as a designer to reach out to your printer when the project begins. Even if the details of the design are sketchy, no project has ever been made worse by an early conversation with its printer.

If, on the other hand, the printer has not been chosen when the design phase begins, it's up to you to help your client make the decision. Explaining that choosing a printer early in the process is in everyone's best interests usually goes a long way toward getting clients to decide.

To Supervise or Not to Supervise

Often clients have no clue about printers and will defer to the designer either to make suggestions or to handle the entire printing process. This level of responsibility then becomes a blessing and a curse. The blessing comes in the form of allowing you to work with printers you know (generally a good thing) and to legitimately mark up their services to the client in exchange for your time and energy involved in supervising the whole job. Markups of 10 percent to 15 percent of a total print budget are not uncommon for designers who handle the print side, but commissions, like most things in life, are negotiable. Furthermore, if you take such a commission by marking up a print job, you owe it to your client to disclose the amount of the markup before the job begins.

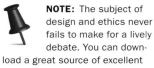

NOTE: The subject of design and ethics never fails to make for a lively debate. You can download a great source of excellent PDFs on the subject for free by visiting the American Institute of Graphic Design (AIGA) Web site at www.aiga.org/content.cfm/design-business-and-ethics.

On the downside, taking responsibility for supervising the print job can haunt your days if the work goes badly. Cost overruns and mistakes become your responsibility in the eyes of your client even if you're not at fault. As such, establishing a clear line of communication with your printer becomes even more important than before.

I resume the subject of printing at the end of this chapter. For now, remember that good design is good communication and good communication is good design.

Begin the Beguine

In 1935 Cole Porter wrote a song for the Broadway musical *Jubilee* called "Begin the Beguine." For years I wondered what a beguine was and why someone would write a popular song about it. After doing some digging, I learned that a beguine is a rumba-like ballroom dance that originated in the French West Indies. But what does a rumba have to do with designing a CD package? you might logically ask.

A dance, as I see it, is a series of steps. You move one foot in front of the other, each one leading the dancers through a variety of gestures and motions to reach its proper end. A design workflow is another kind of dance. In our case I'm talking about a series of steps or phases performed by the designer and client that, if performed properly, also leads to a successful end. There's the parallel.

Assuming you've spoken to your printer and hammered out the details of your project in advance, you're now ready to take the next step of setting up your hardware and software color and selecting a color workflow.

Color Settings and Calibration

As a trainer I'm constantly amazed by how many designers work day in and day out with a monitor or display that's uncalibrated. Not that monitor calibration alone ensures predictable color output, but without it, my guess is as good as yours when it comes to knowing what that printed piece will look like when it returns from the printer.

Years ago Adobe's Russell Brown gave me one piece of advice I'll always cherish: Buy a tool to calibrate the monitor. At the time this meant popping for a puck-like thingy that cost about $350. Biting the bullet, I bought an Eye-One Display colorimeter from Swiss color specialists Gretag Macbeth (Figure 9.2). Using the Eye-One Display is surprisingly easy. Once you install the Eye-One Match software, you plug the Eye-One Display into any USB port for power. After launching the software, you're asked to first calibrate the device by placing it on a flat, dark surface.

Figure 9.2 To find out more about this specific color calibrator, visit www.xrite.com/product_overview.aspx?ID-788.

After self-calibrating, the software offers a choice of an Easy or Advanced setting. I use Advanced, which isn't really *that* advanced, and then sit back and watch the software's light show over the next few minutes as it reads different colors projected by the display. For best results, run the colorimeter in a completely dark room. When it's over, you'll be presented with a "before" and "after" comparison of your monitor. Chances are if you've never calibrated your display, the results will be dramatic.

Figure 9.3 A worker preparing animal skins as parchment or vellum.

Figure 9.4 Johannes Gutenberg.

A Brief History of Paper

Historians track the beginning of paper to around 3000 BC, a time at which stalks of local plants such as papyrus and mulberry were cooked into a pulp, flattened into thin sheets, and spread onto mesh to dry in the sun. These pulps, known as *tapa*, have been found all over the world, and even today tapa is still used in remote regions of the Himalayas and Southeast Asia to produce paper.

Sometime after the fall of Rome, tapa was replaced by animal skins as the preferred surface for writing. This material, known as *vellum*, was quite popular until the Arabic art of papermaking came to the West in the eighth century (Figure 9.3). By way of the Muslim conquest of Spain, the English word *ream* (meaning 500 sheets) is derived through Spanish and French from the Arabic word *rizmah* that translates as "a bundle."

Both Spain and Italy claim to be the first to manufacture paper in Europe. One of the first paper mills in Europe was in Valencia. Some scholars claim that the Arabs built the Valencia mill about 1009 AD. Papermaking continued under Moorish rule until 1244 when the Moors were expelled. From there, papermaking began to gradually spread across Christian Europe.

Before books became books as we now know them, parchment scrolls were used to record people's thoughts. Sequestered in dank *scriptoriums*, or copying rooms, monks or other religious leaders huddled over scrolls made from treated animals skins called *parchment* or *vellum* with pen and ink, laboriously hand-writing manuscripts. This process could take months or years to complete, particularly if occasional mistakes were made.

Sometime around the second century AD, books were no longer written only on scrolls or sheets but in a bound format known as *codex*. Typically books of this kind also included small illustrations or rubrics that were carved from wood blocks and pressed by hand into the book's surface.

By the middle ages a new writing surface developed using old rags and bits of clothing, which were in large supply because of the scourge of plague, or Black Death, that had overtaken much of Europe. The process consisted of boiling the linens with lye until they broke down into fibers that could be transformed into a suitable material for writing or printing.

Then along came Gutenberg. Johannes Gensfleisch zur Laden zum Gutenberg (c. 1398–1468), a goldsmith and youngest son of a successful businessman, is credited with the invention of movable type (Figure 9.4). Although the Chinese had actually developed movable clay type hundreds of years before Gutenberg, young Johannes was the first to create and use metal type in his crude press, an adaptation of a contraption used for pressing nearby Rhine grapes into wine (Figure 9.5).

With a loan of 800 guilders from moneylender Johann Fust, Gutenberg began working on a series of 180 bibles using his new machine. Five years later Gutenberg finished the 42-line-per-page editions that became known as the Gutenberg Bible.

With the advent of movable type and the availability of books, knowledge spread as never before. Among the well educated was a French scientist and naturalist, Rene de Réaumur, who observed in the 1700s how wasps formed durable, lightweight nests from regurgitated wood pulp. Eventually Réaumur's observation led others to begin experimenting with wood as the basis for papermaking, a process still practiced today.

Figure 9.5 The simple press used by Gutenberg with its wooden screw.

Whether you're using the Eye-One Display or not, you should heed the following recommendations when calibrating any display:

NOTE: D50 will look yellow and dull on your monitor unless you're in a dark room.

- White point should be set to D50 (or 5000K) if you're a printer or pre-press operator working in a sufficiently dim environment. D65 (or 6500K) is recommended for everyone else.
- Display luminance is recommended at 150 candelas per square meter (sometimes written as cd/m^2) for dim environments and up to 300 candelas per square meter for brighter environments. Beware of making your display too bright, because you want to leave some headroom to bump up the brightness setting as the backlight on your display ages and gets dimmer. This may mean modifying your environment to lower ambient brightness, and then you can set display luminance a bit lower as well.
- Gamma should be set at 1.8 for all Apple displays (including Cinema displays and laptops), regardless of whether they're connected to a Mac or PC. All other displays should be set to a gamma of 2.2.
- Also pay attention to the working environment and lighting conditions, because this is perhaps the single biggest cause of color-matching problems. Room ambient should be dim, ideally less than 20 lux. (If you don't know a lux from a lox, a typical office environment using fluorescent lighting is around 400 lux and sometimes higher.) Pitch black is best, but who besides bats want to work day in and day out in total darkness? On the flip side, if your environment is brighter than 60 lux, then forget about doing serious color work, let alone soft-proofing.

- Be aware that working near open windows, where the amount of light and the associated color temperature changes throughout the day, is also an impediment to doing serious color work. Remember, the key to color management is consistency, and nothing is less consistent than daylight.

Since buying my Eye-One Display a few years ago, Gretag Macbeth was bought by X-Rite, which in turn also purchased color giant Pantone. At a cost of between $200 to $250, the Eye-One Display 2 is an essential purchase for any serious designer. For about $100, Pantone also sells the Huey Pro, a smaller calibration device geared toward the average user who wants a calibrated display on the cheap. Despite receiving favorable reviews since its initial release, do yourself a favor and step up to the Eye-One Display if you care about color. For those in the market for a new display, NEC's SpectraView monitors come bundled with color software and a hardware colorimeter, providing excellent results for serious users.

Choosing the Proper Workflow

To effectively manage color appearances in Creative Suite 3, you must first select an appropriate color workflow. Use Table 9.1, (adapted from Adobe's excellent file available at www.adobe.com/designcenter/creativesuite/articles/cs3ip_colorworkflow.pdf) to select the workflow that best represents your particular project.

As you can see from Table 9.1, the workflow decision for web designers and publishers is simple. RGB (a transmissive color model) is the only workflow that makes sense for on-screen display. RGB is also the way to go if you're a photographer printing to an ink-jet or other desktop color printer.

For graphic designers whose work will be printed on a commercial press, the choice of workflow becomes less clear. This is because they can follow two

Table 9.1 Choosing a Workflow Based on Your Type of Work

IF YOU ARE A...	WORKING IN THIS MARKET...	SENDING TO THE FOLLOWING DEVICE...	USE THIS RECOMMENDED WORKFLOW...
Prepress professional	Traditional and digital commercial printing	Printing press (for example, offset, Flexo, or Gravure), digital printing press	CMYK Commercial Print Workflow or Mixed RGB and CMYK Print Workflow
Graphic designer	Commercial printing, publishing	Printing press	CMYK Commercial Print Workflow
	Internet publishing, Web-based or computer-based training	Onscreen display	Web Publishing RGB Workflow
Digital photo professional	Photography	Photo lab, RGB printer	RGB Photo Print Workflow

approaches. The first, and more traditional, approach is to convert all images to a CMYK color space (in Photoshop, for example, choose Image > Mode > CMYK) before placing files into InDesign or Illustrator or when printing directly from Photoshop. Working this way, the designer can approximate how images will appear when printed on paper or other reflective substrates. Working in an all-CMYK workflow (Figure 9.6) seems to make sense when printing to a CMYK device, but this comes at a price. CMYK files are larger than RGB files because of their four individual cyan, magenta, yellow, and black component channels. Plus, many of the most useful Photoshop filters and Illustrator effects work only with RGB images. If this flexibility is important to you, then an all-CMYK workflow necessitates that you do all preliminary work in an RGB environment before converting those same files to CMYK for final output.

If you're used to working this way and have become weary of managing and converting RGB files to CMYK, then now is the time to consider using a mixed RGB-CMYK approach (Figure 9.7). In this scenario, all images and graphics that begin as RGB stay in RGB throughout the entire design process. This means designers no longer must manage two sets of files and be encumbered by the hassle that doing so involves. It also means that at the end of the design process, the designer must deliver a converted, press-ready CMYK PDF to the printer for final output.

If using a mixed RGB-CMYK workflow sounds a bit like heresy to you, chances are you have two major questions on your mind. The first is, how does the designer know what an image will look like in print when placing only RGB images or graphics? The second is, how can printers make last-minute file corrections when all they have to work with is a PDF instead of native InDesign or Illustrator documents? Granted, both are legitimate questions, but if I told you now, you might stop reading here. So instead, please hang in here and follow along with this chapter's CD packaging project for the answer.

Synchronizing Color Settings

In Chapter 1, "Getting Started," we visited Adobe Bridge to look at this new and powerful centerpiece of Creative Suite 3. Among the many strengths of Bridge is its one-button ability to synchronize color settings across Photoshop, InDesign, Illustrator, and Acrobat. There's much more to getting consistent color output. But if you use Bridge for nothing else, do yourself a huge favor and take advantage of at least this one key feature.

Using the synchronize feature is pretty straightforward. When you click the Synchronize Color Setting button, you'll see a dialog that offers a choice of available settings. You can add more settings by clicking Show Expanded List Of

NOTE: A number of desktop printers use cyan, magenta, yellow, and black ink sets. Because of this, designers often assume they should be sending CMYK data to these printers for best results. As logical as this sounds, the fact is that for best results an RGB color space should be used for all desktop printer output. The reason? The CMYK colorants in desktop printers (especially inkjets) have a much wider gamut than the CMYK inks used on offset presses. The printer drivers for these printers take advantage of that wider gamut, allowing for more vibrant output.

Figure 9.6 Follow a CMYK workflow in Creative Suite 3 to preserve color values throughout the workflow to final four-color press.

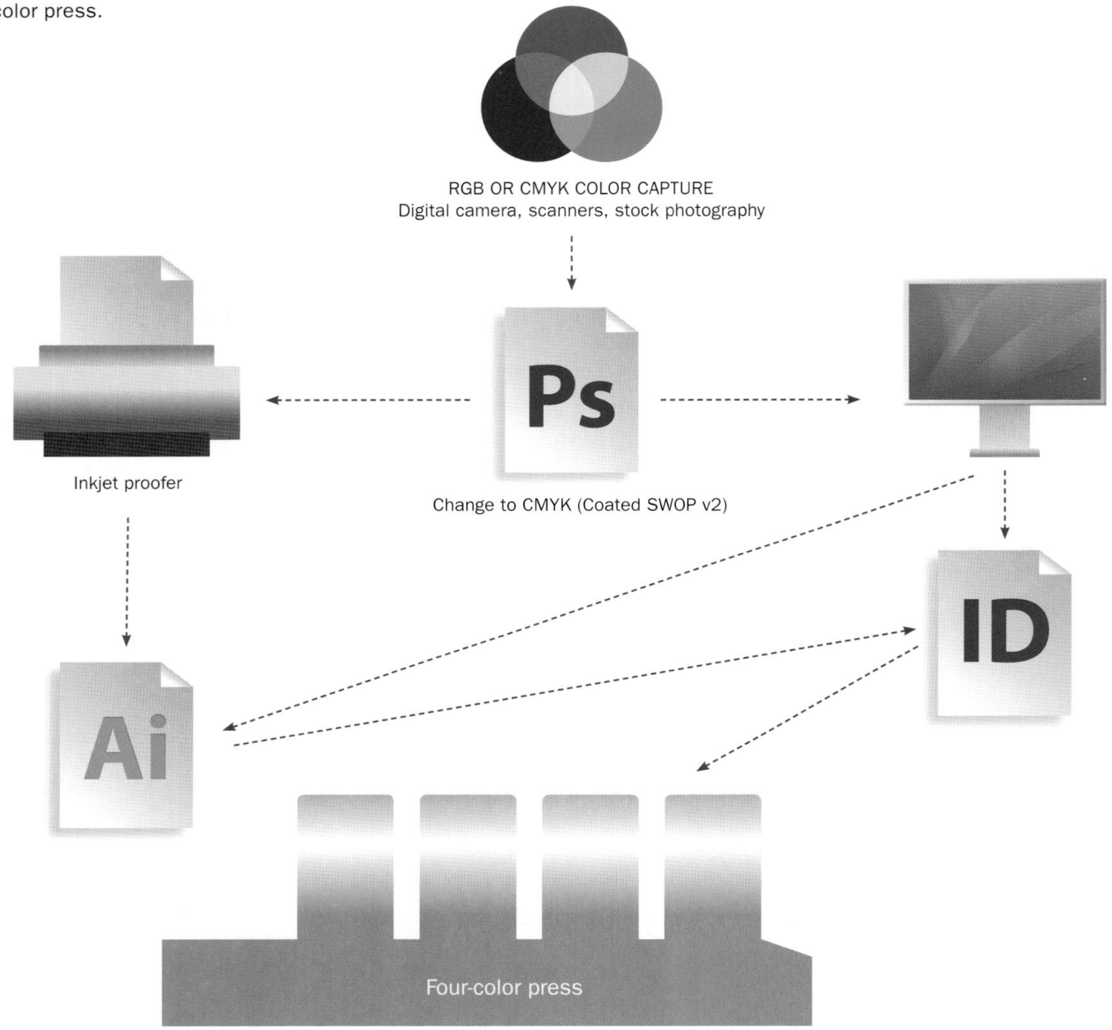

RGB OR CMYK COLOR CAPTURE
Digital camera, scanners, stock photography

Ps

Inkjet proofer

Change to CMYK (Coated SWOP v2)

Ai

ID

Four-color press

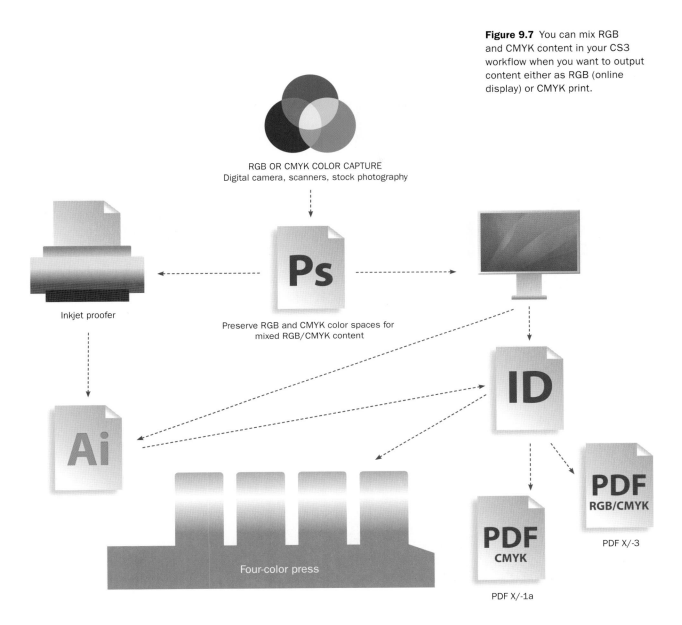

Figure 9.7 You can mix RGB and CMYK content in your CS3 workflow when you want to output content either as RGB (online display) or CMYK print.

RGB OR CMYK COLOR CAPTURE
Digital camera, scanners, stock photography

Inkjet proofer

Preserve RGB and CMYK color spaces for mixed RGB/CMYK content

Four-color press

PDF CMYK

PDF X/-1a

PDF RGB/CMYK

PDF X/-3

Color Settings Files. Once you've chosen the correct setting, click Apply. And what are the correct settings for a print project? you may reasonably ask. The answer, like the subject of color management itself, is rather complicated, but my suggestion is to start with the North American General Purpose 2 settings and go from there (Figure 9.8).

By choosing color settings in Bridge, you're in turn selecting the appropriate working space in Photoshop, Illustrator, InDesign, and Acrobat (Figure 9.9). Doing so further guarantees that you'll be working in the correct workflow for your project.

Figure 9.8 Use Bridge to synchronize color settings across the various components in Creative Suite 3.

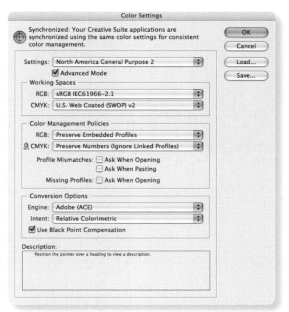

Figure 9.9 More options for synchronizing color settings are available.

Figure 9.10 You'll use an RGB workflow to create this CD jewel box and label.

Designing a CD Package

When staring down the barrel of any new project, the designer's job is to understand, visually interpret, and communicate the project. Although perhaps obvious, it's not unusual for designers to try to force their own artistic will on the project. Having done this myself more than once, I know from experience that rarely does this approach lead to the best result. Maybe this style of "subdue the prey" works for others, but whenever I'm involved with a project and it's not happening, it's usually because I'm trying too hard to tell the project how it should look instead of letting it tell me.

In this project, you'll learn how to listen to the material (and by listen I mean both with your ears and eyes) and transform it into a handsome CD jewel box and label (Figure 9.10). The entire project will be created using an RGB workflow until the final file is converted to a press-ready PDF for commercial printing.

Look to the Content

The CD is a collection of recent music composed by two close friends of mine, Hans and Ernst Ströer. The brothers live with their families outside Munich and have been playing and composing music for years separately and together.

When deciding on a design direction for this project, I first sat down and listened closely to the music. The songs (all orchestral) were clean and well-structured; they were not overproduced like a lot of music. After a couple of listens, it was clear that the design should also be simple and open—new, but not trendy.

Photoshop, InDesign, or Illustrator?

When approaching any project, one of the first questions designers face when using Creative Suite 3 is deciding in which component to begin. In the old days, it was easier to know when to use Photoshop, Illustrator, or InDesign. Nowa-days, with the feature overlap of the three products, it's often hard to know where to start. In my case, I knew that I wanted to use flat areas of color, so my first choice was Illustrator. Of course, application choice is often dictated by which program one knows best (or at all), but this time Illustrator made the most sense. (For more insight, see "Choosing the Right Tool for the Job" in Chapter 1, "Getting Started.")

TIP: If you find yourself setting type or using vector shapes in Photoshop, you'll see the best results by saving your file not as a native Photoshop .psd file but as a Photoshop .pdf. This is because the PSD format is completely pixel-based. All objects must be rasterized when output from .psd files. PDF, on the other hand, supports both pixels and rasters, which is why Adobe recommends its use when type or vector shapes are involved.

After kicking around in Illustrator for an hour or so, it dawned on me that InDesign would make more sense because of its table feature. Although the CD has no tables per se, I realized that the table feature would be the most efficient way to create the grid I needed for the front panel.

So when should I use Photoshop? you might reasonably ask. Although Photo-shop has come a long way in its relatively short life span, keep in mind that its primary job is as an image editor, not a page layout program. This is not to say that I've never used Photoshop to design and lay out a document; I have. But in those cases it has been for one-page book covers (not jackets with flaps) where type setting was minimal (Figure 9.11). In those cases it was because Photoshop allowed me to set display type using effects such as inner shadows or bevels and embossing that were not available in InDesign. Today, with the advent of InDesign CS3 and its powerful effects, if I were to do those same projects again, I'd probably stick with InDesign the whole way.

Setting Up the Front Panel

Chapter 4, "Creating Newsletters and Forms," and Chapter 7, "Designing Annual Reports," showed you how the table features in InDesign can make short work out of organizing data into neat rows and columns of information. Yet if you think more about tables, you'll realize that a table is simply a group of boxes (called *cells*) that can be filled with anything. This fact comes in quite handy

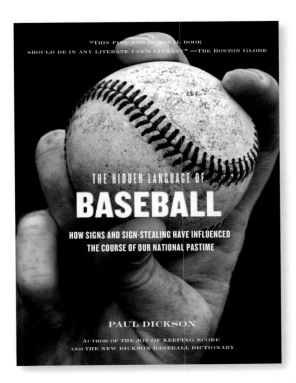

Figure 9.11 These covers were designed using Photoshop but now you can do many of the same effects in InDesign CS3.

when your design is mostly that; a matrix of little colored boxes. Before you insert your table, you need to set up the document itself. Fortunately, InDesign makes this a snap, too:

1. In InDesign, choose File > New, and select Compact Disc from the Page Size pop-up menu (Figure 9.12).
2. Set pages to 1, deselect Facing Pages, and add a bleed on all four sides of 0p9 (0.125 inches).
3. Click OK.

The next step is to set your InDesign preferences. Setting preferences when a document is open applies those preferences to only the open document. Afterward, you'll customize InDesign to support your RGB to CMYK workflow.

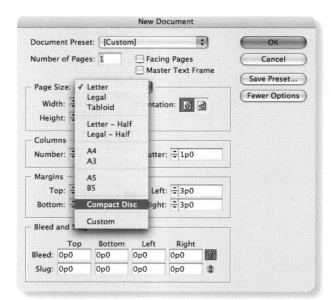

Figure 9.12 You can specify Compact Disc as your page size.

Tell Me More Lies

According to Chris Murphy, coauthor of *Real World Color Management, Second Edition* (Peachpit Press, 2004), "Designers hate being told the truth. They like pretty images. So designers prefer leaving Simulate Paper Color unchecked even though it's less accurate. Selecting Simulate Paper Color is more accurate because it accounts for the yellowness of most paper and the fact that paper isn't pure white, but rather a little darker than that. Pre-press folks, conversely, typically prefer knowing the truth and will choose to have Simulate Paper Color checked. However, in all honesty, since designers aren't often doing side by side comparisons from screen to print, it's okay to not choose Simulate Paper Color, and instead rely on the fact that human vision is adaptive."

"Furthermore," says Murphy, "the U.S. Web Coated (SWOP) v2 profile is getting a little long in the tooth. The data used to describe that print condition has been adjusted slightly for how we print today on #5 ground wood (typical magazines and publications) paper or on #3 sheets (high-quality magazines and publications). You can find free downloadable profiles at www.swop.org. Specifically created for soft proofing, you'll notice that the Simulate Paper Color is much more realistic when using these profiles. In addition, when converting from RGB to CMYK, you'll find the color separations are a little better as well, particularly with respect to blues and the fact there is a slightly higher GCR (Gray Color Removal) being used."

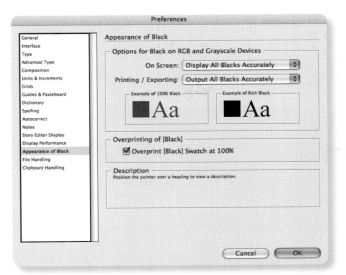

Figure 9.13 Set the preferences for your document.

1. Choose InDesign > Preferences > Appearance Of Black (Mac OS) or Edit > Preferences > Appearance Of Black (Windows).
2. Set both the on-screen and printing/exporting options to display and output all blacks accurately (Figure 9.13).
3. Click OK to apply your preference settings.

Finally, you'll need to adjust your InDesign view settings to allow *soft-proofing* (on-screen simulation) of your RGB document. By working this way, you'll be able to approximate how your CD package will appear when printed to a CMYK output device such as a commercial four-color press.

1. Choose View > Proof Colors.
2. Choose View > Proof Setup > Custom.
3. In the Customize Proof Condition dialog, select Simulate Black Ink (Figure 9.14).
4. Click OK.

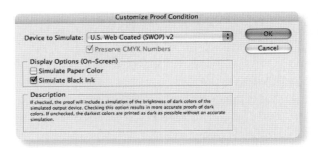

Figure 9.14 Simulate black ink so you can review an accurate version on screen.

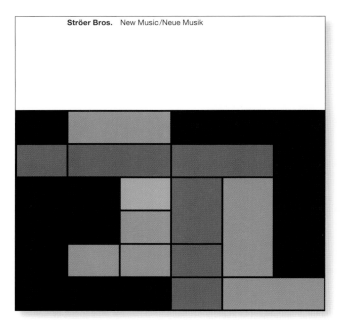

Figure 9.15 The front panel for the CD case.

With all these settings now behind you, you're ready to dive in and create the front panel for the jewel box. To see how the panel will look when you've finished, refer to Figure 9.15.

Designing the Front Panel

A popular phrase among photographers these days when talking about composition is the rule of thirds. Simply put, the rule suggests that a photo (or composition) be divided into three rows and three columns and that the objects of greatest interest rest at the intersection of these imaginary grid lines. Now go back to Chapter 1, "Getting Started," and look at Da Vinci's *The Last Supper*. Here you'll see how a similar concept of thirds (the Golden Mean or Section) was applied more than 500 years ago, well before the invention of photography. In the case of the CD front panel, you'll use the rule of thirds to define the basic composition of the layout:

1. Choose Layout > Create Guides.
2. Set the number of rows to 3 and the gutter to 0 (Figure 9.16).
3. In the Options section, set Fit Guides To Page. If you have no margins, then fitting to margins will do the same thing.
4. Click OK to return to the InDesign layout.

Figure 9.16 Begin the composition by setting the number of rows and the gutter.

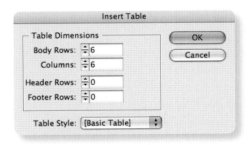

Figure 9.17 Set your table dimensions up in the Insert Table dialog.

Now that your page is divided into three even rows, you'll use the guide at 9p6 as the top of your table:

1. Using the Type tool, click the guide at 9p6, and drag a frame from the top-left corner to the bottom-right corner of your page. Do not enter the bleed area; you'll deal with that once we're done.
2. With your text cursor blinking, choose Table > Insert Table.
3. Enter six rows and six columns in the Table Dimensions section of the Insert Table dialog (Figure 9.17).

4. Click OK. Although the default table will fit properly in width, you'll need to stretch it to the bottom of the page and then apply a black stroke on all grid lines.

5. Again, with the Type tool, place your double-arrowed pointer on the outside bottom stroke of the table and pull to the page bottom, holding down the Shift key to equally expand the height of all cells (Figure 9.18).

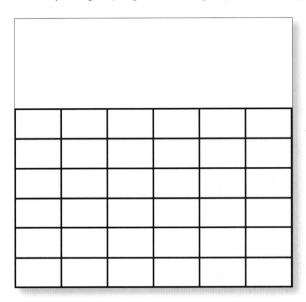

Figure 9.18 Expand the height of all cells in the table.

6. Now place the pointer in the top-left corner of the expanded table. Click when you see a diagonal arrow, which selects the entire table.

7. In the Stroke panel, set the stroke weight to 2 pts and the color to Black. Now you're ready to begin filling the table cells with color.

8. With the Type tool blinking in a cell, press the Esc key to select the cell (double-clicking Esc selects the cell's contents). Once the cell is selected, choose a swatch from the Swatch panel, or mix a custom color from the Color panel. Use the Merge Cell command (Table > Merge Cells) to join two or more cells into one.

Keep experimenting. You can always unmerge cells or even split cells vertically or horizontally to create other configurations. What's nice about this design is that no drawing skill is required. You need only a sense of shape and balance and an idea about how colors relate. This is not to say that coming up with a good-looking design is a snap. I easily spent two hours working back and forth in kuler

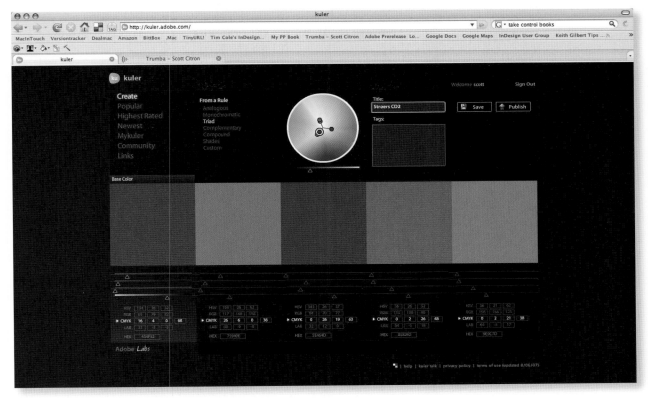

Figure 9.19 Using kuler, you can find nicely balanced tones quickly.

(http://kuler.adobe.com), playing with different possibilities, until I wound up with something I liked (Figure 9.19). Still, for those who fret over what to put on the page, often all it takes is the simple play of shapes and colors to create an effective design.

Once you're done, you'll need to add a black bleed to the left, right, and bottom sides of the front panel. The bleed ensures that no sliver of white paper appears by mistake in the event the layout is not trimmed accurately. Here's the simplest way to do this:

1. Create a frame where the top edge (the Y coordinate) is even with the top edge of your table, but snaps into the bleed area on the left, right, and bottom sides. Fill the frame with Black and choose Object > Arrange > Send to Back.
2. Add the line of title text at the top of the panel as a last step once your grid is finished. Note how the copy aligns flush left to the right edge of the first column from the left (Figure 9.20).

TIP: When using kuler to choose colors, make sure you're working with the RGB sliders. Once you've settled on the color group you like, use kuler to export the swatches in the .ase file format (Adobe Swatch Exchange). To load your swatches for use in InDesign, go to the Swatches panel menu, and choose Load Swatches.

NOTE: If you carefully examine Figure 9.20, you'll notice that the black matrix of the table grid extends into the 0p9 bleed area of the document. This was done by adding a simple black rectangle the size of the grid plus the bleed and sending it to the back. Adding bleeds to artwork is an important step to avoid problems once paper is trimmed to its final dimension.

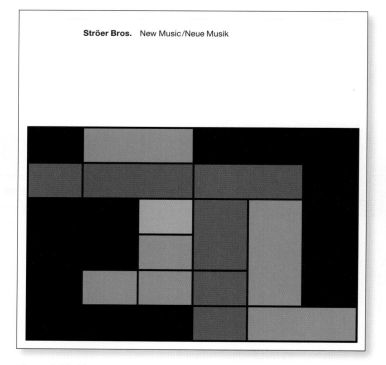

Ströer Bros.   New Music/Neue Musik

Figure 9.20 Line up the text on the grid for a clean design.

Designing the Tray Card

Now that the front panel is done, you can use that file to create the tray card for the back panel. The tray card is the artwork on the back and sides of the jewel case. The dimensions are basically the same, with the addition of the two narrow side panels that wrap around. You'll use the front panel card to create the tray card (Figure 9.21):

1. Save your working file as **Front_Panel_End.idd**. Then, with the file open choose File > Save As.
2. Rename the new file **Tray_Card.indd**, and click Save.
3. To add the two narrow side panels, choose File > Document Setup. Note that the current width is 28p4.
4. Click to insert your pointer directly after 28p4, and type **+3p** with no spaces (Figure 9.22).
5. Click More Options, and add a 3p slug on all four sides. You'll use this area outside the layout to draw fold marks for the side panels.
6. Click OK to close the dialog.

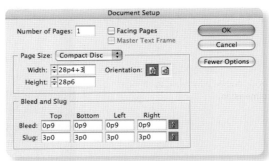

Figure 9.22 Set up your document with a width of 28p4+3p.

Figure 9.21 Create the tray card by adding two side panels first.

Back in the layout you'll see that the width has been increased by 1p6 on both sides of the original layout. This is because 1p6 + 1p6 = 3p. If you're working in inches, 3p is equal to 0.5 inches.

Adding Margins and Columns

Now that you have the tray card document size established, you'll add margins and columns to create the finished layout:

1. Choose Layout > Margins And Columns.
2. Set the left and right margins to 3p.
3. Set Columns to 3 (Figure 9.23).
4. Click OK to apply the settings.

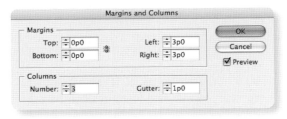

Figure 9.23 Next, set up the margins and columns.

Returning to the layout you'll see that the margins you added will be used to indicate the side panels. The three columns will be used for text. At this point, select the table grid and delete it. Also delete the black bleed frame from behind.

The next step is to place guides for the two side panels. Each panel is 1p6 wide or 0.25 inches from the left and right sides.

1. Drag a ruler guide from the left until its *x* coordinate is 1p6. Be sure to drag the guide from outside the actual page area so the guide extends through the bleed, through the slug, and on to the pasteboard. Or press and hold Command (Mac OS) or Control (Windows) to create a spread guide regardless of where you release your mouse button.
2. Drag another ruler guide until it snaps to the far right edge of the page. The guide's *x* coordinate should read 31p4.
3. To easily calculate where the guide should be placed, insert your pointer in the *x* coordinate field directly after the 31p4 value, type **−1p6** (Figure 9.24), and press Return (Mac OS) or Enter (Windows).

Figure 9.24 Change the *x* coordinate for greater precision.

Notice how the guide has moved to the left the exact amount and that its *x* coordinate is now 29p10.

Creating the Fold Marks

Creating fold marks for the two side panels is the last step to preparing the layout before actually bringing in the final colors, text, and other design elements. Although this can be done manually without much effort, this time you'll use a script that will automate the process in seconds.

Locate the script named **Make Fold Marks on Guides.jsx** in the Chapter 9 folder at www.peachpit.com/prodesignCS3. For the script to work, you must place it in the Scripts Panel folder in the Adobe InDesign CS3 component folder.

Drag the **Guides.jsx** file to /Applications/Adobe InDesign CS3/Scripts/Scripts Panel/Samples/Javascript/ (Mac OS) or to Users\[**username**]\AppData\Roaming\Adobe\InDesign\[**Version**]\Scripts (Windows).

Then follow these steps:

1. Choose Window > Automation > Scripts, and open the Javascripts folder (Figure 9.25).
2. To use the script, double-click it in the Scripts panel. If you have other guides on your page, the script will place dashed lines on all of them, but

deleting those you don't want is a lot faster than manually creating fold marks for those you do want.

3. With all the marks in place, finish laying out the tray card either by following my example or by creating your own.

Most of the work from this point on is self-explanatory, with one exception. To properly create the text that runs vertically on the left and right side panels, follow these instructions:

4. With the Type tool, create a text frame, and type your text.

5. To center the text vertically in the frame, select the Selection tool, and then hold down Option (Mac OS) or Alt (Windows) while double-clicking the text frame to open the Text Frame Options dialog.

6. In Text Frame Options, choose Vertical Justification > Align > Center.

At this point, your text may look centered vertically but in fact may not be. This is because vertical alignment is based on what's called the *first baseline offset*. By default, first baseline offset is set to Ascent, which means that the first baseline in your frame is vertically centering the text based on the ascenders of the font you're using. (If you've forgotten what an ascender is, refer to Chapter 2, "Creating Effective Typography.") Because a font's ascenders are typically taller than other characters, any text that's set as all caps, for example, will be set slightly lower than center. To fix this problem, select the Baseline Options tab and choose Cap Height from the First Baseline Offset option (Figure 9.26).

7. Rotate the side panel text frames 90° and −90°, and position the frames accordingly as a last step.

Figure 9.25 Scripts can help save you a lot of time.

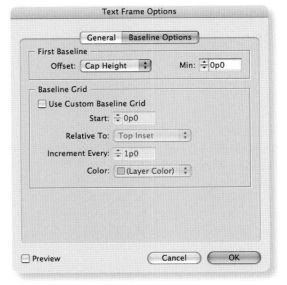

Figure 9.26 Pick Cap Height to fix the problem with the baseline.

Figure 9.27 The final version of the tray card.

To see my version of the tray card, refer to the file named **Tray_Card_End.indd** (Figure 9.27).

Creating the CD Label

The final stage of this project involves designing the CD label (Figure 9.28). Here you'll start with a template and modify it as needed. Before choosing a template, check to make sure how the artwork will be printed. Some processes print all the way to the inner spindle hole, and others don't. You'll also need to know what kind of printing process will be used. Some processes support only simple silk-screen printing of one or two colors; other, most sophisticated and costly, processes are able to print four or even five or more colors at a time.

When creating a series of pieces intended to be presented together in a package such as a CD, there's a fine line between maintaining a consistent design theme

Figure 9.28 The final step of the project...the CD label.

and drifting too far from the central theme as to seem disconnected. I tend to enjoy this part of the design process, because it allows me to spin off a few related ideas without straying too far from home.

In the case of the CD, you can see that I've continued with the rule of thirds concept that runs through the front panel and CD tray designs. To mix it up a bit, I've introduced a traditional floral pattern that overlays the top third of the label. Introducing an element like this is what I like to call a *design surprise*. In other words, the designer establishes a certain design concept or direction and then breaks the convention by introducing a surprise element. When done correctly, these kinds of visual surprises lend richness and texture to a design and keep it from becoming stale or predictable. The following steps will show you how to work with the pattern file:

NOTE: For a large area of black that makes up the lower two-thirds of the disk, I would typically use a rich black (C60, M40, Y40, K100), but in this case we're safer using 100 percent black ink. This is because we have small type knocking out as white, and the chance of misregistration in the printing process could end up creating blurry text. By printing with 100 percent black, we sacrifice the richness of rich black but avoid the risk of making our copy hard to read or unsharp, a reasonable trade. And CD-printing processes such as silkscreen will apply a fairly heavy black ink, unlike the anemic offset process black.

1. To find the CD template from InDesign, choose Help > Welcome Screen.
2. In the Welcome Screen, select Create New From Template. This takes you back to Bridge and displays all the available InDesign templates (Figure 9.29).
3. Double-click the folder named Cd-Dvd. Inside you'll find four templates.
4. Double-click the file named **DVD Label.indd** to open an untitled copy of the file.
5. With the Untitled file open, choose File > Save. Save the file, and name it **CD_Label.indd**.
6. Select and delete the two placeholder text frames.
7. Choose File > Place and navigate to the **36 Arts and Crafts.ai** file in the Chapter 9 Links folder.
8. Click Open and place the pattern anywhere on your page.
9. With the pattern still selected, choose Edit > Cut to place the file on the clipboard.
10. Select the embedded 1(2)1.jpg file and choose Edit > Paste Into. This will replace the existing image with the Illustrator pattern.
11. Fill the selected circular frame with Black.

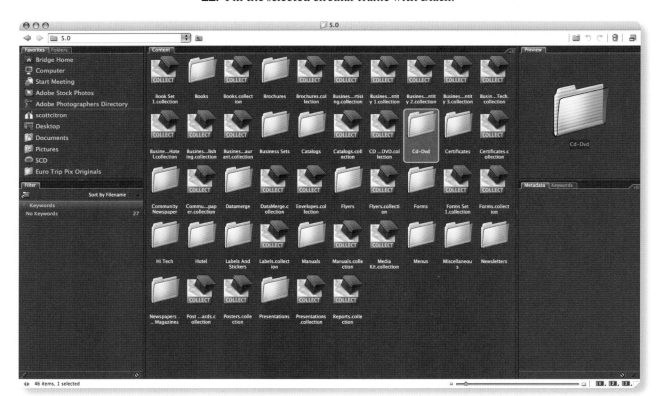

Figure 9.29 Numerous templates are available for you to use.

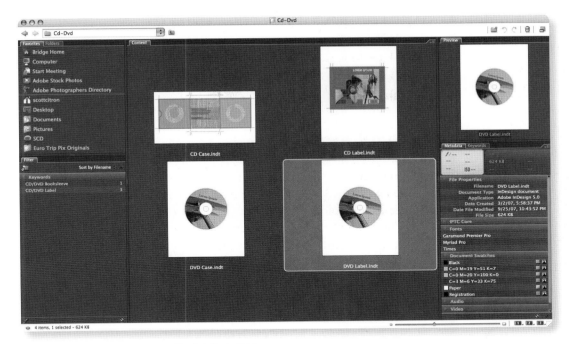

Figure 9.30 You can view many file details in Bridge.

Bridge Breakdown

Bridge offers many features for searching for files not available otherwise through the Mac OS Finder or through Windows Explorer. For example, with multipage templates Bridge lets you cycle through and preview all the pages in the template, a feature not available when viewing InDesign .indd files. Also, once a file is selected in Bridge, the Metadata panel located to the far right (Figure 9.30) displays a number of attributes about the file. For example, in this file we can get a glimpse of file properties, fonts, and swatches that are used.

12. With the frame still selected, choose Object > Select > Content. This will select the frame that contains the pattern.
13. With the pattern frame selected, fill the frame with any color you choose (don't worry if you don't see your colored fill, you'll fix that in the next step).
14. Double click to toggle to the Direct Selection tool. With the pattern now selected, choose Object > Effects > Transparency (Figure 9.31).
15. Set the blend mode for the graphic to Multiply, which will now reveal your color.

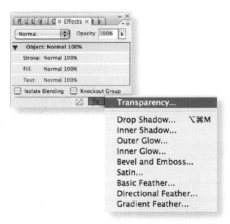

Figure 9.31 To access the Effects panel, either click the FX button at the bottom of the Control panel or click the button in the Effects panel (shown here).

16. Choose Object > Select > Container to toggle to the frame that contains the pattern. Using the Selection tool, click and drag from the solid center dot to reposition the pattern to the upper third of the CD.

Of final note is the list of songs. To place the text choose File > Place and navigate to the file named **Songs.txt** in the folder for Chapter 9. Note how the track number is a lighter weight than the track name it precedes and how the gray dot leader and the track running time are yet again another style. Breaking down the text shows how three character styles (track number, dot leader, and track running time) have been applied in one paragraph style (the track name). Also note how the running times align on the colons by way of a decimal tab stop (Figure 9.32).

Although this kind of formatting could be applied manually because it involves only a few lines of copy, I've set it up as a nested style so you can again see this powerful feature of InDesign (for an introduction to nested styles, see "Creating and Nesting Character Styles" in Chapter 4, "Creating Newsletters and Forms").

To view the nested style, open the file named **CD_Label.indd** in the Chapter 9 folder. With the file open, double click the Track Title paragraph style in the Paragraph Styles panel. Inside the panel, select the Drop Caps and Nested Styles options. When you have pages and pages of complex formatting as in a book or a magazine, taking the time to set up nested styles will reward you mightily for your effort. To see how these nested styles were created, open the Paragraph Styles panel, double-click the Track Title style, and examine the Drop Caps and Nested Styles panel (Figure 9.33). Take a few minutes to deconstruct the structure of the style, paying close attention to the character styles that are embedded, or nested, within.

Figure 9.32 You can apply the various character styles as one paragraph style (track name).

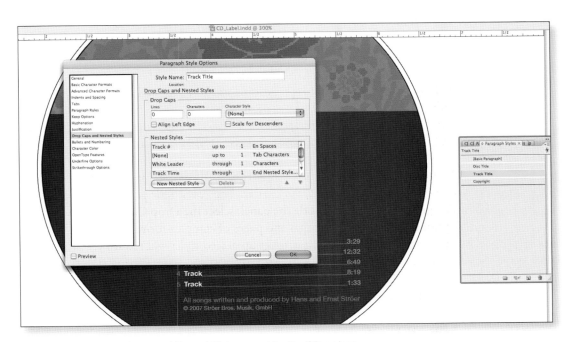

Figure 9.33 The Drop Caps and Nested Styles panel for the CD project.

Papermaking and Printing in the New Millennium

Nearly 90 percent of all paper today is made from trees, particularly softwood or coniferous trees. These trees are grown specifically to be harvested by paper and wood products companies. Once the trees are collected, they are brought to mills where their bark is often stripped by high-pressure water jets prior to grinding or chopping the raw material into small chunks. Chemicals are sometimes added to encourage this process, and bleaches are also used to whiten the pulp.

This pulp eventually becomes a thick slurry that, suspended in tremendous amounts of water, is fed onto huge wire mesh surfaces for further processing into paper.

The process of printing has come a long way in the thousands of years since the Chinese first began pressing ink-coated incised blocks into crude substrates and surfaces. Today most printing is either offset lithography (books, magazines, newspapers), flexography (packaging, labels, relief printing, mainly for catalogs), screen printing (T-shirts to floor tiles), rotogravure (magazines and packaging,) ink-jet (used for everything from applying mailing addresses to direct-mail pieces to fine art reproduction), hot wax dye transfer, and laser printing.

Offset, the most common of all techniques today, works because of the lithographic process that exploits the principle that water and oil don't mix. Thus, an impression of the page is made on a flexible metal plate whose surface is specially treated to attract ink. Conversely, those areas that are to remain ink-free do so by picking up a film of water from rollers suspended in a nearby tank. Once the plate is inked, its impression is transferred to a flexible rubber blanket (the offset cylinder), which in turn contacts the paper running through the press (Figure 9.34).

What makes the offset process so compelling is that paper can be fed at high speed from a roll, making it perfect for newspapers and other volume printing.

Once paper comes out of the press, there's often several more processes in store before trimming or binding. Among those steps might be embossing, debossing, UV coating, foil stamping, die cutting, or varnishing. Each of these additional steps naturally adds to the cost of the final piece, yet not without lending a special tactile or visual quality as well.

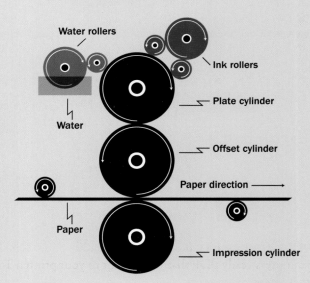

Figure 9.34 This drawing demonstrates the simplicity of the offset lithographic process.

Proofing Your Work

Although the CD project in this chapter is intended to be printed commercially, you may want to print to a desktop printer instead if you need to create only a few CDs for friends and family. The other reason to print to your local desktop printer would be, of course, to create what's called a *hard proof* of your work.

If this is the case, I highly recommend you spend an hour with Adobe's senior creative director, Russell Brown. On his Web site at www.russellbrown.com/tips_tech.html (Figure 9.35), you'll find three great video tutorials for setting color in Photoshop, Illustrator, and InDesign and for printing to Xerox and Epson printers. I suggest watching the videos in order, starting with Photoshop, through Illustrator, and finally InDesign. Although these videos cover CS2, they are still relevant to current software.

Figure 9.35 The Russell Brown Show Web site is an excellent resource of tips, tricks, tutorials, and Creative Suite links.

Once you've proofed the project and made any final changes, it's time to create your press-ready PDF that will be sent to your printer. To create the PDF, follow these steps:

1. Choose File > Export > PDF.
2. In the PDF Export Options dialog, choose the PDF/X-1a preset (Figure 9.36).
3. Turn on the View PDF After Exporting setting.
4. Turn on all marks and bleeds (Figure 9.37) as well.
5. Click Export to create the final PDF.

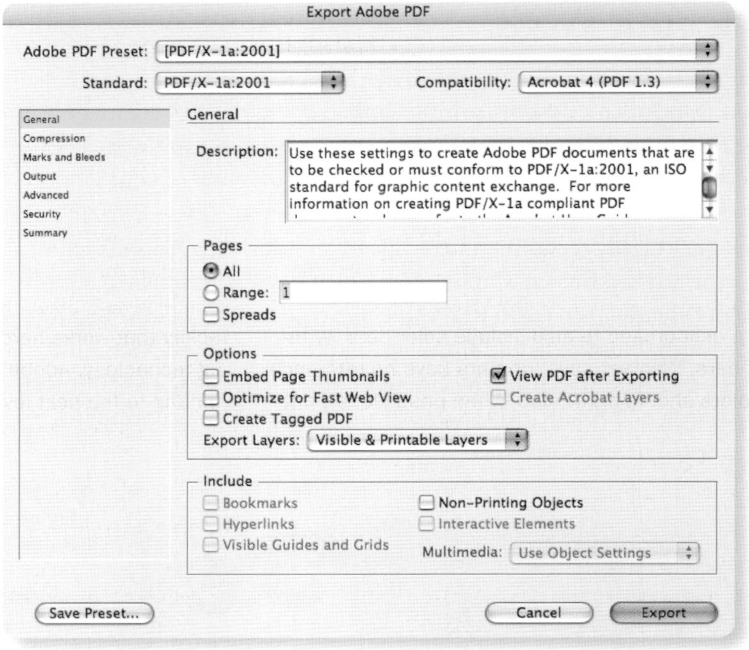

Figure 9.36 Create a press-ready PDF for your completed CD project.

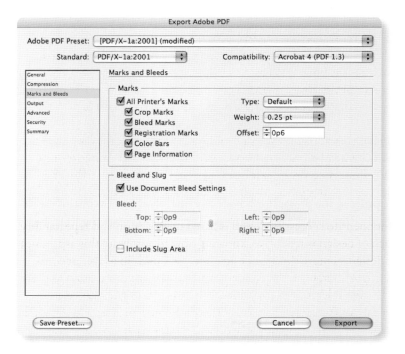

Figure 9.37 You'll want to include marks and bleeds in the export.

According to James Wamser, Adobe Certified Instructor and Print Specialist at Sells Printing in Milwaukee, Wisconsin, the most important ingredient to a successful print job begins with communication between designers and print specialists.

Sells clients who choose to submit their own color proofs are encouraged to also include color bars. Without color bars, Wamser says, printers have no reference to how colors should print. Also, when possible, a printer's template should be used for special packaging such as CDs. Templates include guides that indicate folds, live area, and bleed.

James also recommends to all Sells clients that to ensure the most trouble-free output they use a PDF workflow instead of sending native files. Another option that's gaining traction at Sells is PDF X-4, which supports live transparency, unlike PDF/X-1a, which is a flattened file format. PDF/X-4 along with the Adobe PDF Print Engine has proven to be very successful, eliminating potential transparency and flattening issues. Their excellent work aside, Sells prides itself as a cutting edge facility that works hard to stay abreast of the latest printing technology. Adobe's PDF Print Engine, which takes printing to the next level, is how Sells and its clients benefit by using the PDF/X-4 file format.

The biggest problem when clients insist on sending native files is missing fonts and graphics. PDF files when prepared correctly, streamline the printing process, while providing more consistent and reliable results.

Project Wrap-Up and Conclusion

Throughout this book, you'll recognize a common theme: successful design is the result of the intersection of type, color, and space. It's that easy, and that hard. Throughout the book and again in this chapter I've tried to show how, by leveraging the simple beauty of good type, harmonious color, and strong layout, the often-overwhelming process of design can be made manageable.

My other wish is that you've noticed that despite the wealth of sophisticated tools available in Creative Suite 3, you needn't use every filter in Photoshop, every brush in Illustrator, or every font in InDesign. Instead, good design is rooted in the consistent application of a handful of core techniques.

The last component to successful design is based on precision and repeatability. Because much of design is repetitive, knowing how to automate this aspect not only allows designers more time for design but also builds in a layer of consistency. By taking advantage of styles, scripts, presets, and actions, much of the drudgery of design is left to the computer. Whereas you might start to complain every time a client asks to see her book with a different typeface, I doubt you'll hear a whimper from the computer when you redefine a paragraph style.

It's that easy. And that hard.

Index